Age in the Welfare State

The overwhelming costs of providing for aging populations have brought many welfare states to the brink of insolvency. Now is the time to ask: how did we get here? *Age in the Welfare State* explains how it came to pass that some nations give the lion's share of social benefits to the elderly, while others do more to protect children and working-age adults. A sweeping work of historically and sociologically informed political science, *Age in the Welfare State* offers a surprising challenge to the conventional wisdom that welfare state policies are a result of either pressure-group politics or the ideologies of parties in power. This vividly written and exhaustively documented work draws on in-depth case studies of family, labor-market, and pension policy making in Italy and the Netherlands, as well as broader cross-sectional analysis of spending patterns in twenty OECD countries. Scholars of social policy and comparative politics, practitioners, and policy makers will be challenged by this book's startlingly new insights about the historical roots of current welfare state predicaments.

Julia Lynch is Assistant Professor of Political Science at the University of Pennsylvania. Her recent dissertation, on which this book is based, garnered the Gabriel Almond prize of the American Political Science Association for the best dissertation in comparative politics. Professor Lynch was previously a scholar in the Robert Wood Johnson Health Policy Scholars program at Harvard University, and she has been a visiting researcher at the European University Institute in Florence and the Luxembourg Income Study project in Luxembourg.

Cambridge Studies in Comparative Politics

General Editor
Margaret Levi   *University of Washington, Seattle*

Assistant General Editor
Stephen Hanson   *University of Washington, Seattle*

Associate Editors
Robert H. Bates   *Harvard University*
Helen Milner   *Princeton University*
Frances Rosenbluth   *Yale University*
Susan Stokes   *University of Chicago*
Sidney Tarrow   *Cornell University*
Kathleen Thelen   *Northwestern University*
Erik Wibbels   *University of Washington, Seattle*

Other Books in the Series

Continued after Index

Age in the Welfare State

THE ORIGINS OF SOCIAL SPENDING ON PENSIONERS, WORKERS, AND CHILDREN

JULIA LYNCH

University of Pennsylvania

CAMBRIDGE
UNIVERSITY PRESS

CAMBRIDGE UNIVERSITY PRESS
Cambridge, New York, Melbourne, Madrid, Cape Town, Singapore, São Paulo

Cambridge University Press
40 West 20th Street, New York, NY 10011-4211, USA

www.cambridge.org
Information on this title: www.cambridge.org/9780521849982

First published 2006

Printed in the United States of America

A catalog record for this publication is available from the British Library.

Library of Congress Cataloging in Publication Data

Lynch, Julia, 1970–
Age in the welfare state : the origins of social spending on pensioners, workers, and
children / Julia Lynch.
  p. cm. – (Cambridge studies in comparative politics)
Includes bibliographical references (p.) and index.
ISBN-13: 978-0-521-84998-2 (hardback)
ISBN-10: 0-521-84998-5 (hardback)
ISBN-13: 978-0-521-61516-7 (pbk.)
ISBN-10: 0-521-61516-X (pbk.)
1. Public welfare – Cross-cultural studies.   2. Age groups – Government policy –
Cross-cultural studies.   3. Age discrimination – Cross-cultural studies.
4. Patronage, Political – Cross-cultural studies.   I. Title.   II. Series.
HV51.L96   2006
362 – dc22   2006004116

ISBN-13   978-0-521-84998-2 hardback
ISBN-10   0-521-84998-5 hardback

ISBN-13   978-0-521-61516-7 paperback
ISBN-10   0-521-61516-X paperback

In memory of Rue Bunzelman Deutsch

Contents

Tables and Figures

x

Tables and Figures

Figures

Abbreviations

ISTAT   Istituto Nazionale di Statistica (national statistical agency)
PCI   Partido Comunista Italiano (Communist Party of Italy)
(P)DS   (Partido) Democratici di Sinistra (Democratic Party of the Left, formerly PCI)
PSI   Partido Socialista Italiano (Socialist Party of Italy)
TS   *trattamenti speciali* (special unemployment insurance benefits)
UIL   Unione Italiana del Lavoro (Centrist labor union confederation)

The Netherlands

ABW   Algemene Bijstandswet (Unemployment Assistance Act)
AKW   Algemene Kinderbijslagswet (General Family Allowance Act)
AOW   Algemene Ourderdomswet (General Old-Age Pensions Act)
ARP   Anti-Revolutionaire Partij (Protestant Reform Party)
CBS   Centraal Bureau voor de Statistiek (national statistical agency)
CDA   Christen Democratisch Appel (Christian Democratic Appeal, formed in 1980 from merger of Catholic and Protestant parties)
CNV   Christelijk Nationaal Vakverbond (Catholic trade union confederation)
FNV   Federatie Nederlandse Vakbeweging (largest Dutch trade union confederation)
JWG   Jeugdwerkgarantiewet (Youth Work Guarantee Law)
KVP   Katholieke Volkspartij (Catholic Peoples' Party)
NVV   Nederlands Verbond van Vakverenigingen (Socialist trade union confederation, merged to form part of FNV in 1981)
PPR   Politieke Partij Radicalen (Radical Party)
PvdA   Partij van de Arbeid (Labor Party)
RWW   Rijksgroepsregeling voor Werkloze Werknemers (Unemployment Assistance Act)
SER   Sociaal-Economische Raad (Socio-Economic Council)
SVB   Sociale Verzekeringsbank (Social Insurance Bank)
VUT   Vervroegde Uittreding (private early retirement pension provision)
WAO   Wet op de Arbeidsongeschiktheidsverzekering (Disablement Insurance Act)
WIW   Wet Inschakeling Werkzoekenden (Job-Seekers Employment Act)
WW   Wet Werkloosheidsvoorziening (Unemployment Insurance Act)

Abbreviations

WWV   Wijziging Wet Werkloosheidsvoorziening (Extended Unemployment Insurance Act)

International

ILO   International Labour Office
IMF   International Monetary Fund
LIS   Luxembourg Income Study project
OECD   Organization for Economic Cooperation and Development

Miscellaneous

ENSR   Elderly/Non-elderly Spending Ratio
GDP   Gross Domestic Product

Country Abbreviations Used in Figures

AUS   Australia
AUT   Austria
BEL   Belgium
CAN   Canada
DEN   Denmark
FRA   France
FIN   Finland
GER   Germany
GRE   Greece
IRE   Ireland
ITA   Italy
JPN   Japan
LUX   Luxembourg
NET   Netherlands
NOR   Norway
NZL   New Zealand
POR   Portugal
SPA   Spain
SWE   Sweden
UK   United Kingdom
US   United States

Acknowledgments

This book has been many years in the making, the vast majority of which have been enjoyable. I attribute this in large part to the fact that it was truly a joint effort. It would not have been possible for me to research, write, or complete it without the invaluable contributions of various funding institutions, mentors, colleagues, friends, and family.

I owe deep intellectual debts to many: to Gøsta Esping-Andersen, who set me on the right track; to John Zysman, Jonah Levy, and Henry Brady, who gave me the right tools and showed me how to use them; to Maurizio Ferrera and Tim Smeeding, who always showed faith and backed it up with good works; and especially to Karen Anderson and Sara Watson, who have always been generous and who just keep getting smarter every year. Numerous colleagues – among them Melani Cammett, Andrea Campbell, Anna Grzymala-Busse, Katie Carman, Evan Lieberman, Lauren Morris MacLean, Paul Pierson, Mark Vail, Rob Weiner, Christa van Wijnbergen, and Daniel Ziblatt – gave intelligent feedback at crucial moments. I cannot thank these wonderful people enough.

Field work for this project was financed with a National Science Foundation Graduate Research Fellowship, a Social Science Research Council International Dissertation Field Research Fellowship, and an Alan Sharlin Memorial Award from the Institute for International Studies at the University of California, Berkeley. Financial support during writing and rewriting came from another Sharlin Award and a John L. Simpson Memorial Research Fellowship, also administered by the Institute for International Studies at Berkeley, and from a most generous fellowship from the Robert Wood Johnson Health Policy Scholars program.

While in Italy, I relied heavily on the kindness of the European University Institute in Florence. Since my first venture to Italy in 1993, the faculty, staff, and researchers of the EUI have provided me with a home away from home and a vibrant intellectual community. The Robert Schuman Centre's 1998–9 European Forum on "Recasting European Welfare States" provided an ideal environment for testing out new ideas during my stay in Italy and beyond. I would particularly like to thank Stefano Bartolini and Martin Rhodes for making the resources of the EUI available to me on repeated occasions.

My research in Italy would not have been possible without the support of Maurizio Ferrera, whose kindness, generosity, and belief in the project has sustained me through many rough patches. I would also like to thank Marino Regini and Daniele Franco, as well as librarians Peter Kennealy at the EUI, Oreste Bazzichi at Confindustria, and Mila Scarlatti at the Centro Studi CISL. Aedin Doris, Jackie Gordon, Ann-Louise Lauridsen, Dan Oakey, Jacobien Rutgers, and Joanna Swajcowska supplied moral and immoral support at crucial moments during my Italian sojourns.

In the Netherlands, Anton Hemerijck was a welcoming beacon, setting me up with logistical support from the University of Leiden and providing me with the feedback and intellectual support necessary to research a case study effectively in a short period of time. The staff of the library at the Ministry of Social Welfare and the experts gathered at the Hugo Sinzheimer Institute in Amsterdam amazed me with their patience and expertise. Nelleke van Deusen-Scholl and Heleen Mastenbroek managed to teach me workable Dutch in a period of about five months, a feat that shall never cease to amaze me. Karen Anderson, Jacobien Rutgers, and Bauke Visser helped to make my time in the Netherlands pleasant as well as productive.

Logistical support in the final phases has come from my terrific TS-CS guru, Ben Goodrich; from Todor Enev, whose deeply intelligent data sleuthing makes the term "research assistant" utterly inadequate; and from Melanie Daglian, whose positive energy made preparing the final manuscript an enjoyable task. Tom and Emma were there at the beginning and saw it through to the end. There are no two better friends with whom to go through life. Last, this book is dedicated to my very special grandmother, Rue Bunzelman Deutsch. As we both got older, she became my partner in crime, showing me that sometimes the true meaning of intergenerational solidarity comes down to poking fun at the middle generation.

Philadelphia, Pennsylvania
November 2005

1

Introduction

Welfare states work better for some age groups than for others. Social programs in the United States and Italy, for example, do little to raise children out of poverty, but elderly citizens are made better off by the substantial benefits available to them. In other countries, such as Norway and Portugal, senior citizens' incomes on average are lower than in the United States or Italy, but low-income workers, families with children, and the long-term unemployed receive significant support from the welfare state. Across the industrialized countries, social programs such as public pensions, family allowances, and benefits for the unemployed vary significantly, with consequences for the well-being of different age groups in the population.

This book asks how social policies in rich democracies buffer and channel risks for the aged, the young, and working-age adults. What do different welfare states do for their elderly and non-elderly citizens? Why does the age orientation of social policies vary from country to country and over time? And what are the political consequences of different strategies for redistributing resources across different age groups in society? How and why welfare states distribute resources to different age groups is linked to broader questions of theory in comparative politics: What are the important dimensions of similarity and difference among different modes of economic regulation? Which actors impact political-economic outcomes? What is the relative importance of social and economic structures, political practices, and institutional legacies in determining the policies pursued in different countries?

The welfare state's role in caring for young people and the elderly plays an important part in political debates about welfare reform. An alleged elderly bias in American social spending has, during recent years, nourished intense political debates about generational equity. In many European countries,

1

relatively high incomes from pensions and increasing rates of child poverty provide a fertile environment for the emergence of a parallel discussion. Unequal benefits for the old and the young provide ammunition for those who advocate providing more support for people at all stages of the life course, but also for those who wish to cut existing benefits in the name of intergenerational equity. These inequalities also serve as a reminder that welfare states can differ objectively and dramatically in their ability to insure diverse age groups in society against risks such as poverty, ill health, or social exclusion.

This book begins with an analysis of social spending patterns in twenty industrialized democracies. Welfare states do in fact differ quantifiably in the age orientation of their social policies. The first half of the book establishes a strategy for conceptualizing and measuring these differences (chapter 2), and then explores a series of competing hypotheses about why countries might vary in the age orientation of their social policy regimes (chapter 3). The second half of the book amplifies and tests these rival hypotheses systematically using paired case studies. Case studies of the development of three key social programs in Italy and the Netherlands – family allowances (chapter 4), unemployment benefits (chapter 5), and old-age pensions (chapter 6) – demonstrate the path by which two countries, sharing a set of common ideological orientations and facing similar labor market and demographic conditions in the immediate postwar period, arrived at welfare states that allocate very different roles to the state in distributing resources across generations.

Why Study the Age Orientation of Welfare States?

Welfare states vary in the extent to which they protect older and younger citizens. But traditional theories of welfare state development neither notice nor explain this variation. If welfare state scholars have until now preferred to focus on the cross-class, cross-occupation, or cross-gender distribution carried out by social policies, why should we now be concerned with the age profile of welfare states? Put simply, it is because changing socio-economic conditions mean that how welfare states cover the risks associated with different stages of the life course has become more important.

Advanced industrialized societies today are aging. At the same time, labor markets are changing, and family structures evolving. The male-breadwinner model of social organization, premised upon stable, lifelong employment for men, has given way to more frequent or longer periods of unemployment. Families, long called upon to provide for needs not met in the marketplace or by the state, are stretched to new limits. But this is occurring just as their capacity to respond is reduced by increasing female employment outside the home, divorce, and changing fertility patterns. In the context of current demographic, labor market, and family changes, how welfare states address the risks faced by people at different stages in the life course affects both citizens' lives and the capacity of national economies to adapt to new conditions.

Demographic, social, and economic transformations confronting even the most "traditional" of Western societies affect the foundations of the political economic orders established in the period after the Second World War. How will welfare state institutions, which were created under radically different demographic, social, and economic circumstances, respond to these changes? How well will traditional institutions of social policy buffer citizens as they adapt their lives to the new social risks associated with changing work patterns and family demands? Will political sponsors of the welfare state be able to balance pressure from constituencies to both maintain established entitlements and meet new needs?

To evaluate how welfare states will stand up to these new pressures, we need to understand how they address the risks encountered by people at different stages in the life course. Quite apart from normative concerns about intergenerational justice, it is worth understanding how welfare states treat different age groups because this affects crucially the decisions individuals make about labor market participation, family organization, and investment and savings strategies. When welfare states direct resources toward families with children, for example, it can affect fertility rates, female labor force participation, and the professional preparedness of young adults. The division of labor among family, market, and state in caring for young children or the frail elderly may affect both women's emancipation and the quality of care provided. The structure and extent of public pension systems of course has consequences for labor costs and financial markets, but can also set limits on the speed and flexibility with which welfare states retool to meet new needs that affect adults during their working years. In sum, the capacity of welfare states to respond to new challenges depends critically on a characteristic that has received almost no attention in the literature on comparative social policy: the age orientation of social policies.

Why Does Age Orientation Vary? Some Preliminary Evidence and Hypotheses

The age-orientation of social policies, as chapter 2 demonstrates in some detail, varies dramatically across advanced industrialized countries and in ways that upset our traditional notions of family relationships among different types of welfare states. Figure 1.1 shows the average for the years 1985 to 2000 of the ratio of direct social expenditures on the elderly (pensions and services for the elderly) to spending on the non-elderly (unemployment benefits, active labor market policy, family allowances, and family services), adjusted for the relative size of elderly and non-elderly populations in each of twenty OECD (Organization for Economic Cooperation and Development) countries. I call this measure the Elderly/Non-elderly Spending Ratio, or ENSR. It allows us to estimate the relative weight of spending on the elderly – people aged sixty-five and above or in formal retirement – versus that on working-age adults and children. This spending measure is of course only an approximation of the full range of services and benefits offered to different groups, many of which we consider in more depth in chapter 2. But the ENSR serves to introduce us to the range of variation across countries in the age orientation of social policies.

The most striking feature of the age orientation of welfare states is its transgression of the boundaries set by Esping-Andersen's (1990) seminal division of advanced countries into three "worlds" of welfare capitalism. The least elderly-oriented countries among the twenty OECD nations considered here are a mix of his "Liberal," "Conservative-Corporatist," and "Social Democratic" regimes. At the same time, two of Esping-Andersen's Liberal regimes, the United States and Japan, are clearly among the most elderly-oriented. Likewise, Conservative-Corporatist regimes run the gamut from relatively youth-oriented Belgium and the Netherlands to elderly-oriented Italy and Austria. The lack of correspondence between the ENSR and Esping-Andersen's key concept, decommodification, is easy to see in Figure 1.2. The relief from market forces that social policies provide is surely an important measure of the welfare state. But it is not enough to ask how much welfare states decommodify; we must also ask whom they decommodify.

Alternative typologies fare no better when confronted with the data on age orientation. "Christian Democratic" welfare states (van Kersbergen 1995) are as likely to be youth-oriented (the Netherlands) or age-neutral (Germany) as they are to throw their support to the elderly (Italy).

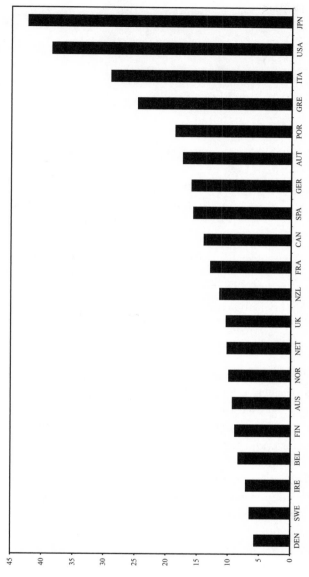

Figure 1.1 Elderly/non-elderly spending ratio (ENSR), average 1985–2000. *Sources:* Spending data from OECD 2004; demographic data from OECD 2003b.

5

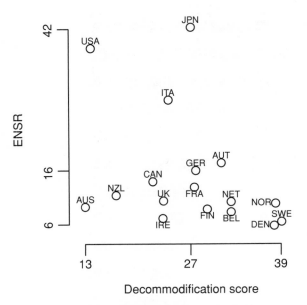

Figure 1.2   Age orientation and decommodification. *Sources:* Spending data from OECD 2004; demographic data from OECD 2003b; decommodification scores from Esping-Anderson 1990.

Neither do Mediterranean countries cluster neatly, contrary to scholarship suggesting a distinctive Southern European welfare state type (Leibfried 1992; Ferrera 1996c; Rhodes 1997). Italy and Greece look like classic "pensioner states" (Esping-Andersen 1997), but Portugal resembles Canada, the United Kingdom, and Germany more closely than it does its Southern European neighbors. The weak correspondence between the age orientation of social policy regimes and welfare state "worlds" or "families" suggests that there is an important dimension of variation among different kinds of welfare states that familiar typologies do not capture.

If standard typologies of welfare state outcomes do not correspond to the variation we've observed, it should not surprise us that the causes of divergent welfare state characteristics typically cited in the literature also fail to predict differing age orientations. As the bivariate scatter plots in Figures 1.3 to 1.5 suggest, neither the demographic structure of a country's population, its wealth or "level of development," nor the overall size of the welfare state predict consistently how welfare states will allocate resources to the elderly and non-elderly in their populations. Figure 1.5 does show an inverse relationship between total social spending and the age orientation

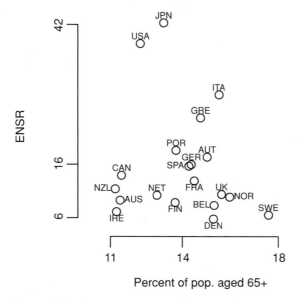

Figure 1.3 Age orientation and demographic structure. *Source:* See Fig. 1.1.

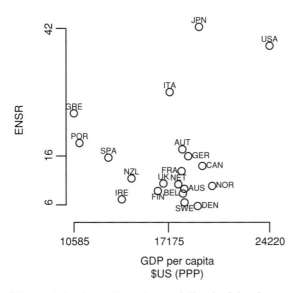

Figure 1.4 Age orientation and "level of development." *Sources:* Spending data from OECD 2004; demographic and GDP per capita data from OECD 2003b.

7

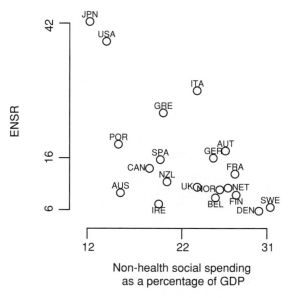

Figure 1.5 Age orientation and total welfare state "effort." *Sources:* Total non-health social expenditure data from OECD 2004; demographic data from OECD 2003b.

of the welfare state (bigger welfare states tend to be less elderly-oriented), but the presence of two very elderly-oriented outliers makes the relationship seem much stronger than it might be for the remaining countries. These data reveal the important point that there are both small (Japan) and large (Italy) elderly-oriented welfare states, and both small (Ireland) and large (Sweden) youth-oriented welfare states. At the same time, classic "power resources" variables, such as the strength of organized labor, employers' preferences, and the relative power of Left and Christian Democratic political parties, fall short of explaining differences in the age orientation of welfare states, as we see in chapter 3.

Why don't classic theories of welfare state development explain these outcomes? Some scholars have posited that the demographic structure of a population affects welfare state policies. In particular, the elderly are said to have distinctive needs and distinctive preferences that drive welfare state spending (see, e.g., Wilensky 1975; Pampel and Williamson 1989; Thomson 1989, 1993). These authors argue that traditional welfare state theories miss an important set of political actors, the elderly, because they focus too narrowly on class-based actors. A major aim of this book is to test this hypothesis about the political influence of demographic groups. Can different mixes of welfare benefits for the young and old across countries and across time be explained by pressure from welfare state constituencies in the form of age-based lobbies?

The criticism that standard welfare state theories ignore nonclass actors has merit, but shifting the focus to the role of age-based actors does not account for diverging welfare state age profiles. Two far more important problems in the comparative welfare state literature need to be addressed before it can be made to account adequately for the outcome that we are trying to explain. First, the prevailing view of politicians as largely motivated by programmatic goals must be revised to take into account nuances in the varieties of political competition. Second, we must consider how the institutional environment within which electoral competition takes place shapes welfare state regimes.

Explaining Variation in Age Orientation: The Argument in Brief

If welfare states vary in surprising ways in their protection of older and younger age groups in the population, how can we explain this variation? Why do some welfare states emphasize protection for risks during childhood and the working life, while others focus more on covering needs in old age? This book argues that two types of institutions explain this variation: the structure of welfare state programs enacted in the early twentieth century – occupationalist or citizenship-based – and the dominant mode of political competition in a polity, particularistic or programmatic.

First, as we see in chapter 3, the structure of early welfare state programs affects the populations (labor market "insiders" vs. "outsiders") that are covered by public welfare programs. Since these populations take on distinctive age profiles with the development over time of both public and private social insurance schemes, the choice of which population to cover strongly influences the eventual age orientation of social policy regimes. Second, the type of political competition characteristic of a party system affects the development of welfare state programs in the post–World War II period and determines whether elderly-oriented occupationalist welfare regimes can "switch tracks" by adding more youth-oriented citizenship-based programs. The policy studies in chapters 4 through 6 reveal affinities between particularistic politics and fragmented occupationalist social insurance regimes that make program structure and the mode of political competition extremely difficult to uncouple. In sum, this book argues that patterns of partisan competition and social policy structures interact over time to produce durable, mutually reinforcing constellations of social policies that mature into either elderly-oriented or more youth-oriented welfare states.

Two Watersheds of Welfare State Formation

At the heart of the distinction between groups of countries with similar age orientations lie two historical bifurcations in the paths of social policy development. The first split, the basic genetic division between citizenship-based and occupational regimes, occurred in the late nineteenth and early twentieth centuries, when modern states grappled with new social and political problems arising from industrialization. A second watershed occurred in the decades around the Second World War, when most countries with occupationalist welfare systems considered adopting citizenship-based social policy regimes, but only a select group actually took concrete steps in this direction.

The initial split between citizenship-based and occupational social welfare regimes had profound consequences for the eventual age orientation of welfare spending.[1] In the countries adopting citizenship-based regimes (the Scandinavian and British Commonwealth countries), public welfare provisions developed in the gaps not covered by mutual-aid programs run by labor unions. State welfare spending supplemented preexisting private occupational benefits, and so focused on the risks most likely to be encountered by people who were not covered by mutualist benefits. In Manow's (1997) terminology, such welfare regimes "compensated" for the gaps in private coverage, offering benefits for children, women, and elderly citizens without pensions. Citizenship-based regimes contained the seeds of programs that would later develop into the mainstays of youth-oriented welfare states: support for mothers and children, and comprehensive social assistance for those with weak ties to the labor market.

---

[1] It should be noted that in practice many welfare states mix citizenship-based and occupationalist program types. Even prior to World War II, Sweden, for example, had a pension system that combined a flat-rate citizenship-based benefit with a supplementary contributory tier offering benefits graded according to occupation. However, throughout this book I label welfare programs that have a substantial component that is available to citizens regardless of occupation or contributory history as "citizenship-based," to distinguish them from programs in which there is no universal or means-tested entitlement independent of labor market status.

Introduction

In those countries that eventually became more elderly-oriented, labor movements in the late nineteenth century relinquished control over autonomous forms of social insurance to the state. Public social insurance programs thus built on the framework of occupational programs that unions had constructed to benefit their own members. This technique of "upgrading" private occupational social insurance schemes by transforming them into state-run programs (Manow 1997) resulted in public welfare benefits that focused almost entirely on the needs of people with close ties to the labor market. In these states, social protection for groups outside the labor market remained the province of nonstate actors, primarily families and charities. Protection for people affiliated with the core labor market was provided by the state, setting the stage for elderly-oriented welfare spending in much of Continental Europe, the United States, and Japan as core work forces aged dramatically in the 1970s and 1980s. Thus, the structure of welfare programs initiated in the late nineteenth and early twentieth centuries laid the groundwork for different types of spending, resulting in a basic division between youth-oriented universalist and means-tested welfare states, on the one hand, and more elderly-oriented occupationalist regimes, on the other.

A second watershed in welfare state development, in the decades around World War II, introduced further variation into the structure of welfare state regimes, and hence into the age-orientation of welfare spending in different countries. During and immediately after the Second World War, most countries with occupationalist welfare states considered legislative proposals to introduce substantial elements of the citizenship-based, Beveridgean model pioneered in victorious Britain (Ferrera 1993). Some countries succeeded in this agenda, introducing forms of citizenship-based coverage for children, women, and others with weak ties to the labor market. Other states, however, did not, and continued on a path toward growing expenditures on an aging core work force and occupational pensioners, with minimal coverage for the rest of the population.

How can we account for the persistence of occupationalism in some countries and the introduction of more youth-oriented citizenship-based welfare policies in others after World War II? The opposing slopes of this second watershed are characterized by different modes of political competition prevalent in different countries. The countries that did not adopt universal programs in the 1930s through 1960s shared a particularistic mode of political competition that inhibited the development of substantial universal welfare programs. As the years passed, highly fragmented social security

11

programs continued to provide resources for clientelist politicians and to obscure the costs of political clientelism, resulting in a self-reinforcing cycle of particularistic politics, fragmented occupational welfare programs, and elderly-oriented spending.

Italy and the Netherlands: Contrasting Case Studies

The case studies of Italian and Dutch social policies in chapters 4 through 6 illustrate the "mechanism of reproduction" (see Thelen 1999; Pierson 2000) that has sustained these path-dependent welfare policy outcomes after World War II. Both Italy and the Netherlands had pure occupationalist welfare regimes before World War II, and in both countries after the war official reform commissions (the D'Aragona Commission in Italy, the van Rhijn Commission in the Netherlands) advocated moving to a universalist, citizenship-based system. Other similarities, too, lead us to expect that the Netherlands and Italy would follow a similar path after the war. Both countries belong to Esping-Andersen's (1990) Conservative-Corporatist world of welfare; in both countries the major expansion of the welfare state in the postwar period was carried out under coalitions dominated by Christian Democratic parties; and in both countries labor relations regimes were characterized by numerically weak unions and sporadic tripartite concertation. Yet Italy has a highly elderly-oriented, occupational welfare system, whereas the Netherlands is quite youth-oriented and characterized by a mix of occupational and citizenship-based programs. The Netherlands succeeded in implementing a number of new universalist welfare programs after World War II, while Italy, despite repeated attempts to do so, did not. As a result, the Netherlands entered the 1990s with a far more youth-oriented welfare system than did Italy.

Why did Italy remain a strongly occupationalist welfare regime, while the Netherlands adopted many citizenship-based programs? The key to understanding this difference is the very different ways that political competition has been organized in the two countries for much of the postwar period. Italian politics has been characterized by an extremely high degree of political particularism. By contrast, politics in the Netherlands has tended toward the programmatic end of the spectrum. This difference in the mode of political competition between Italy and the Netherlands explains why the Netherlands adopted citizenship-based welfare programs, such as universal pensions, universal family allowances, and a basic social minimum, while Italy did not.

Introduction

Clientelism and occupationalism interacted to prevent Italian social reformers from introducing the citizenship-based welfare regime envisioned by the D'Aragona Commission in 1947. Politicians associated with both the Christian Democratic Party and the Italian Left were influenced by the atmosphere of particularistic political competition to block the harmonization of pension benefits and the introduction of universal public pensions in Italy – not just in 1947, but also at least once in every decade since. Clientelist politicians also resisted the development of neutral state capacities such as effective taxation, which in turn stymied attempts to introduce universal benefits for children, the unemployed, and the elderly. And the complexity of occupationalist programs made it difficult for either the public or policy experts to see the results when politicians offered selective benefits in return for votes.

If in Italy the combination of fragmented, occupational welfare programs and particularistic political competition derailed attempts to introduce new universal social programs after the Second World War, the opposite was true in the Netherlands. There neutral state capacities such as universal taxation made it possible to introduce citizenship-based programs fairly easily. The ability to levy and collect taxes on the self-employed and farmers, in particular, secured labor and the Left's support for agreements that introduced universal family allowances and pensions.

The simplicity and transparency of universal programs in turn made it difficult for politicians to exchange highly targeted benefits for votes. In fact, once programs were universalized, it became impossible to increase benefits for one group without increases for all recipients. In the case of family allowances and unemployment benefits, this led to a gradual escalation of benefits, and when high unemployment hit in the mid-1970s, costs for these programs soared as the number of beneficiaries increased dramatically. In the case of public pensions, the sheer size of a program dedicated to providing a decent standard of living for the entire elderly population, combined with the ease with which future outlays could be predicted, made many potential advocates of higher pensions think twice before demanding benefit increases. The simplicity and transparency of citizenship-based social programs tended to increase pressure for spending in the benefit categories that did not provide full income replacement over a long period – generally youth-oriented programs, such as family allowances or unemployment insurance – and reduced the pressure to grant large increases in more expensive benefit categories such as old-age insurance.

13

The case studies in chapters 4 through 6 highlight three distinct mechanisms by which the structure of welfare state programs and the mode of political competition combine to affect the age orientation of social policies. First, the distinction between occupational and citizenship-based welfare programs determines how politicians can use welfare benefits as tender in the competition for votes, and thus alters politicians' preferences about the level of various types of benefits. Second, the structure of social programs affects how salient different types of benefits are to potential recipients, and how visible are the effects of decisions about where to allocate resources. Finally, the mode of political competition affects the resources available to politicians and policy makers who might wish to expand particular social programs.

This essentially institutionalist explanation for the variation in the age orientation of welfare states poses a challenge to the existing literature on comparative social policy on three fronts. First, the argument presented here demands that welfare state outcomes be analyzed in relation to other public policies. In particular, the link between tax systems and welfare benefits is revealed to be a crucial one, which affects both the kind of welfare benefits that constituencies demand and what politicians can offer to meet that demand. Second, this book argues that politicians matter for welfare state outcomes not so much because of their ideological orientations but because of the way they compete for votes and office. Finally, this argument downplays the role of welfare state constituencies in bringing about the policies that benefit them, and asserts instead the causal primacy of long-term processes and interactions between program structure and politicians' behavior. In other words, it supports a sharp distinction between welfare state regimes as the revealed preferences of powerful social groups, and policies as outcomes of institutionally structured processes of political interaction.

2

Measuring the Age of Welfare

Welfare states clearly work to transfer resources between age groups, not least through pay-as-you-go old-age pensions, which account for one-fifth to one-half of total social spending in most countries of the OECD. But the elderly in different countries benefit to varying extents not only from cross-national differences in the generosity of pension benefits, but also from differences in other policy areas, such as housing and health care. Similarly, working-age adults and children benefit from a variety of programs financed by the population at large, including education, publicly provided child care, and income supports.[1]

The concept of intergenerational justice has prompted a robust theoretical literature, but little empirical investigation.[2] In particular, we know very little about how social provisions for different age groups vary across welfare state types, across countries, or across time. Because so little is known about the age-distributive properties of social policies, it is dangerous to conclude that "the contemporary welfare state in capitalist democracies is largely a *welfare state for the elderly*" (Myles 1989). Nor can we be sure that, as some have argued, a single "selfish generation" that reached adulthood just after the Second World War has tailored welfare state spending for its own purposes (Thomson 1993). Without reliable measures of the age orientation of social policies across nations and over time, it is impossible to know to what extent contemporary welfare states are biased toward the elderly of particular generations, toward successive cohorts of the elderly, or even *if* they are uniformly biased toward the elderly rather than the young.

---

[1] This chapter is based substantially on Lynch 2001.
[2] See, e.g., Daniels 1988; Johnson, Conrad, and Thomson 1989; and Laslett and Fishkin 1992.

15

In this chapter we consider a series of indicators of the age orientation of social policies. The resulting rankings group countries quite consistently according to how a variety of social policy instruments – direct expenditures on social insurance programs, labor market policies, education, and health care, as well as indirect tax expenditures and housing policies – allocate resources to different age groups. The most consistently elderly-oriented welfare states in the sample of OECD countries considered here are Japan, Italy, Greece, the United States, Spain, and Austria. The most youth-oriented are the Scandinavian countries, the Netherlands, and the English-speaking countries other than the United States. A group of Continental European countries – Germany, France, Belgium, Luxembourg, and Portugal – occupies the middle ground. Because these groupings of countries are so consistent across policy areas, it is possible to develop a simple measure of the age orientation of social policy regimes that uses just a few pieces of readily available aggregate social spending data.

But given that families often share resources across generations, or purchase private insurance that acts as a form of resource transfer across the life course, is the age orientation of *state* policies really the form of intergenerational transfer with which we should be most concerned? And are aggregate spending measures really the best way to capture the variation in state policies?

Determining the age orientation of individual social policies can be difficult since policies often have effects, and reflect priorities, other than those most obviously indicated in statutes. Early retirement provisions in Italy that allowed female public-sector workers to retire at full pay after only fifteen years of service are a good example. One could interpret these "retirement" benefits not as a transfer to the elderly, but rather as family policy camouflaged for a context in which direct subsidies to working mothers were unacceptable to politically powerful religious forces (Saraceno 1994, 70). Because policies may reflect hidden priorities of policy makers and may benefit more than one specified target group, it is risky to draw conclusions about who social programs are really intended to help based solely on spending data, without going deeper into the political struggles behind the policies' implementation. This chapter works with aggregate spending data to sketch a preliminary portrait of policy priorities; case studies in chapters 4 through 6 flesh out this sketch.

Welfare transfers taking place within the state sphere are likely to be closely intertwined with intergenerational transfers that take place within families and in the context of private markets. Still, state policies toward

16

different age groups are important even if they do not reflect the total output of the state-market-family nexus for particular age groups. The distributional consequences of effecting intergenerational transfers via families, markets, or the state are not neutral. Welfare states take on distinctly different purposes when redistribution is limited to transfers within families, rather than between families; and power structures within families are also likely to reflect resource flows directed by the state.

It is tempting to allow the family to continue to serve as a black box obscuring the importance of state-sponsored redistribution to different age groups. Intergenerational ties and resource sharing within families are supposed to be the glue that prevents an explosion of tensions between age groups similar to the global upheavals of 1968. But the structure of pay-as-you-go social insurance programs may provide a simpler explanation for the current quiescence of younger cohorts in the face of elderly-oriented welfare state spending. When populations and real wages are both growing, transfers from the young to the old appear to be nothing more than transfers across the life course – younger people pay for benefits that they themselves will receive as they age. Under these circumstances, politicization of differences in welfare spending on different age groups is unlikely. As demographic and economic growth both slow, however, there is pressure to balance social insurance budgets by increasing contributions now and cutting benefits in the future. The potential for politicization of conflicts between age groups over the apportionment of state resources becomes important under these circumstances, though interpersonal ties between generations may mitigate the effects somewhat. Again, it is worth investigating the age priorities of state spending because these priorities have a political impact, even when buffered by the resources of families.

The State of the Art: Work on the Generational Effects of Welfare Policy to Date

Two main strategies for measuring the generational effects of welfare policies are in evidence in the existing literature: "generational accounting," which emerged in the 1990s as the major form of economic research on aging and social policy at the macro level, and an older body of sociological work that sought to evaluate the effects of social policies on the life chances of different age groups.

Generational accounting models (see, e.g., Kotlikoff and Liebfritz 1998) evaluate current tax structures and benefit patterns to calculate the lifetime tax-benefit position of specific age cohorts in a given country. Applying a standard discount rate, these models sum the total remaining lifetime taxes versus total remaining lifetime benefits in order to arrive at a figure known as a generational account for a person of a given age. For a person around retirement age, the generational account will generally be low or negative, since recent retirees have paid most of the taxes they will pay in their lifetime and are about to receive a large infusion of benefits in the form of a pension. Following the same logic, a person at age thirty will tend to have a much higher generational account: a lifetime of income taxes lies ahead, while the education benefit has already passed and the pension benefit is far in the future. Calculating the generational account for a person born today will indicate the overall lifetime tax-benefit position of a newborn, assuming no change in tax or benefit structures.

Generational accounting provides a useful comparative baseline for assessing the impact of present tax and transfer programs on different cohorts, but the highly aggregate nature of the accounts makes interpretation difficult. The combination in one measure of all tax and benefit programs, not just those relevant to social protection, makes it hard to individuate the effects of welfare policy per se. Furthermore, the use of discount rates means that accounts for any given age group are highly sensitive to the value of the most proximate tax or benefit program. A third limitation of the generational accounting technique is that accounts for all age groups assume constant tax and transfer policies. This means that for the generational accounts to reflect real aggregate gains (or losses) for a given age group compared with any other, policies would have to remain unchanged from the date of birth of the oldest cohort until the date of death of the youngest. While generational accounts are useful for comparing the lifetime tax-benefit position of newborns across countries *were policies to remain unchanged*, they are of little utility (as Kotlikoff and Liebfritz are careful to point out) in comparing the lifetime accounts of generations that have actually lived through, or expect to live through, a great deal of policy change.

The generational accounting framework is concerned with the question of generations, strictly speaking, not age groups. These concepts are related but distinct. Public policies may be neutral with respect to generations – that is, they do not effect significant transfers between groups of citizens born at different points in time – but at the same time are biased toward a particular age group. A purely contributory pension system, into which people make payments when they are young and out of which they draw

18

benefits when they are old, would fall into this category. Conversely, one could imagine an age-neutral policy that effects large intergenerational transfers – for example, deficit spending resulting from a tax cut that is carefully designed to affect levies on wage income and pension income in equal measure.

In policy-making circles, generational accounting techniques and claims about intergenerational justice have come to dominate on those occasions when the age orientation of social policy regimes is under discussion. But social policies are not static, and the distribution of resources among different age groups, not among different generations, is often at the heart of political conflict over the welfare state. Hence analysis of the age orientation of welfare states should ideally clarify the distribution of resources across age groups, as well as across generations.

Some important work in this area has been undertaken. O'Higgins (1988) offered a comparison of the treatment of elders and children in ten OECD countries, with direct expenditure and some tax data for the period 1960 to 1985. But while this contribution was an important first step toward the goal of measuring the age orientation of social policy, a restricted sample size and highly aggregate spending data limited the analysis. Meyer and Moon (1988) and Jencks and Torrey (1988) expanded the categories of analysis beyond the confines of social insurance spending but, as did O'Higgins (1988) and Pampel (1994), compared the situations of only the elderly and children, leaving out the middle ground of adulthood, where contemporary welfare states have had such widely varying success in adjusting to changes in employment and family patterns. More recently, Castles and Ferrera (1996) usefully consider the age-distributive effects of the housing/pension policy complex, but are hampered in the conclusions they can draw by the small number of cases and the limited set of policies that they discuss. Despite a growing interest in the relationship between demographic change and social welfare systems, major lacunae remain in our understanding of how social policies work to transfer resources across age groups and generations.

Measuring the Age Orientation of Social Policy

The remainder of this chapter is dedicated to evaluating in as much depth and breadth as possible the distribution of public social policy resources to different age groups in twenty highly industrialized democracies. Many different kinds of public policies affect the distribution of public resources to different age groups. Zoning regulations specifying minimum housing lot sizes, state subsidies of credit markets, and policies designed to stimulate the employment of youth or older job candidates are just a few examples. So a truly comprehensive measure of how states distribute resources across age groups would need to consider the totality of policy arenas and instruments through which states might act to channel resources to different age groups.

This chapter focuses, more modestly, on the distribution of benefits to different age groups carried out through three key areas of public policy: direct social expenditures on social insurance benefits, education, and health care; tax expenditures on welfare-substituting goods; and housing policies. Only public spending and private spending that is mandated by law (e.g., occupational pension schemes in France) are included.

The age categories employed throughout this analysis are *elderly* and *non-elderly*. These categories are rather ungainly as compared with seniors and children, or labor market participants versus dependents. But they are useful because public debates so often posit a trade-off between continuing to support the elderly at a high level and devoting resources to other kinds of needs in the non-elderly population. The definition of the relevant age groups is compelled as well by the considerable overlap between the well-being of children and non-elderly adults, and the scant similarity between the well-being of seniors and of their children's and grandchildren's age groups. Cross-nationally, poverty rates among seniors, after taking into account both taxes and social benefits, are not highly correlated with the same measure for either children ($r = .67$) or non-elderly adults ($r = .59$). However, post-tax, post-transfer poverty rates for children and non-elderly adults are quite highly correlated ($r = .89$), with the relationship particularly strong where poverty is concentrated among families with large numbers of children.[3] Working-age adults and children experience similar risks of poverty and receive similar degrees of protection from the welfare state, while the elderly are often in a category all their own. Using elderly and non-elderly as our basic age categories also responds to the practical demands of working with social expenditure data. While in most countries social benefits are paid directly to elderly persons and not to their adult children, transfers intended for children (e.g., child allowances, day care subsidies, funds for school fees or books) are always given to the parents and are considered part of the parent's income, not the child's.

---

[3] Poverty rates are the percentage of individuals in each age group living in households with size-adjusted disposable income (after taxes and transfers) below 50 percent of the country median. Author's calculations from Luxembourg Income Study data.

Table 2.1 *Public spending on the elderly, per person aged 65+, as a percentage of GDP per capita*

Australia	37.0
Japan	44.5
Portugal	45.0
Canada	45.2
United Kingdom	46.5
Ireland	46.8
United States	49.5
Norway	58.4
New Zealand	58.8
Spain	60.7
Denmark	61.5
Sweden	62.3
Belgium	63.8
Netherlands	65.6
Finland	70.2
Germany	70.7
Greece	74.0
France	84.1
Italy	90.4
Austria	91.4

Sources: Spending data from OECD 2004; GDP and demographic data from OECD 2003b.

The Age Orientation of Direct Social Expenditures

The distribution of spending on social programs providing cash benefits and services for different age groups in the population is the most basic measure of the age orientation of a country's social policies, and also the easiest measure to construct. For a few categories of direct expenditures (notably, disability benefits, health care, and housing) the age orientation of spending is not immediately apparent. But a wide range of cash benefits and social services do have obvious age orientations. Spending on services for the elderly and pensions for old age and survivors constitutes the core of elderly-oriented social spending. Spending on unemployment benefits and active labor market policies, as well as occupational injury and sickness programs, are the core benefits aimed specifically at working-age adults. Family allowances, services for families (e.g., child care), and education are the main items geared toward children.

Tables 2.1 through 2.6 illustrate the relative importance accorded to elderly-oriented, worker-oriented, and child-oriented social spending in

21

Table 2.2 *Public spending on unemployment and active labor market policies, per registered unemployed, as a percentage of GDP per capita*

Sweden	170
Denmark	144
Netherlands	122
Finland	91.3
Belgium	88.7
Norway	82.6
Austria	77.9
Ireland	76.5
Germany	71.0
New Zealand	70.1
France	64.2
Canada	46.1
Portugal	45.5
Australia	43.6
Spain	38.9
Italy	37.5
United Kingdom	35.8
Japan	34.4
Greece	21.0
United States	20.9

Sources: Expenditure data from OECD 2004; GDP and unemployment data from OECD 2003b.

Table 2.3 *Public spending on occupational injury and sickness programs per member of the civilian labor force, as a percentage of GDP per capita*

Sweden	4.31
New Zealand	3.98
Netherlands	3.79
Ireland	3.26
France	2.27
Germany	1.62
United States	0.65
United Kingdom	0.65
Japan	0.51

Sources: Expenditure data from OECD 2004; GDP data from OECD 2003b; labor force data from OECD, *Labour Force Statistics.*

Table 2.4 *Public spending on cash benefits and services for families, per person under 15, as a percentage of GDP per capita*

Sweden	22.9
Denmark	19.4
Finland	18.0
Austria	17.7
Norway	16.5
Belgium	13.0
France	12.9
Germany	12.0
United Kingdom	11.8
New Zealand	10.2
Australia	8.92
Netherlands	8.44
Greece	7.16
Ireland	6.47
Italy	5.46
Portugal	4.72
Canada	3.41
Japan	2.43
United States	2.43
Spain	1.64

Sources: Expenditure data from OECD 2004; demographic and GDP data from OECD 2003b.

different countries. Total expenditures in each category are adjusted for the size of the beneficiary pool and expressed as a percentage of the nation's per capita gross domestic product (GDP). These figures are then averaged over the period 1985–2000.[4] Data aggregated across time of course obscure the dynamics of welfare state change during a period when many regimes were subject to reform and retrenchment. But period averages remain useful for visualizing the basic parameters of spending on different age groups.

Per capita direct public expenditures on the elderly (Table 2.1), in the form of services and pensions for retirees and survivors, vary from a low of 38 percent of GDP per capita in Australia to a high of 92 percent in Austria. Generally speaking, the public occupationalist pension systems of Continental Europe spend the most per person, while the low-spending welfare states of the English-speaking world and recent developers Japan

[4] The OECD Social Expenditure Database (OECD 2004) contains only spotty information on family policies and active labor market policies prior to 1985.

Table 2.5 *Public education spending, per person aged 0–20, as a percentage of GDP per capita (average 1985–2000)*

Denmark	33.4
Sweden	31.2
Norway	29.9
Canada	23.0
New Zealand	21.5
United Kingdom	19.2
Ireland	18.8
United States	17.2
Australia	17.2
Japan	15.9
Italy	11.6
Germany	11.3
Netherlands	9.31
Finland	4.69
France	3.41
Austria	1.83
Belgium	0.57
Spain	0.11
Portugal	0.11
Greece	0.04

Sources: Expenditure data from OECD 2003a; GDP and demographic data from OECD 2003b.

and Portugal spend the least on the elderly. Scandinavian welfare states, contrary to their reputation as big spenders, actually spend only moderately on the elderly on a per capita basis.

The key spending category for working-age adults, spending on active and passive labor market programs per registered unemployed person (Table 2.2), ranges from a high of well over one and a half times the GDP per capita in Denmark and Sweden to a low of just over 20 percent of GDP per capita in the United States and Greece. Standardizing aggregate unemployment expenditure figures by the number of registered unemployed, rather than by the number of unemployment insurance beneficiaries, allows for an estimate of the extension as well as the level of unemployment benefits. Countries that have high numbers of uninsured unemployed people (e.g., first-time job seekers) or that spend very little on unemployment benefits and active labor market policies will have low per capita spending, and vice versa.

Table 2.6 *Per capita health spending ratios*

Country (year)	Spending ratio (65+/0–64)	Source of health spending	Country (year)	Spending ratio (65+/0–64)	Source of health spending
U.S. (1987)	8.9	Public only	Finland (1990)	4.0	Public and private
Japan (1997)	4.9	Public only	Netherlands (1994)	3.9	Public and private
U.S. (1995)	4.6	Public and private	U.K. (1997)	3.4	Public and private
Ireland (1979)	4.5	Public only	France (1991)	3.0	Public and private
Canada (2000)	4.5	Public only	Sweden (1990)	2.8	Public and private
New Zealand (1998)	4.3	Public only	Germany (1994)	2.7	Public only
Denmark (1983)	4.1	Public only	Italy (1983)	2.2	Public only
Australia (1989)	4.0	Public and private	Portugal (1993)	1.7	Public and private

Sources: OECD 1998; 2003b; U.S. "public only" figure calculated from Waldo, Sonnerfeld, MacKusick, and Arnett 1989.

Labor market supports may of course be targeted at quite different age groups across countries and across time. For example, in 1996 Germany introduced an extension of unemployment benefits for workers transitioning into retirement, while at the same time reducing the period of eligibility for younger workers. OECD figures on active labor market policy spending include outlays for early retirement "for labor market reasons," as well as youth job training programs. A detailed survey of the beneficiaries of labor market policies could be undertaken in order to "allocate" spending to categories of older and younger workers (chapter 5 undertakes such a study for Italy and the Netherlands). For the present, it is enough to note that countries vary widely in their average generosity toward the unemployed, even taking into account programs that do not find their way into comparisons of the replacement rates of standard unemployment insurance benefits.

The Scandinavian countries resume their accustomed position as welfare leaders when we turn to labor market policy spending directed toward working-age adults. But the Nordic countries are not alone in allocating resources generously to the unemployed; the Netherlands and Belgium are also among the top five in this regard. Ireland, New Zealand, and Canada belie their reputation as residualist Anglo-Saxon welfare states, appearing squarely in the middle of the pack on labor market spending per unemployed person. Spain, Italy, and Greece, which spend lavishly on programs for the elderly, have among the least generous welfare states for the unemployed. The data for occupational health and safety expenditures (Table 2.3) are spottier, but display a similar pattern.

Direct expenditures on benefits for families with children (Table 2.4) – child allowances and services such as child care, public summer camps, or mothers' aides – follow a pattern similar to benefits geared toward participants in the labor market. (The main exceptions are Canada and the Netherlands, which rank substantially lower on spending per child than they do on labor market policy spending, and Australia, which ranks higher.) The overall similarity in the country rankings for spending on labor market supports and on families is perhaps surprising. There is no inherent link between the two types of policies other than the fact that they are both aimed at non-elderly beneficiaries. Perhaps one could make the case that spending on children is a form of labor market support if it allows women to enter the work force, as in Sweden and Norway. Yet some of the welfare states of Continental Europe not renowned for their efforts to support female labor force participation nevertheless spend quite generously on families with children. Spending on families with working-age heads, both with and without children, seems to follow similar patterns, which quite evidently differ from the pattern of spending on the elderly.

But not all direct public spending on families with children comes through the paradigmatic social insurance institutions of the welfare state. Education spending, which is often ignored in comparative studies of the welfare state, undoubtedly "counts" as social spending, albeit of a different kind, and is clearly focused on the non-elderly. Table 2.5 shows public expenditures on primary, secondary, and tertiary education per school-age person, as a percentage of GDP per capita, averaged over the period 1992–8.[5] Perhaps even more than is the case for social insurance programs, it is difficult to know whether public spending on school construction, teachers' salaries, or high-end scientific equipment is really a good measure of how much education is being provided to a nation's children and young adults. In the United States, for example, education spending is

[5] These are the years for which cross-national and cross-time comparable data are available from the OECD.

concentrated at the tertiary level, reflecting a strong emphasis on research technology rather than on teachers and classrooms for primary and secondary school students. Caution in interpreting these data is clearly required. Still, the figures for per capita education spending highlight the general tendency for countries that are elderly-oriented in the field of social insurance to spend relatively little on the non-elderly in the form of education, and vice versa.

Health spending, like education spending, is a very large component of social spending in OECD countries, ranging from 20 to 40 percent of total social spending, or around 5 to 8 percent of GDP in 1998 (OECD 2003b).[6] Health spending per capita on the elderly and non-elderly, like social insurance and education spending, varies in important ways across countries. While in some countries providing an adequate standard of care to children and pregnant women is the most basic test of the health system, elsewhere either health benefits are not publicly provided at all to non-poor, non-elderly citizens or access to specific benefits varies by age group. In still other countries, where health care is a universal benefit, in practice rationing may lead to unequal emphases on treatment for elderly and non-elderly patients.

What is an appropriate age-sensitive measure of public health spending? The OECD has collected from many of its member countries statistics on health care spending by age group (see Table 2.6). It bears emphasizing, however, that these statistics are incomplete, widely disparate in terms of the years and populations covered, and in some cases include private as well as public health spending. For those countries where the per capita spending ratio reported by the OECD includes both public and private health spending, we can make the simplifying assumption that per capita health spending ratios by age groups are the same in both the public and private health sectors. Because private health expenditures are a very small portion of the total in most countries, this assumption is in most cases unproblematic. In the United States, where private health spending is important and serves a younger population than do the publicly provided Medicare and Medicaid programs, per capita spending ratios for both public only and public and private health expenditures are shown.

While per capita health expenditures on elderly and non-elderly groups continue to highlight the United States and Japan as among the most

---

[6] Note that with the exception of this paragraph, I use the term "total" social expenditures throughout this book to refer only to nonhealth expenditures.

elderly-biased countries, Italy appears dramatically more youth-oriented in its health spending than in other areas of the welfare system. France and Germany also seem to be more youth-oriented than one might have guessed based on the social insurance expenditure data. The Scandinavian countries, on the other hand, give more emphasis than expected to older patients. Given the diversity of measurement techniques and sources used in deriving the health spending ratios, and the problematic nature of health spending as a measure of health care emphasis for different age groups (Meyer and Moon 1988), how seriously should one take the per capita health spending ratio as a measure of the age orientation of health policy?

Some support for the measure is provided by the observation that the very low figures observed for Italy and Portugal correspond to a known property of Southern European welfare states: universalist health systems counter the fragmentation and stratification characteristic of other areas of social provision in these systems (Ferrera 1996c; Gough 1996).[7] One need not rely solely on the per capita health spending ratio as a measure of age orientation in health policy, though. Changes in infant mortality rates can be used to evaluate whether the per capita health spending ratio reflects real differences in the distribution of health resources to elderly and non-elderly populations. Infant mortality is sensitive to levels of prenatal care and health status of pregnant women. If changes in infant mortality are inversely related to per capita health spending ratios, we can be more confident in the validity of the health spending ratio as a measure of age orientation of health policy. In fact, when controlling for the wealth of a nation, a lower per capita health spending ratio (i.e., more spending on the non-elderly relative to the elderly) is strongly associated with declines in infant mortality.[8]

[7] On the other hand, recent changes to the Italian health system exempt elderly people, regardless of income, from many co-payments. This suggests that even within an exceptionally age-neutral health subsystem there may be pressures toward conformity with the overall elderly bias of social provision in Italy.

[8] GDP per capita is used as an instrument for the level of infant mortality at the start of the period under study. Results of the OLS regression with percentage change in infant mortality 1985–98 as the dependent variable are as follows:

	Coefficient	Standard error
Constant	−8.936	1.238
Health spending ratio	0.898	0.251
GDP per capita, 1985 (millions $US PPP)	0.110	0.099

This result lends credence to the claim that per capita health spending ratios are a good measure of the emphasis of different welfare states on health care for elderly and non-elderly populations. It further suggests that case studies of the development of health programs may be useful in illuminating the causal processes behind the development of particular age orientations in social policy regimes: health policies in Southern European countries may well be exceptions that prove the rule when compared with other kinds of social programs.

Summarizing the Age Orientation of Direct Expenditures

So far we have considered the relative generosity of direct public expenditures for a variety of social needs – income supports and services for the elderly, the unemployed, and families with children, as well as education and health care – in OECD countries. And we have detected some evidence that across different policy areas, countries are consistent in the way that they allocate resources to different age groups in their populations. Clearly, some countries spend more on services and others more on cash benefits; some more on active labor market policies and others more on unemployment benefits; some try to ensure equality of access via education, some through the labor market; and others equality of outcome via income supports. Among those countries that spend a lot on their non-elderly populations, some allocate more resources to children and others to working-age adults. Leaving aside these finer distinctions, however, a global measure of the age orientation of all direct social spending can give us valuable information about policy priorities with regard to different age groups in different countries. Such a measure based on direct expenditures, if it is consistent with what we know about how other policy instruments treat different age groups, also offers a highly tractable way to analyze the age orientation of welfare states.

Let us construct a measure that is a summary comparison of public social insurance expenditures on the elderly (aged 65+ or in formal retirement) and expenditures on the non-elderly (children and adults aged 0–64 and not in formal retirement). We can call this measure the Elderly/Non-elderly Spending Ratio, or ENSR. Several types of direct expenditures must unfortunately be excluded from this measure. The largest is cash benefits for the disabled, which accounts for between 2 and 11 percent of direct social expenditures excluding health care in OECD countries (OECD 2003b).

Table 2.7 *Elderly/non-elderly spending ratio (ENSR) (average 1985–2000)*

Denmark	5.75
Sweden	6.50
Ireland	7.11
Belgium	8.32
Finland	8.86
Australia	9.29
Norway	9.89
Netherlands	10.2
United Kingdom	10.4
New Zealand	11.4
France	12.9
Canada	14.0
Spain	15.7
Germany	16.0
Austria	17.4
Portugal	18.6
Greece	24.7
Italy	28.9
United States	38.5
Japan	42.3

Sources: Spending data from OECD 2004; demographic data from OECD 2003b.

Disability pensions are converted into retirement pensions upon reaching the retirement age in some countries, which means that virtually 100 percent of this category could be safely designated as non-elderly spending. But in other countries disability pensions can be cumulated with retirement pensions, complicating our accounting. Similarly, in most countries it is not possible to track the age of beneficiaries of social transfers for housing. Cash benefits are probably one of the least important determinants of housing outcomes, though, so we consider housing policy separately from direct social expenditures. Finally, a paucity of reliable data on occupational injury and sickness spending as well as public health spending leads us to exclude these categories from the ENSR. Given the difficulties in interpreting aggregate public education spending, it seems wise to compare a measure that does not include it with one that does.

Table 2.7 shows values of the ENSR for twenty OECD countries, averaged over the years 1985 through 1998. Non-elderly expenditures include payments for unemployment benefits (including early retirement for labor market reasons), active labor market policies, family cash benefits, and services for families. Elderly expenditures are those for old-age pensions (including early retirement for non–labor market reasons), survivors' pensions, and services for the elderly and disabled (primarily nursing homes). Spending on the elderly is divided by the number in the population aged 65 or more; spending for families with children and spending on active and passive labor market policies are divided by the population aged less than 65.

The numerical values for the ENSR represent, in a strict sense, a spending ratio. But it is inadvisable to conclude from the ENSR that, for example, the United States spent almost forty times as much on the elderly as on the non-elderly on a per capita basis, while Denmark spent only five times as much. In the first place, this basic measure is not a complete survey of expenditures in all areas. Second, while almost all elderly people living in OECD countries have access to some form of public pension, not all persons under age 65 are, at any given time, receiving benefits such as child allowances or unemployment insurance.[9] Furthermore, the value to the individuals concerned of different types of payments may not be captured by the magnitude of spending. Supports for children and working-age adults typically aim to supplement market incomes or replace them for a short period of time. All other things being equal, we would not expect them to be as costly on aggregate as old-age pensions, which provide a year-round replacement for market income.

Incorporating per capita education spending figures into the basic ENSR, as in Table 2.8, reduces both the levels and the variation across countries considerably from the basic ENSR. Education spending is large enough to buffer the effects of other social spending even for the countries that spend least on their schools. The major shift in ENSR rankings after including education spending occurs in Japan, which seems to spend heavily enough on education to modify its strong elderly orientation in the field of social insurance.

Raw per capita spending on different categories of beneficiaries such as the elderly or the unemployed, the ratio of health spending on different age groups, the basic ENSR, and the ENSR with per capita education

---

[9] An alternative measure using the number of children and the unemployed as the divisor for non-elderly expenditures can be constructed, but it is more difficult to interpret and does not yield significantly different results. Only Austria ranks significantly differently (less elderly-oriented) using this measure.

Table 2.8 *ENSR with education spending
(average 1985–2000)*

Denmark	0.32
Ireland	0.40
Netherlands	0.40
Sweden	0.44
Norway	0.44
Australia	0.53
New Zealand	0.56
Belgium	0.65
Canada	0.70
Finland	0.72
Germany	0.75
United Kingdom	0.76
Japan	0.83
Portugal	0.87
Austria	0.97
France	1.07
United States	1.24
Italy	1.66
Spain	1.72
Greece	2.53

Sources: Expenditure data from OECD 2003a; 2004;
demographic data from OECD 2003b.

expenditures all present slightly different views of the variety of social policy orientations across OECD countries, through the lens of direct expenditures. Those countries clustered at the middle of the spectrum on the basic ENSR measure seem to employ different combinations of policies in order to attain a generally age-balanced policy profile. However, with the possible exception of health care, these measures of different policy expenditure combinations generally point toward the same conclusions: Italy, Greece, the United States, and Japan are heavily elderly-oriented countries, with Spain, Portugal, and Austria not far behind in most respects. On the other hand, the Netherlands, the Scandinavian countries, and some of the Anglo-Saxon world (the United Kingdom, Ireland, Canada, and New Zealand) provide a more balanced repertoire of direct social services and benefits to different age groups in the population.

It is worth emphasizing once again that the age orientation of social spending does not seem to correspond with typologies of welfare states based either on welfare state "effort" (the level of aggregate social spending) or welfare state "worlds." High-spending countries may be either elderly-oriented (Italy) or quite youth-oriented (the United Kingdom); low-spending countries may also be elderly-oriented (the United States) or youth-oriented (Australia). Most strikingly, many of Esping-Andersen's Liberal countries, which score low on his decommodification index because of the presence of means-tested benefits, are as youth-oriented as the truly universalist countries of Scandinavia. High spending and even the decommodifying power of the welfare state do not then divide the youth-oriented from the elderly-oriented welfare states. Rather, the age-orientation of the welfare state depends on the target of social spending, on *who* gets decommodified.

Refining the Measure: Taxes and the "Hidden Welfare State"

Direct expenditures on welfare goods tell one story about the extent to which different age groups benefit from current social programs. But social policy is made up of more than direct welfare expenditures (Howard 1997). Tax systems both effectively reduce social spending, through taxes on cash benefits, and increase it, through tax expenditures on major social programs. The distributive effects of specific tax policies are notoriously difficult to interpret, which is of course one reason why they play such a prominent role in social policy. Good household-level tax and transfer data would be the most efficient and probably the most accurate way of determining the comprehensive tax-benefit position of different kinds of families. However, even the most rigorously standardized comparative micro-data sets[10] contain limited (and not terribly reliable) information on taxes paid by households. Until better household-level data become available, aggregate tax expenditure data provide the best estimates available of the age orientation of tax policies.

Very significant perils confront those analysts who would compare tax expenditure data across countries and across policy areas within a given country (Adema, Pearson, Einerhard, et al. 1997). Adema et al. provide some of the only truly comparable data on tax expenditures on social welfare programs in OECD countries, reported here in Table 2.9. Of the six nations included in their study, only the United States and the United Kingdom

---

[10] The Luxembourg Income Study project and European Community Household Panel are two sources of pre- and post-tax household income for OECD countries.

33

Table 2.9 *Social-fiscal measures as a percentage of GDP, 1993*

Country	Total social-fiscal measures (% of GDP)	Direct social expenditures (% of GDP)	Direct taxes and social contributions paid on transfer income	Social-fiscal measures on old-age benefits (% of GDP)
Denmark	0.08	30.5	3.91	0.08
Germany	0.86	28.7	2.57	0.08
Netherlands	0.76	30.6	5.86	0.68
Sweden	0.20	38.3	5.31	0.20
U.K.	3.03	23.4	0.19	2.68
U.S. (federal level only)	2.00	15.0	0.08	0.85

Source: Adema et al. 1997.

have tax expenditures on social policy that are significant compared with the magnitude of direct social expenditures. This is true even taking into account the effective reduction in direct expenditures due to direct taxation of social benefits, which can amount to around 3 to 6 percent in Northern European countries. For example, even after tax clawbacks on income such as pensions and unemployment insurance, Germany still spends roughly 26 percent of GDP on direct spending for social programs, as compared with less than 1 percent on indirect spending (tax expenditures).

Happily, the countries where tax expenditures on social policy *are* significant compared with direct expenditures report quite comprehensively on tax expenditures. As a result, it is possible to confirm whether the social policy delivered through taxation mechanisms in these countries has the same general age orientation as policy carried out through direct expenditures. Despite the risks inherent in comparing tax expenditure data across different policy areas and different countries, it is worth examining the tax expenditure figures for those countries where they may be expected to play a large part in social policy: the United States, the United Kingdom, Canada, and Australia. How much goes to the elderly in the form of tax expenditures on private pensions or special health insurance programs?[11] How much do

---

[11] Classifying all tax expenditures on private pensions as an elderly expenditure is admittedly somewhat arbitrary, since the age of the average beneficiary will depend on whether the tax relief is granted at the time of the payment into the pension plan or at the time of liquidation of the pension. Since most countries do both, it is very difficult to judge which is the most reasonable assumption on balance. For the sake of consistency, I choose to

Table 2.10 *Tax expenditures on the elderly and non-elderly (billions of national currency)*

| Country | | Tax expenditures on: | | | |
	Old age	Unemployment, labor market	Education	Family allowances, child care	ENSR for tax expenditures
U.S. (1995)	89,885	7,245	2,785	8,735	4.79
U.K. (1993–4)	18,120	3,500	550	1,450	3.29
Canada (1992)	17,390	4,471	954	2,945	2.08
Australia (1993–4)	46,423	1,530	21	182	26.8

Source: OECD 1996.

families and young people gain from tax exemptions on unemployment benefits, child care, or family allowances? Table 2.10 allows for some very tentative judgments along these lines.

Adema et al.'s data on tax expenditures in the United States, United Kingdom, Canada, and Australia provide an interesting complement to the direct-expenditure measures of the age orientation of social policy in these Liberal welfare states. Australia saw a sharp decrease in the share of *direct* public expenditures devoted to the elderly following privatization of its public pension system in 1986. The data in Table 2.10, which reveal a very large imbalance in favor of the elderly in *indirect* social benefits, indicate that the overall balance between age groups may not have changed all that much in Australia since 1986. Rather, subsidization of the elderly seems to be increasingly undertaken through the tax system, while support for the non-elderly continues to flow through direct expenditures. A time series in tax expenditures dating from before the pension reform would be invaluable in confirming or refuting this possibility.

If the relative youth orientation of the Australian system may be explained away by the continued presence of policy aids for the elderly in the form of tax benefits, the opposite seems to be true of Britain. Britain in 1993 reported tax expenditures on social policy on the order of 3 percent of GDP, while its direct social expenditures were around 23 percent of GDP. So the relatively youth-oriented social policy orientation indicated by the ENSR for direct expenditures in the United Kingdom is not canceled

---

classify tax expenditures on private pensions as elderly-oriented, but it is well to keep in mind that these tax expenditures may also have an immediate impact on the disposable income of non-elderly persons.

35

out, as in Australia, by large tax expenditures that heavily favor the elderly. While it is true that subsidies for private pensions make up the lion's share of tax expenditures in Britain, the disparity between elderly-targeted and youth-targeted tax expenditures is not nearly so great as in Australia. In Britain there are significant tax expenditures on items of interest to the non-elderly, particularly in the area of labor market supports. A similar pattern may be observed in Canada, where, as O'Higgins (1988) observes, the rather average social policy emphasis on young people in the sphere of direct expenditures is countered by generous tax policies in the area of labor market supports and family allowances.

Scholarship on tax expenditures in the United States (Longman 1987; Howard 1997) tends to confirm O'Higgins's assertion that tax expenditures do not tell a significantly different story from direct expenditures. The introduction and expansion of the Earned Income Tax Credit has shifted the weight of tax policy in the United States somewhat away from the extreme elderly bias observable in both direct expenditures and the rest of the tax system. Still, the emphasis on the elderly in U.S. tax policy is strong, particularly in the fields of housing and private pensions, and certainly does not counterbalance the extreme elderly orientation of direct expenditures.

In sum, the best available information on tax expenditures for social policy points in the same direction as the information on direct expenditures. With the possible exception of Australia, which also had an ambiguous ranking based on the ENSR for direct expenditures, tax data confirm the relative age orientation of different welfare states derived from measures of direct expenditures alone.

Refining the Measure: Housing Policy Patterns and Outcomes

The final refinement of the measure of age orientation refers to the housing sector. As noted above, tax expenditures on housing and housing-related debt are, in most OECD countries, the largest tax expenditure on individuals. At the same time, direct public expenditures on housing are relatively meager. In fact, housing policy in OECD countries is carried out through a wide variety of policy instruments, ranging from local zoning regulations to intervention in credit markets to contractor and developer subsidies to land purchases to direct housing allowances to taxation of imputed rent. Since many of these policies work in opposite directions, it is difficult to develop a measure of the age orientation of housing policy based on regulations and statutes alone.

But housing policy is an important component of social welfare policy, both because of its direct effects on quality of life, and because of its implications for lifetime savings and attitudes toward other welfare programs (Kemeny 1980, 1981; Castles and Ferrera 1996). Most comparative welfare state researchers abandon the search for a comparative measure of housing policy, instead using a single quantitative measure of housing policy outcomes: aggregate levels of home ownership. This measure is problematic, however, for two reasons. First, and most obviously, aggregate home ownership statistics obscure differences in home ownership rates among different age groups in the population. Second, an emphasis on ownership rates alone ignores the extent to which home ownership is promoted as the most desired form of housing tenure.

Using housing tenure data from the Luxembourg Income Study (LIS), I evaluate how well governments live up to their stated housing goals, and how this varies across age groups in the population. I derive the country's housing policy goals from secondary literature (Boleat 1985; Balchin 1996) and from the responses of housing policy officials to a survey conducted by the European Union (EU) on housing policy priorities (Dumon 1992). For some countries, the housing policy priority is to promote home ownership among the widest possible swath of the population. For others, the priority is to guarantee a minimum of fairness in the rental sector, either through direct public provision of rental housing or through protection of renters' rights in private markets. Table 2.11 shows the policy focus (home ownership vs. rental), overall home ownership rates (including cooperative housing), and the difference in home ownership rates among elderly (over 55-year-old) and young (25- to 34-year-old) adults, for those countries for which data were available.

What do these home ownership outcomes imply about housing policy inputs? I assume that home ownership rates among different age groups are determined by a range of housing policy inputs, including government regulation of credit markets and policies that increase the availability of low-cost homes for private ownership, increase the availability of low-interest and low-down-payment loans for first-time home buyers, and encourage home ownership through fiscal instruments targeted at lower income homeowners. These kinds of policies will increase levels of home ownership among young people, who tend to be asset-poor and income-poor relative

37

Table 2.11 *Housing policy orientations (late 1980s to early 1990s)*

	Policy focus	Aggregate home ownership rate	Elderly-youth difference in ownership rates		Policy focus	Aggregate home ownership rate	Elderly-youth difference in ownership rates
NET	Rent	33.7	3.60	LUX	Own	69.6	21.5
DEN	Rent	59.9	5.50	BEL	Own	68.8	21.8
SWE	Rent	57.7	6.10	FIN	Own	75.2	23.5
GER	Rent	42.8	15.6	CAN	Own	68.0	27.4
AUT	Rent	49.7	16.3	FRA	Own	59.1	33.7
				AUS	Own	73.9	33.9
				US	Own	66.7	37.7
				SPA	Own	72.2	41.1
				ITA	Own	59.1	41.8

Sources: Policy focus and aggregate home ownership: Balchin 1996; Dumon 1992; elderly-youth difference: author's calculations from LIS data (Wave IV).

to older people. These types of policies will thus tend to reduce the differences in relative levels of home ownership between the young and the old.

Table 2.11 reveals that countries with similar housing policy goals vary substantially in the degree to which these goals are achieved for different age groups. For example, among those countries where home ownership is not a stated priority, Austria and Germany stand out for the large differences in home ownership rates between younger and older populations. The Netherlands, Denmark, and Sweden, on the other hand, as in other areas of social policy, show more balanced results for different age groups. Among countries where home ownership *is* an explicit goal of housing policy, the United States, Spain, and Italy clearly have achieved that goal to a much greater extent for their elderly citizens than for young people. And although I was not able to calculate home ownership rates by age group for Japan, Boleat (1985, 403) reports a similar age variation in tenure: overall, 60 percent of Japanese households own their homes, while this is true for only 17 percent of households headed by persons under 29, and 46 percent of 30- to 49-year-olds. Belgium, Finland, and Canada show differences in ownership rates that probably reflect these countries' efforts to encourage home ownership among young people. Again, home ownership patterns support the picture painted by the basic ENSR: the United States, Austria, Japan,

Italy, and Spain tend to have among the most elderly-oriented housing policy regimes, while the Netherlands, Sweden, and Denmark have among the most age-neutral housing policies. Once again, Australia fits uneasily into the overall scheme, and we lack data for the United Kingdom, Ireland, and New Zealand that might help to confirm whether the age orientation of housing policy, as in direct expenditures, is a dimension that cuts across the traditional Liberal welfare state group.

Conclusion

This chapter has presented a variety of measures of the age orientation of social policy, based on direct expenditures, tax expenditures, and housing policy. While each measure presents a slightly different picture, taken together they reinforce one another. This triangulation of measures permits us to conclude with some confidence that countries do vary in the amount of emphasis they place on helping their elderly versus non-elderly populations through public social policies, and vary in consistent ways. In particular, we note that the most youth-oriented social policy regimes belong to the Scandinavian and British Commonwealth countries, while the most elderly-oriented countries are a more diverse group, encompassing parts of Continental Europe (Italy, Greece, Spain, Austria), the United States, and Japan. Furthermore, the ENSR measure based on direct expenditures alone appears to approximate rather well the age orientation of social policy more generally across countries.

O'Higgins (1988) identifies a generalized pattern in OECD countries of expansion of welfare benefits for families in the 1950s, with retrenchment in these areas and growth in the pension sector from the 1960s through the mid-1980s. His findings accord with Thomson's (1993) hypothesis that a "selfish generation" has captured welfare policy across the OECD, designing welfare states to meet the needs of their steadily aging cohort. However, the data presented here show much greater variety in social policy orientation than is suggested by O'Higgins or Thomson. While the elderly bias in some countries is indeed acute, in other countries younger age groups enjoy significant benefits – although whether this has occurred through the political action of age-based constituencies or as a result of other processes remains to be seen.

The remainder of this book focuses on identifying the causal processes that generate the diversity of public policy orientations toward different age groups that we have observed here. To what extent are differences in the age orientation of social policies the result of conscious policies designed to privilege certain age groups or generations over others? How much do these policy differences reflect societal attitudes about the relative neediness or deservingness of different age groups? Do they in fact spring from the interaction of political actors seeking to protect interests that are defined by age at all?

3

Age and the Welfare State

THEORIES AND HYPOTHESES

Chapter 2 revealed wide variation among industrialized countries in the relative emphases that governments place on social protection for elderly and non-elderly population groups. But the age orientation of social policies varies across countries in ways that are quite unexpected given what the scholarly literature on comparative social policy tells us about how welfare states develop. Esping-Andersen's (1990) three welfare regime types do not separate neatly into youth-oriented, elderly-oriented, and age-neutral welfare states, as we might expect. And basic country attributes such as aggregate levels of welfare spending or the size of the elderly population tell us even less about the probable age orientation of a given welfare state.

This chapter looks systematically at a variety of potential explanations for why the industrialized countries in this study display such different social policy age orientations. Scholars have called on a variety of structural, cultural, political, and institutional features of nation-states to explain divergent patterns of welfare state development. These existing theories about welfare state development were not designed explicitly to explain the age orientation of social policies. But, as we have seen, age orientation is a fundamental aspect of how welfare states redistribute resources, with consequences for labor and financial markets, family structures, fertility, and so on. So it is fair to expect that these classic explanatory paradigms should be able to account for this important aspect of what welfare states do and how they do it.

Yet existing paradigms do not perform well when confronted with the task of explaining variation in the age orientation of welfare states. And with good reason. The age structure of the population, ideologies about redistribution across the life course, and the political power of groups with age-related policy agendas fail to explain variation in the age orientation of

41

welfare states precisely because the age orientation of social policies is not, in fact, related to social structural, partisan, or institutional features that are in any straightforward way linked to age. Rather, the distinct age profiles of social policy regimes are a largely unintended consequence of how welfare state programs are structured, and how politicians typically compete within a party system. The second half of the chapter presents an alternative explanation for the variation in age profiles of social policy regimes, arguing that early choices about the structure of welfare programs combine with distinctive modes of political competition in different countries to account for the development over time of differing age orientations.

Classical Explanations for Variation in Welfare State Outcomes

The comparative political economy literature has elaborated a variety of explanations for why welfare states vary in their form and function, some of which could yield insights into the sources of cross-national variation in the age orientation of social policies. *Modernization* approaches identify economic and demographic "development" as the keys to understanding how much, and what, welfare states do. One subtype of this argument deserves special attention: the political impact of pensioner lobbies and elderly voters, "gray power," has been hypothesized to affect welfare state spending in important ways. Welfare state *familialism*, often linked to the preferences of Christian Democratic political actors, may also be related to the age orientation of social policies. *Power resources*, namely, the strength of class-based actors such as Social Democratic parties, unions, and employers, tell us a great deal about why welfare states vary along dimensions not related to age. To the extent that social spending on different age groups has equity implications, left power resources may also be important predictors of the age orientation of welfare states. Employer preferences, the subject of a current wave of scholarship in comparative political economy, may also explain why welfare states develop a particularly elderly-oriented or youth-oriented repertoire of social policies. Finally, *institutionalist* approaches that argue for the impact of constitutional structures, forms of interest intermediation, or state capacities all offer insights that could help explain why the age orientation of social policies varies from country to country.

Each of these classical approaches can add something to our understanding of why some countries devote the lion's share of their welfare resources to the elderly, while others focus more on the needs of working-age adults and children. A fuller explanation of the age orientation of welfare states, though, requires attention to both the political and institutional contexts within which political entrepreneurs forge links to potential constituencies of the welfare state. The second part of this chapter lays out such an explanation. First, let us consider how far classical welfare state theories can take us toward understanding why nations vary in the age orientation of their social spending.

Modernization

Developmentalist approaches to explaining the growth of the welfare state (see, e.g., Wilensky 1975; Flora and Heidenheimer 1981; Flora and Alber 1983; Flora 1986; Myles 1989) argue that the arrival of industrial society creates both new social needs and the resources with which to meet these needs. Of special relevance to the problem of understanding the age orientation of welfare states is the contention in many such accounts that industrial capitalism creates particularly pressing needs among the elderly, as it creates a new class of inactive elderly persons: retirees. This development in turn drives the expansion of benefits for the elderly. According to this logic, welfare states develop primarily to protect the elderly because the needs of the elderly are (1) the first to emerge on a large scale in industrialized society and (2) the most remote from the traditional concerns of care-giving institutions such as the family, poor laws, or private charity. Such assumptions are in fact echoed in policy discussions surrounding the implementation of pension schemes, where debate often focuses on the uniquely deserving character of the elderly or on the impracticality of relying on families to provide the necessary income support.

Welfare state policies do not, however, appear in practice to develop in response to a temporal primacy of the needs of elderly people. It is true that most industrialized countries adopted old-age insurance programs before either unemployment insurance or family allowances. But in most states the first public welfare benefits to be introduced were either poverty alleviation programs, targeted at children and adults as well as the elderly, or sickness and occupational injury insurance benefits for current workers (Flora and Alber 1981). Neither do benefits for the elderly come first in the sense of being a higher priority. If this were the case, we would expect countries with lower levels of aggregate welfare spending to be the most elderly-oriented, while only high-spending welfare states would be able to afford the "luxury" of youth-oriented social programs. However, elderly-oriented

43

countries with high levels of social spending as a percentage of GDP (e.g., Italy) coexist with small, youth-oriented welfare states (e.g., Ireland).

Gray Power

Even if there is no mechanical correspondence between economic and demographic development and elderly-oriented welfare spending, it still seems plausible that the age structure of populations could affect the direction of welfare state spending via the political power of the elderly. Some theorists argue that growing state spending on pensions is a result of the influence of *gray power*: large blocs of elderly voters with well-defined policy preferences. In one of the first quantitative cross-national studies of the welfare state, Wilensky (1975) argued that elderly populations influence the development of welfare state spending because large elderly populations create both a need for more welfare spending and a political constituency to fight for the allocation of resources. Pampel and Williamson (1989) likewise found that in democratic countries the "political pressure of a large aged population" is an important influence on spending. Thomson (1989) posited the aging of a politically powerful "welfare generation" as the driving force behind the growing emphasis of welfare states on programs for the elderly versus programs for children from the 1970s onward.

More recently, Pierson (1994) and Campbell (2003) examine the impact of the elderly on welfare state retrenchment. Both argue that policy legacies shape the interests and capacities of elderly constituencies of the welfare state, and in so doing constrain subsequent policy making. Pierson specifies a set of micro-foundations underlying his argument about policy legacies. Voters exhibit a powerful negativity bias, fighting retrenchment of "their" programs at almost any cost; and politicians use strategies of blame avoidance to get around the resistance of constituencies to policy retrenchment. These micro-foundations suggest that the preferences of numerous and highly motivated elderly voters regarding pension programs lie at the heart of the politics of welfare reform.

But gray power still falls far short of predicting when, where, and why one might observe a bias toward the elderly or the young in welfare spending. If the size of the elderly population, and thus its electoral strength, were a good predictor of the age orientation of social spending, we would expect to see all countries becoming more elderly-oriented with the passage of time. But analysis of spending data over time reveals that nine of the twenty countries

Theories and Hypotheses

Table 3.1 *Percent change in ENSR, 1960–2000*

Country	Percent change since 1960
Finland	−80
Australia	−70
Portugal	−58
Denmark	−56
Austria	−53
New Zealand	−52
Ireland	−32
Germany	−20
Netherlands	−6
Greece	17
France	23
Italy	42
Sweden	49
Spain	50
Norway	76
Belgium	86
United Kingdom	92
United States	104
Canada	116
Japan	799

Notes: The reference period for Portugal is 1977–2000; Greece 1962–2000; Spain 1967–2000; Belgium and U.S. 1960–99; U.K. 1960–98; and Japan 1970–2000.

Sources: Spending data: OECD 2004; demographic data: OECD 2003b.

in this study have in fact become *more* youth-oriented between 1980 and 2000 (see Table 3.1).

Why does the gray power hypothesis fall so far short of the expectations generated in the literature on comparative welfare state spending? The first reason is an almost trivial one: there is no general agreement on what kind of welfare spending the elderly should, let alone do, prefer. Wilensky (1975) and Pampel and Williamson (1989) originally surmised that the elderly would favor elderly-oriented spending. But in 1990 Wilensky reversed himself, asserting that elderly voters are in fact more altruistic in their policy preferences and are naturally inclined to support state subsidies for families with children (Wilensky 1990). By 1993 Williamson and Pampel were likewise less convinced that the elderly would support more pension spending in all political contexts. The disagreement about what the elderly want could be resolved empirically, but the existing literature on this subject is rather thin outside the United States.

A second problem with the gray power approach is less trivial. It assumes that voters know what they want and communicate their desires upward to politicians, who then act on their constituencies' policy preferences. Pierson's (1994) work, for example, casts doubt on this model, but ultimately does not reject it. Pierson has a persuasive account of how policy feedback and politicians' behavior affect voters' behavior. He emphasizes both the demobilizing effects of politicians' efforts to frame policy changes in a positive light and the capacity of earlier policy decisions to shape how welfare state beneficiaries organize themselves politically. But Pierson remains tied to a view of political preference formation in which, at any given time, the beneficiary/voter takes stock of a full range of policy options and expresses a preference, and it is once again up to the politicians to dissuade, dissemble, and deceive the voters into accepting retrenchment.

A well-established literature exists, however, indicating that policy preferences get their start among political leaders, and are only subsequently taken up by mass publics. Converse (1964) and Zaller (1992) make the strongest case for elite leadership of public opinion, but others (Arnold 1990; Gerber and Jackson 1993), too, argue that elites form opinions prior to their constituencies on at least some issues some of the time. Research on framing (e.g., Gilens 1999) and agenda-setting (e.g., Baumgartner and Jones 1993) further suggests that voters do not select their policy preferences from among a complete set of all plausible options, but rather take their cues about what is possible and desirable from politicians. The gray power approach forgets to ask what *politicians* want, how they communicate these preferences to the electorate, and how the electorate's choices are constrained by the shape of elite opinion and strategy.

Familialism

Modernization and gray power approaches focus on the politics of need: welfare states respond to new needs, especially among the elderly, in proportion to the level of need and/or the political power of those who are (or will be) in need. A different strand of research shifts the focus to the ability and propensity of other societal actors to provide for needs without recourse to public social programs. Recent scholarship suggests that deeply held societal values that are reflected in family structures and religious orientations can affect welfare state outcomes. Both family structures and religious doctrines could plausibly be held to shape the political positions of various actors when it comes to issues of intergenerational equity and the proper role of family versus state in caring for the needy at different stages in the life course. In particular, the dominance of Catholic social doctrine in some Continental European countries and the persistence of multigenerational family structures in Southern Europe and Japan have been set forth as explanations for the elderly-orientation of these welfare states.

Van Kersbergen (1995) argues that Christian social doctrine has distinctive effects on social policy outputs. On its face, the strength of Christian or Catholic social values in different countries is a weak explanation for variation in age orientation: Christian democratic countries such as Italy, the Netherlands, Belgium, Germany, Austria, and Portugal share a cause (Christian social doctrine) but vary widely on the effect (age orientation). Still, key tenets of Christian social doctrine, including a focus on families as the primary providers of social assistance, and on a family structure revolving around a male breadwinner, have been mustered to explain both very high child allowances and unemployment benefits in the Netherlands (Bussemaker 1992) and very low benefits for young people in Italy (Saraceno 1994). Given these conflicting claims, it seems wise to investigate the sources from which cultural ideas about appropriate care for different age groups are drawn. But even a close reading of the Catholic encyclicals most explicitly dedicated to the social policy issues, *Rerum novarum* (Leo XIII 1891) and *Quadragesimo anno* (Pius XI 1931), reveals no preference, explicit or implicit, for social provision for one age group over another. The empirical evidence that Christian or Catholic cultural values cause distinctive age orientations in social policies then seems rather thin.

The ideas contained in Christian social doctrine very likely do matter for welfare state outcomes, and even for the age orientation of welfare states. They may play an important role in informing the policy choices pursued by various political actors, including but not limited to Christian Democratic parties and Church lobbyists. However, the degree to which Catholic-dominated welfare states differ in their treatment of different age groups is striking. Thus, the influence of Catholic familialism on welfare state outcomes must be conceived of in terms of the variety of legitimating ideas about social policy that could plausibly be supported by Catholic doctrines, and the selection of ideas that eventually become influential in a given polity. In other words, if we wish to understand why Catholic countries have such different profiles of distribution across age groups, we must try to figure out why different tenets of social Catholicism are emphasized in different settings, and what are the pathways by which these values filter into the policy-making arena.

Other scholarship emphasizes the importance of family structures themselves for social policy outcomes (see Jurado and Naldini 1996). According to many observers of Southern European politics, in particular, the prevalence of multigenerational families and a pervasive familialist orientation in these countries accounts for the underdevelopment of public policies ranging from child care to social services to unemployment benefits. This argument could apply to the Japanese case as well, where multigenerational families are also relatively common.

It is certainly plausible that cohesive extended families engaging in extensive intrafamilial resource sharing make it possible for Southern European countries to sustain high levels of unemployment without falling prey to debilitating social conflict between labor market "insiders" (primarily older, male workers and pensioners) and "outsiders" (younger, female workers and the unemployed). It is far from clear, however, that family structures are the cause of limited benefits for working-age adults and children in Southern European countries, rather than the other way around. True, Southern European social policies rely on extended family structures to a greater extent than in other countries (Millar and Warman 1996; Naldini 2003). But, at least in the Italian case, this is a rather recent phenomenon. The tendency for social legislation to focus on the family as primary caregiver and source of income support is, according to Addis (1998) and Saraceno (1999 interview), a result of increasing demands and decreasing welfare state resources, rather than a result of the impact of a familialist culture.

Indeed, research in other areas of welfare state provision suggests exercising caution before drawing a direct causal link between extended family structures, on the one hand, and public policy outputs, on the other. Jurado (2002) demonstrates that the family structure most characteristic of Southern European societies, the long permanence of adult children in their parents' households, is caused by characteristics of housing and labor markets in Southern Europe, rather than by the socio-cultural features more commonly assumed to be the culprit. Similarly, research on public attitudes toward family policies in Italy reveals that respondents who agree most whole-heartedly with "traditional" family values are also those who are most supportive of strong state intervention on behalf of family values (Palomba 1995). Extended family structures and a Catholic culture emphasizing the subsidiarity principle – leaving the family to its own devices – are not enough to explain the relative paucity of state welfare provisions for younger people in Southern Europe.

Power Resources

Since the 1980s many of the most influential studies seeking to explain variations in welfare states' timing, size, structure, and performance have been grounded in the study of the political power of the working class and, more recently, employers. Power resources approaches argue that welfare state outcomes can be explained by the political strength of class-based political actors. In its more traditional formulation, the emphasis is on working-class actors alone (see Stephens 1979; Korpi 1983; Esping-Andersen 1985; Myles 1989). Highly developed welfare states that reduce income inequality are, in this account, the result of the political strength of representatives of the wage-earning classes, who use the political arena to combat market dynamics. More recent work in the power resources tradition highlights the importance of employers' preferences (Swenson 2002; Mares 2003) or of coalitions between working and middle classes (see Baldwin 1990; Esping-Andersen 1990), but shares with earlier analyses a focus on how the power of class-based actors affects policy outcomes.

Whether left power resources can adequately explain the observed variation in social policy age orientations is ultimately an empirical question. All other things being equal, we might expect working-class political actors not to prefer elderly-oriented social spending, which concentrates benefits on one group rather than spreading them in a more egalitarian fashion across the population. But in practice, the Left has often preferred programs that are highly decommodifying for older citizens but not younger ones, especially when the alternative is a welfare state that is equally mean toward all. Social programs linked to occupational performance tend to generate more elderly-oriented spending than citizenship-based programs do, and Social Democratic and union actors in some contexts *now* prefer universalist social policies to occupationalist ones. But there is no reason to think that political actors on the Left had this in mind when they advocated for particular program designs. In fact, there is ample evidence that the very nonoccupational welfare state structures that have over the course of the twentieth century matured into rather youth-oriented systems were imposed against the will of Social Democratic actors (see Baldwin 1990; Swenson 2002).

We can ask a similar set of questions about employers. What kinds of policies do they prefer? What would these policies imply for the age orientation of social spending? And did employers in fact get the policies they wanted? One hypothesis suggests that relatively youth-oriented policies in the small, open economies of Scandinavia, the Benelux countries, Austria, and Ireland are the result of employers' distinctive preferences for universalist social policies in these countries. While increasing economic openness within countries over time does not uniformly coincide with more youth-oriented social spending (see Fig. 3.1), it is worth exploring the possibility that there might be a causal connection between the preferences of employers in small, open economies and the age orientation of the social policies in these countries.

Employers' product-market strategies (Estevez-Abe, Iverson, and Soskice 2001) are collinear neither with economic openness nor with age orientation. But it seems plausible that employers in small, open economies might prefer universalistic, tax-financed social programs to occupationally based programs. The former would reduce employers' direct nonwage labor costs, while the latter would impose costs that employers could not pass on to consumers without decreasing their international competitiveness. Let us for a moment accept the premise that, on balance, employers in small, open economies will prefer citizenship-based social policies to occupational social insurance. Demonstrating that employers' preferences are responsible for the age orientation of welfare states in these countries then relies on showing that employers' preferences were decisive in both the decision to introduce citizenship-based social policies in the small, open economies around the turn of the twentieth century and the decision to introduce new universalistic programs in those countries that had occupational social insurance systems entering World War II.

The first of these two claims is plausible, at least for the Scandinavian countries. Export-oriented (agrarian) employers in Denmark, Sweden, and Finland seem to have preferred citizenship-based programs. And in alliance with Liberals, their policies won out over those of the Social Democrats, who advocated occupationally based benefits (Baldwin 1990, chapter 1; Kangas, in press). The second claim, that a shift to more universalistic social policies in some countries after the Second World War resulted from employers' preferences in these countries, is less tenable.

As Katzenstein remarks in his authoritative tract on the political economies of small states, "domestic compensation...responds primarily to the logic of domestic politics; it is not a deliberate response to

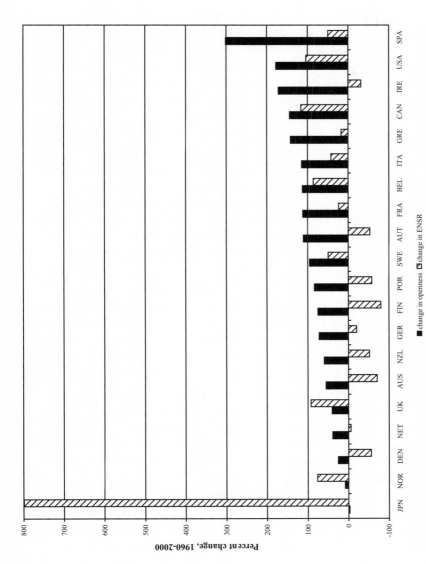

Figure 3.1 Change in economic openness and age orientation, 1960–2000. *Note:* Openness is ratio of exports plus imports to GDP. Germany openness is for 1970–2000; Greece ENSR is for 1970–2000; Japan ENSR is for 1962–2000; Portugal ENSR is for 1977–2000; Spain ENSR is for 1967–2000; UK ENSR is for 1970–2000; and U.S. and Belgium ENSR is for 1960–99. *Sources:* Openness: Heston, Summers, and Aten 2002; ENSR: spending data: OECD 2004; demographic data: OECD 2003b.

51

the logic of the international economy" (1985, 133–4). A shared open-ness to international markets certainly cannot explain why Austrian and Belgian employers might have preferred to compensate for economic open-ness via occupationalist welfare programs, while Scandinavian employers chose universalist ones earlier in the century. Furthermore, if Katzenstein is correct that employers in Belgium and Austria were more able than in Scandinavia to impose their demands on "a labor movement too weak to dictate its own terms" (173), it then follows that *occupationalist* pro-grams in Belgium and Austria are more plausibly the result of employers' preferences.

The genesis of the initial split between occupationalist and citizenship-based welfare states in the early twentieth century is less at issue here than the persistence of these institutional choices over the course of the next cen-tury. The claim that employers might have been responsible for the shape of social policies in small, open economies at the turn of the century tells us little about this persistence, which, as we shall see, is crucial to the even-tual age orientation of welfare states. It is possible that in some countries where citizenship-based social policies are of long standing (e.g., Sweden), employer interests, reaffirmed over the course of the twentieth century, locked these policies into place (for such an argument, see Swenson 2002). But the case studies of social policy development in the Netherlands in the post–World War II period (chapters 4 through 6) do not support the inter-pretation that employers' interests drove the transition from occupationalist to universalist policies in that particular small, open economy. Generalizing from either Sweden or the Netherlands to the effects of employers' pref-erences in all of the small, open economies seems risky in the absence of detailed cross-case historiographical evidence.

Regardless of whether the focus is on the working class or on employ-ers, the very logic of power resources analysis brings to the fore issues that are helpful in formulating alternative hypotheses. The power resources approach assumes that the policy preferences of class-based actors are deducible from their positions in the productive system. But the interests of wage earners and employers can be powerfully affected by a variety of other conditions. Mares (2001), for example, argues that employers' preferences about pension reform are conditional on the percentage of social expendi-tures currently allocated to pensions. It is reasonable to presume that savvy class representatives, like all good politicians, will advance policy demands that seem feasible and likely to produce desired results given the extant polit-ical and policy environment. Class interests in the abstract thus seem to be a poor predictor of the policy demands that are likely to emanate even from relatively homogenous class-based political actors.

Power resources approaches also tend to assume an unrealistic degree of homogeneity of interests within working-class-based organizations. This is especially relevant for the study of age-related spending priorities, since most working-class organizations encompass both older and younger workers. Parties and unions are cross-age coalitions, and as such may adopt contradictory or difference-minimizing positions on issues related to intergenerational distribution in an attempt to hold together overlapping class- and age-generated cleavages (see Anderson and Lynch 2003; Natali and Rhodes 2004). So even if we could deduce the age-related policy preferences of working-class organizations from their class origins (which seems unlikely), the internal dynamics and external environments of parties and unions would still affect the welfare policy positions that they advocate.

Institutions

Political institutions constitute one important aspect of the environment for class-based (and other) political actors. A range of political institutions, from neo-corporatist bargaining structures to electoral systems to judicial review, have been hypothesized to affect the development of welfare policies. Within the comparative social policy literature, attention has been focused on two main types of institutions: constitutional structures (so-called veto points) and neo-corporatist industrial relations.

The literature on constitutional structures (see, e.g., Imergut 1992; Huber, Ragin, and Stephens 1993) argues that features of a nation's formal institutional landscape can determine social policy outcomes by setting up rules of the game that favor certain political actors over others. The expected consequences of different constitutional structures for the age orientation of social policy regimes are not immediately clear. Still, there seems to be no a priori reason to reject the hypothesis that these sorts of institutions could matter. But such a static vision of institutions offers little hope for understanding why the age orientation of social policies changes over time within countries.

There is empirical support for the idea that neo-corporatist institutions may affect the age orientation of social spending (Pampel 1994). But the literature on corporatism and social policy makes bifurcated predictions about the consequences of incorporating organized interest groups directly into policy making. On the one hand, optimists (see, e.g., Katzenstein 1985;

Visser and Hemerijck 1997) view positively the capacity of corporatism to result in policies that are in the general interest, and thus not particularly oriented toward one age group or another. These authors predict that in the presence of corporatist institutions, social policies will be other-regarding, promoting equity across wide segments of the population and compensating societal losers. These beneficial results occur, according to these authors, because neo-corporatist policy-making processes enhance possibilities for trust, long-term engagement, and positive-sum games. Other analysts (e.g., Offe 1981; Olson 1982; Esping-Andersen 1996) express more pessimism about the policy outputs of corporatism. For these authors, corporatism can perniciously link the inherently rent-seeking behavior of organized interests to policy making. This results in public policies that protect labor's, employers', or welfare constituencies' interests narrowly defined, but that do little to advance equity, competitiveness, or long-term economic performance. This viewpoint suggests that corporatism may enhance the capacity of powerful elderly groups to pursue their own policy agendas on aging, to the detriment of other age groups in the population.

Quantitative studies of welfare state outcomes, including aggregate spending, spending in particular program areas, and income inequality, generally support the notion that corporatist institutions result in bigger, more egalitarian welfare states (see, e.g., Esping-Andersen 1990; Hicks and Swank 1992; Hicks and Misra 1993; Birchfield and Crepaz 1998; Crepaz 1998; Bradley, Huber, Moller, et al. 2001). Pampel (1994) even puts forth evidence suggesting that corporatism has a distinctive youth-oriented effect on welfare spending. But the measures of corporatism employed in quantitative cross-national studies leave a great deal to be desired. Scholars who have attempted to define and measure corporatism cross-nationally (see, e.g., Schmitter 1981; Wilensky 1981; Cameron 1984; Lehmbruch 1984; Crouch 1985) disagree about the core concepts that should be included in the term and their range of applicability, resulting in important differences in how different countries are scored from one measure to the next. And many welfare state scholars use measures that do not capture changes over time in the degree or kind of corporatism present in a particular country. Detailed process-tracing analyses of the kind presented in chapters 4 through 6 of this volume are necessary to understand the link between corporatist bargaining structures and the age orientation of social policies.

The Dutch and Italian case studies hint at some connections. In Italy, episodes of tripartite concertation seem to strengthen the hand of broad-based forces within the union movement that have little to lose and much to gain from reining in pension spending. This mechanism may be generalizable to other contexts (Anderson and Lynch 2003 propose such a model). However, more careful qualititative research is necessary to confirm whether either Pampel's (1994) model or Anderson and Lynch's fits the historical evolution of spending in the countries with universalist social policies.

The literatures on veto points and corporatism hold that formal institutions – in some cases constitutional provisions or laws, in other cases government-sponsored agreements ratified by trade union and employer organizations – affect the age orientation of welfare provisions by enhancing or reducing the bargaining power of particular political actors. A different strain of institutionalism focuses on less formal institutions and on the ways in which these institutions affect both the range of possible policies and the preferences of different political actors. An exemplary work in this vein is Orloff's *The Politics of Pensions* (1993). Orloff argues that three kinds of institutions are particularly important in shaping the development of pension policies in the United States, the United Kingdom, and Canada: state capacities, in particular the ability to tax; the mode of operation of political parties and bureaucracies, either patronage-oriented or programmatic; and feedback effects from earlier policy decisions. Orloff's argument is compelling and anticipates some of the most interesting insights regarding policy feedbacks from Pierson's (1994) work on welfare retrenchment in the United States and the United Kingdom. But it is highly contextualized and difficult to generalize. The core argument of this book concurs with Orloff's in important respects, including its focus on fiscal capacity and the modus operandi of political parties. However, it generalizes these results beyond pension policy, beyond the Anglo-Saxon countries, and beyond the early twentieth century, allowing us to see the results of particular institutional configurations for social policy outcomes in a wide variety of national settings. This book also takes up the gauntlet thrown down by Thelen (1999) and Pierson (2000), investigating closely how institutions reproduce themselves over time and, in so doing, create enduring social policy regimes.

A Path-Dependent Institutionalist Explanation

The remainder of this book argues that path-dependent political and social-policy institutions are the best explanation for the age orientation of welfare state spending. How social programs are organized (along citizenship or occupational lines) and how politicians compete with each other (programmatically or using particularistic appeals to groups of voters) are the key factors that determine patterns of social spending on different age groups. But how are these two factors related to one another, and ultimately to the age orientation of social spending?

To preview: at two critical junctures the welfare states of the industrialized democracies set out on trajectories toward divergent age orientations. From the first critical juncture, in the early twentieth century, two groups of countries emerge with welfare states that are organized according to radically different logics, either citizenship-based or occupationally based. These organizational forms mature into welfare states of different hues. Citizenship-based programs become more youth-oriented with the passage of time, while occupationalist programs contain within them the seeds of elderly-oriented social spending. But in order for these divergent age orientations to develop, countries must maintain their institutional setups well into the postwar period. At a second critical juncture, around the Second World War, the occupationalist camp divides into two further groups: one that maintains occupationally based family allowance and unemployment programs and one that replaces many of its prewar occupationalist programs with citizenship-based ones. This second parting of ways is explained and reinforced by the predominant mode of political competition in these countries, either programmatic or particularistic. The outlines of this argument are illustrated in the form of a branching tree in Figure 3.2.

The structure of core welfare state programs is clearly correlated with the age orientation of welfare states, for reasons that shall become clear shortly. Countries that have universal, citizenship-based provisions for old age, unemployment, and child rearing tend to be more youth-oriented. Quite surprisingly, this is true regardless of the overall size of the welfare state relative to GDP, regardless of whether programs are means-tested or not, and regardless of whether the basic citizenship-based benefit is supplemented by a public occupationalist tier. Occupationally based social programs, on the other hand, tend to generate elderly-oriented welfare states. But the structure of welfare programs is only a partial explanation for why some countries treat some age groups more generously than others. Understanding how the observed correlation between program structure and age orientation develops over time requires identifying the "reproduction mechanisms" (Thelen 1999) that reinforce the choice of program structure entered into at a particular critical juncture. Without this knowledge, we cannot understand why and how early choices about welfare state

56

Theories and Hypotheses

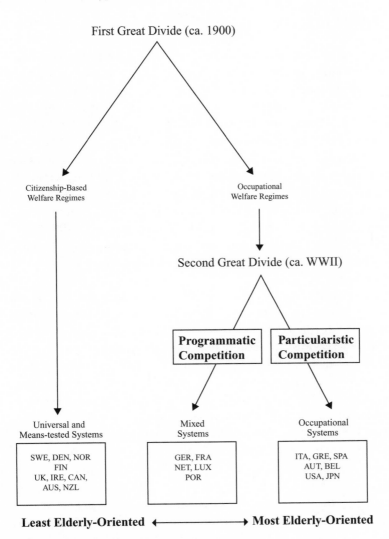

First Great Divide (ca. 1900)

Citizenship-Based
Welfare Regimes

Occupational
Welfare Regimes

Second Great Divide (ca. WWII)

**Programmatic
Competition**

**Particularistic
Competition**

Universal and
Means-tested Systems

SWE, DEN, NOR
FIN
UK, IRE, CAN,
AUS, NZL

Mixed
Systems

GER, FRA
NET, LUX
POR

Occupational
Systems

ITA, GRE, SPA
AUT, BEL
USA, JPN

Least Elderly-Oriented ←—————→ **Most Elderly-Oriented**

Figure 3.2 Watersheds of welfare state formation.

institutions play out over the long run to produce the age orientations we observe today. How political competition is organized in different countries helps to explain why occupational programs persist in some countries but not others – and in turn why some countries with similar welfare program structures in 1900 ended up with very different age orientations at the end of the century.

Citizenship-Based versus Occupational Programs

Let us begin with an assertion: that welfare regimes with occupationalist programs produce elderly-oriented social spending, while welfare regimes with citizenship-based programs produce social spending that favors the young.

We can think about welfare state regimes as lying along a continuum according to the structure of their main social programs. At one end of the continuum we find pure citizenship-based regimes. Here, welfare benefits may be either means-tested or truly universal, but in either case eligibility for these benefits is the same regardless of the person's job title, sector, or labor market status. All citizenship-based systems cover relatively young labor market "outsiders" such as mothers and children, which accounts in large part for their relative youth orientation. Universalist citizenship-based systems also provide protection for workers and pensioners, while means-tested systems typically leave labor-market insiders to procure insurance in the market.

On the other end of the spectrum are pure *occupational* regimes, in which eligibility for and/or the quality of a full spectrum of social benefits varies in accordance with a person's connection to the labor market. Occupational regimes are elderly-oriented because they focus on providing coverage for labor market "insiders." These current or former members of the core work force constitute an aging subpopulation, because of both the increasing difficulty of absorbing younger workers into well-protected sectors of the economy and the increasing lifespan of pensioners.

Figure 3.3 shows twenty welfare states divided into three groups based on the structure of their main pension, family allowance, and basic social assistance benefits in 1970: predominantly citizenship-based, predominantly occupational, or mixed.[1] Countries such as Sweden and the United Kingdom, which top off basic citizenship-based benefits with a much smaller occupational tier, are classified as citizenship-based. These countries are then ranked according to the mean age orientation of their social spending for the period 1985 to 1998. The relationship between welfare state structure and age orientation is clear: citizenship-based welfare regimes are more youth-oriented than occupationalist systems, while welfare states that substantially mix occupationalist and citizenship-based programs have intermediate age orientations as well.

[1] Information on benefits structures from MISSOC 1995; Palme 1990, 77; and Wennemo 1994, 99.

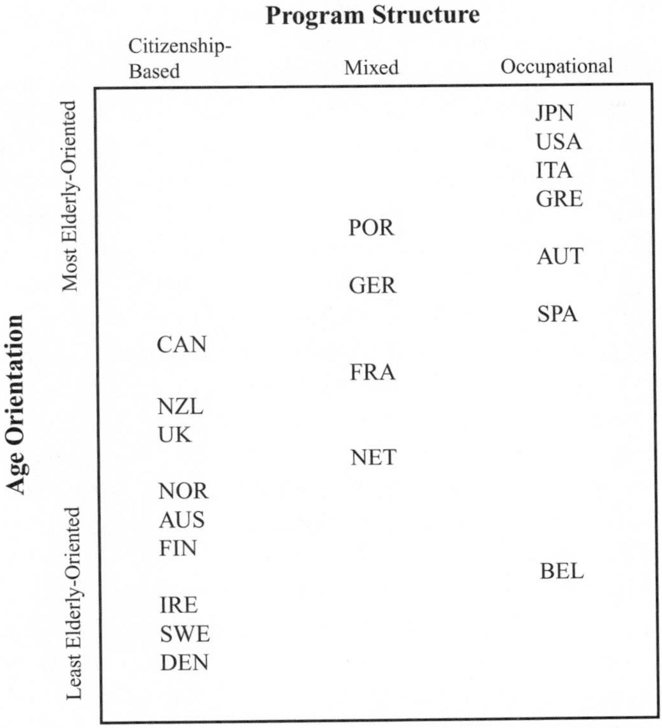

Program Structure

Figure 3.3   Age orientation and welfare state program structure.

The First Critical Juncture

How can we understand the development of this connection between occu-pationalism and pro-elderly spending, and vice versa? The late nineteenth and early twentieth centuries marked the beginning of a rapid phase of welfare state development in the countries of Europe, North America, and the British Commonwealth. There were two fundamentally different ways that welfare states grew up: along either citizenship or occupational lines. Accounting for the success of different organizational models in different countries is a task that has been undertaken elsewhere (see, esp., Baldwin 1990; Ferrera 1993; Manow 1997). Regardless of the precise process that is thought to generate it, these analyses highlight the same outcome: different kinds of welfare state programs that cover very different kinds of people. We can think about the different populations covered by occupationalist and citizenship-based regimes in terms of the distinction between labor market "insiders" and labor market "outsiders."

In citizenship-based systems, the core of the welfare state is made up of programs designed to complement, rather than replace, benefits provided by mutual associations for their members (policies such as old-age and invalidity pensions, unemployment insurance, or health insurance; Manow 1997). As a result, state welfare programs in citizenship-based regimes cover labor market outsiders: people with weak ties to unions and mutual organizations, such as children, abandoned mothers, or the indigent. For example, in the United Kingdom in 1910, outdoor relief (income maintenance programs for the poor of all ages) and noncontributory old-age pensions accounted for 84 percent of all public social welfare spending, while social insurance programs such as those for occupational accidents and disease accounted for only 16 percent, and there were no public provisions for unemployment insurance or occupational pensions (data from Ritter 1983). These work-related programs were instead provided by nonstate actors, namely, Britain's friendly societies.

By contrast, in occupationalist regimes the state takes over from mutualist organizations the job of protecting people with tight links to unions and the labor market: people with long-term, stable employment in insured sectors of the economy, as well as retired workers, people in between jobs, and people with job-related health problems. In other words, state welfare provision focuses on social insurance programs for labor market insiders. In Germany in 1910, for example, 52 percent of the labor force was enrolled in public occupational pensions, 51 percent in public occupationally linked health insurance, and 87 percent in public occupational injury insurance (data from Flora and Alber 1981). But basic social assistance and poverty alleviation were relegated to religious charities, municipalities, and, above all, families. The task of caring for labor market outsiders in occupationalist regimes falls to nonstate actors.

If citizenship-based regimes originated by providing state protection for labor market outsiders, and occupational regimes for labor market insiders, how does this affect the age orientation of these different types of welfare states today? To answer this question, we need to understand how the age composition of these insider and outsider groups changes as welfare states and private insurance markets matured over the course of the twentieth century.

In a schematic citizenship-based regime, beneficiaries of state-provided welfare programs are primarily labor market outsiders: people who do not receive benefits through union schemes, friendly societies, and the like. Because the supply of private old-age insurance was quite limited in the early twentieth century, most former workers fall into this outsider category and rely on the state (and their families) to protect them from poverty in old age. Thus, the majority of the labor market outsiders covered by the public welfare programs in citizenship-based regimes are elderly people who have ceased working. As a result, in the early twentieth century citizenship-based regimes tended to be quite elderly-oriented.

As markets for occupational pension insurance matured, however, more and more of the elderly became covered under employment-based pensions. One of the things that advanced industrial capitalism does rather well is look after retired workers – perhaps, as Myles (1989) argues, because it is in the interest of employers to move older people out of manufacturing jobs to make way for more productive younger workers. In any event, as more and more elderly people gain access to private employment-based pensions, fewer and fewer of them are left as outsiders to be cared for by the state. Once most of the elderly poor are removed from the outsider group, though, citizenship-based regimes become much more youth-oriented. The pool of labor market outsiders who constitute these regimes' core clients becomes dominated by young people: children, the long-term unemployed, single-parent families, and the like. As a result, by the latter part of the twentieth century, citizenship-based welfare regimes were quite youth-oriented.

The reverse transformation occurs in occupationalist welfare regimes. Unlike in citizenship-based regimes, these countries began the twentieth century with fairly youth-oriented welfare states. Social programs covered labor market insiders, leaving outsiders to be cared for by their families and by private and/or religious charities. But in the early twentieth century, as noted above, there were relatively few old people in the insider category that receives state protection, since employment-related old-age pensions were not yet fully developed. As employment-related pensions – which in occupationalist welfare states are publicly provided – grew, retired people became insiders. This means that occupationalist systems grew increasingly elderly-oriented over the course of the twentieth century as pension systems matured. In addition, the aging of the protected core work force has meant that in occupationalist systems, even public programs such as unemployment insurance or disability pensions that should benefit working-age people tend to be skewed toward older workers.

Occupationalist programs lead to more elderly spending, and citizenship-based programs lead to more spending on young people, despite the fact that in the early twentieth century these different types of systems had *opposite* age orientations. This is because as pension systems and labor markets develop and mature, the age structure of labor market insider and outsider groups changes. In interaction with dynamic changes in markets for labor and insurance, static welfare state institutions create a pattern of social policy spending that matures over time to result in the age orientations we observed in the 1990s.

The Second Critical Juncture

But how static are these welfare state institutions, really? Welfare state institutions are often characterized by policy feedback mechanisms that make them rather sticky (Weaver 1986; Pierson 1994). But they can and do change under certain circumstances. We can think about the first critical juncture, the initial choice between occupationalist and citizenship-based regimes in the early twentieth century, as setting countries off on one of two tracks of welfare state development. But an opportunity to switch tracks occurred in the period around the Great Depression and World War II. The 1930s and 1940s were a time of great institutional fluidity, when many advanced industrialized countries had an opportunity to re-evaluate and rebuild their welfare programs after the disasters of the 1920s and 1930s. Wartime conditions aggravated social problems, while in many countries a drive for national unity fostered during World War II contributed to a new push for national social programs. In addition, both public and private insurance programs had been bankrupted throughout much of Europe because of runaway inflation and wartime destruction of property. This presented occupationalist welfare states, in particular, with a prime opportunity to experiment with new forms of social protection.

In most European countries with occupational welfare states, governments commissioned official studies to investigate the feasibility of introducing universal, citizenship-based welfare programs along the lines of the Beveridge Plan in Britain. Such inquiries occurred in France, Belgium, the Netherlands, Austria, Germany, and Italy in the period between 1945 and 1948 (Ferrera 1993). Under the influence of the International Labour Organization (ILO) and policy lessons diffusing from Britain, some countries that before World War II had had purely occupational welfare systems adopted citizenship-based programs, beginning the process of switching tracks. But an equal number of occupationalist regimes stayed the course, despite the conclusions of government advisory panels that encouraged the adoption of British-style universal benefits. How can we explain this divergence in national trajectories after World War II, a divergence that, as we have seen, would have profound consequences for the age profile of welfare regimes?

Programmatic versus Particularistic Political Competition

The opposing slopes of this second watershed, the division between countries that stayed on the occupationalist track and those that began the switch toward the citizenship-based track, are characterized by different modes of political competition. The switchers were all countries where programmatic political competition prevailed, while the countries that did not adopt citizenship-based welfare programs in the 1930s through 1960s shared a particularistic mode of political competition that inhibited the development of substantial universal welfare programs. Clientelist politics and occupationalist welfare programs reinforced each other through a host of mechanisms, as we shall see. But first, let me clarify the distinction between the two modes of political competition.

The mode of political competition varies along a continuum ranging from programmatic to particularistic. *Programmatic competition* occurs when politicians and parties vie for votes by promising to enact policies that they argue will benefit society at large. This type of political competition is characterized by the relatively low degree of selectivity of the beneficiary groups (e.g., entire classes, rather than particular industries, neighborhoods, or ethnic groups). To the extent that policies are designed to benefit somewhat selective groups (e.g., the working class) rather than the public at large, they are justified with reference to coherent political ideologies. A variety of different labels – responsible party government, universalism – have been attached to this phenomenon. In Shefter's seminal work (1994, chapter 2), policy orientation is the polar opposite of patronage orientation. I reject this label because patronage-oriented politicians are no less concerned with policies; they simply care about policies for distributive rather than programmatic reasons.

At the other end of the spectrum of competitive strategies lie particularistic political practices ranging from log rolling, constituency service, and intensive interest group involvement in policy making to an out-and-out exchange of benefits for votes. Particularism occurs when politicians offer tangible benefits to selective groups of voters in return for their votes. Alternative labels for this phenomenon include clientelism and patronage (and sometimes patron-clientelism). There are subtle distinctions between patronage and clientelism, usefully discussed in Piattoni (2001). I use the terms particularism and clientelism interchangeably to denote behaviors that meet the definition offered above. Particularistic politics may or may not be justified rhetorically with reference to political ideologies or the common good. A politician operating in this environment might offer, for example, to introduce favorable public pension legislation affecting workers in a single industry, in the expectation that the beneficiaries of the proposed policies would reward the politician with their votes.

Measuring the mode of political competition in a polity presents a number of challenges. Both programmatic and particularistic modes of political exchange operate in all polities, so what we are really trying to measure is the rough balance of the two. But determining the nature of political appeals is not always straightforward. Piattoni (2001, 6 n. 9) notes, "The most striking feature of mass clientelism is that, in an effort to truly reach the masses, it often works through fairly impersonal means, such as the passage of laws or implementation of measures that favor entire categories of persons."

The wide variety of practices included under the umbrella term make it difficult to establish the extent of particularism in any comprehensive way. And the opprobrium with which many of these practices are viewed makes it difficult to obtain reliable information about the extent to which they occur in any given polity. Still, there is wide agreement about the degree to which political life is dominated by particularistic versus programmatic parties and politicians in the different countries of the OECD. Specialists most often classify Austria, Belgium, Greece, Italy, Japan, Spain, and the United States as possessing distinctively particularistic styles of politics and policy making. France and Portugal occupy a middle ground, while political competition in the remaining countries of Northwestern Europe, Canada, and the Antipodes is primarily programmatic.[2] Corruption rankings such as those summarized for the World Bank in Kaufmann, Kraay, and Mastruzzi (2003) can be combined with other measures of clientelism to triangulate in a situation of imperfect measurement. Corruption rankings generally concur with the intensity of patronage politics noted in case studies. Greece, Italy, Japan, and Belgium suffer from both high levels of corruption and strongly particularistic politics, whereas Austria, the United States, and Spain score somewhat lower on both counts. Some scales report some problems with corruption in Portugal and France, while the remaining countries of

[2] See, e.g., Lyrintzis 1984; Cazorla 1992; Shefter 1994; Cotta 2000; Kitschelt 2000; García and Karakatsanis 2001; and Hopkin 2001.

Northwestern Europe, Canada, Australia, and New Zealand are apparently corruption-free zones. The World Bank corruption ranking index does not measure the same precise phenomenon as do the case-based qualitative characterizations of the mode of political competition, but the consonance of the two measures of closely related phenomena should give us some confidence that the characterizations drawn from the case studies are reliable.

Let us now return to the link between occupationalism and particularism. That such a link exists is clear: each of the countries in the right-hand column of Figure 3.3, that is, the countries with occupationalist welfare states, also appear on our list of predominantly clientelist polities, and none of the countries in which particularistic politics is the norm has anything other than an occupationalist welfare state. There are several reasons why this correspondence occurs. At the most intuitively basic level, occupational programs provide crucial resources for particularistic politicians. Occupationally based social insurance programs plainly lend themselves far more than do universal programs to the kind of fine-grained targeting of incentives on which particularistic political competition thrives (Skocpol 1992; Shefter 1994). Clientelist politicians thus tend to expand welfare policies in ways that enhance their fragmentation and to oppose proposals that would harmonize existing programs.

The complexity of occupational programs vis-à-vis a single, uniform universal benefit also redounds to the benefit of politicians who engage in particularistic targeting of benefits for votes. Multiple, fragmented benefit schemes geared toward different kinds of workers and their dependents generate compartmentalized sets of winners and losers. The costs for society at large of any individual deal with a small slice of the electorate are very hard to see. The aggregate effect of a profusion of micro-legislation targeting benefits toward different groups can confound even professional budgetary analysts, making it difficult to reach consensus on the "real" impact of social policy or of proposed reforms.

The reverse is true for universalistic systems. When a raise for one is a raise for all, programmatically oriented politicians may gain by offering benefit increases to broad swathes of the population, but particularistic politicians, who live by targeting, benefit little. Uniform benefits are also transparent, meaning that both benefits and costs are highly visible. Cost control is easier to obtain in the big-ticket areas, such as pensions, because even defenders of generous benefits must confront spending projections that are easy to calculate and generally agreed on. Universal systems offer neither the targeting nor the opacity that appeal to particularistic politicians.

At a deeper, structural level, particularism and occupational programs are linked because particularistic politicians are unlikely to support the development of neutral state capacities. Neutral state capacities clearly undermine the politics of selective benefits, but without them, universal social policies are nearly impossible to enact. Tax systems are a prime example. Clientelist administration of tax systems often results in ineffective taxation, or outright exemption from taxation, of the self-employed in industry, services, and agriculture. In the absence of effective taxation of these groups, however, social programs must be financed by industrial workers and public employees. This makes it harder, both politically and from a fiscal standpoint, to expand occupational social programs to cover new groups of beneficiaries among the self-employed. Where the self-employed are taxed effectively, on the other hand, it is possible to extend occupational programs to cover the entire population without invoking the ire of industrial workers and the Left. Neutral labor exchanges and nonpreferential administration of social benefits, too, are unlikely to be developed by particularistic politicians. In their absence, nonclientelist politicans in the system refrain from supporting nominally universalist social programs that are likely to be administered selectively.

The shift in political preferences that occurs in the context of particularistic competition is the most subtle, but perhaps the most important, of the mechanisms linking such competition to occupational, and ultimately elderly-oriented, social programs. As we have seen, particularistic political competition tends to undercut support for universal social benefits *even among those politicians and parties who would be ideologically inclined to support them.* In particular, financing general social benefits through payroll taxes often strains the solidaristic impulses of the Left, while a state administration that is colonized by a clientelist opposition may lead the Left to prefer occupational programs where unions retain some control over administration.

One might well ask whether clientelism and occupational social policies could be jointly caused by some third factor. A large small-firm or small-farm sector, weakness of the Left, fears of Communist takeover in the postwar period leading to tolerance for dirty politics, or a societal preference for collectivism versus individualism in both politics and policy are all more or less plausible candidates. Each seems vulnerable to criticism that it does not fit all country cases (e.g., there are many small firms and small farms in the Netherlands, but that country has had a pristine and very effective tax administration for centuries) or that it might be contradicted by another equally plausible explanation (should the Left be weak or strong to encourage clientelism and/or occupationalism?).

Another study linking the large literatures on clientelism and the origins of solidaristic universal social policies would surely be welcome, but this is not that book. I stop by noting that in countries where particularistic political competition prevails, dominant politicians have an interest in preserving or extending occupational fragmentation; that in these countries the basic infrastructure of government necessary for constructing universalistic welfare programs tends to be underdeveloped; and that political support for universal programs is further undermined by clientelist administration of taxes, labor exchanges, and social benefits. Under such circumstances, it hardly seems necessary to ask where clientelism comes from; what matters is that clientelism and occupationalism reinforce each other so strongly, and in so many ways, during the period after World War II when the new global consensus was for universalism. In the presence of particularistic political competition, countries that entered into the second critical juncture with occupationalist social programs are thus unlikely to introduce the new citizenship-based programs that would allow their welfare states to develop in a more youth-oriented direction.

To sum up, the two great divides in welfare state formation represented by our two critical junctures condition the eventual age orientation of social policies. The first divide, the split in the early twentieth century between occupational and citizenship-based regimes, creates divergent age orientations as welfare programs mature: occupationalist regimes become elderly-oriented, while citizenship-based ones are more neutral with respect to age. The second great divide occurs around World War II. Some occupationalist countries reduce the elderly orientation of their welfare spending by becoming mixed systems, adding universal programs to their base of occupational programs. Others remain pure occupational systems and continue to develop highly elderly-oriented spending patterns. This second divide is both facilitated and reinforced by the mode of political competition, programmatic or particularistic, that prevails in these countries.

Conclusion

The next three chapters examine the development of family allowance, unemployment, and old-age pension benefits in Italy and the Netherlands through the early 1990s. These Dutch and Italian case studies flesh out the mechanisms behind the main claim of this book, that the dominant mode of political competition is crucial for the eventual age orientation of social spending. The key conceptual link is the recognition that the mode of political competition reinforces choices about the structure of welfare programs. Joining this intuition to our understanding of how different program structures mature over time to produce different age orientations, it becomes possible to visualize, as in Figure 3.2, a tree-like set of branching pathways by which specific age orientations in social policy emerge.

Italy and the Netherlands both lie on the right-hand path in Figure 3.2, indicating that both had occupational welfare states prior to World War II but followed different trajectories toward their respective age orientations in the postwar period. Of necessity, then, the case material in this book focuses on how universalism and a moderate age orientation may or may not develop during this later period, not how they persist on the left-hand pathway, among those countries that had developed non-occupational, citizenship-based welfare states already in the early twentieth century. The medium-N analysis presented in this chapter helps to make the case that these results generalize to both main branches of the tree.[3] Restricting the case studies in this book to Italy and the Netherlands helps us to hone in on the precise mechanisms that allow for institutional change or persistence and that are so important for the story of how age orientation develops.

Italy and the Netherlands are an appealing, though little-used, pair of country cases for the analysis of welfare states. Esping-Andersen (1990) classifies both as Conservative-Corporatist welfare regimes in structure, even though the Netherlands' very generous unemployment benefits generated an almost Social Democratic decommodification score by 1985. More gendered analyses of social policy would see further similarities in both welfare states' male-breadwinner orientation, which reflects a shared origin in Red-Roman (Social Democratic–Christian Democratic) collaboration in the construction of the welfare state through the 1970s. On more social-structural dimensions, too, Italy and the Netherlands share important similarities. Small businesses and the agricultural sector have long been mainstays of both economies. And while in neither country was the labor movement moribund, in neither did it come to full force. Unionization rates are moderate in both countries, and both Dutch and Italian policy concertation has been episodic during the period since World War II.

---

[3] Further statistical analysis of both cross-sectional and time-series relationships among the potential causal variables outlined here would also be useful, though care must be taken to model the path-dependent aspects of these relationships correctly.

Theories and Hypotheses

Yet social policies in Italy and the Netherlands had very different age profiles by the 1990s. Chapters 4 through 6 explore the institutional features and the political battles that lie behind the persistence of an elderly social policy orientation in occupationalist Italy, and the growth of more youth-oriented policies in the universalist welfare state that developed in the Netherlands after World War II. Four distinct mechanisms of persistence emerge. First, the distinction between occupational and citizenship-based welfare programs alters the costs and benefits to politicians of expanding programs in different ways. Second, program structure affects the salience to the public of different types of benefits, and thus the ability of political actors to mobilize voters around the expansion of particular welfare state programs. Third, the way that social programs are structured affects the degree of transparency surrounding political decisions about spending, which rewards particularistic and programmatic politicians unevenly. Finally, the ability of clientelist politicians to use the welfare state for patronage affects the preferences of other political actors in ways that lead to the preservation of occupationalist systems where political competition is primarily particularistic. The effects of program structure and the mode of political competition work on youth-oriented and elderly-oriented programs in different ways, resulting in a tight bundling of elderly-oriented welfare spending with occupationalist regimes and particularistic politics, and of youth orientation with citizenship-based regimes.

4

Family Allowances

WAGES, TAXES, AND THE APPEAL
TO THE SELF-EMPLOYED

This chapter traces the development of spending on family allowances in Italy and the Netherlands from the end of the Second World War through the early 1990s. Family allowance spending grew dramatically in the Netherlands during the postwar period, contributing to its youth-oriented social policy regime, while in Italy the opposite occurred. A focus of this chapter is the strategic behavior of politicians working within political parties, behavior that interacts with the structure of family allowance programs in Italy and the Netherlands to determine spending outcomes. The way that family allowance programs are structured – along universalist lines in the Netherlands and occupationally based in Italy – is in turn an outgrowth of the competitive strategies of politicians. At the same time, the structure of family allowance programs sets the parameters for future growth of benefits by altering both politicians' and potential constituencies' perceptions of the benefits to be gained by either increasing benefit levels across the board or extending family allowances to new constituencies in a piecemeal fashion.

Family allowances are an important indicator of the age orientation of social policies because they are usually the largest public expenditure item for families with children, even in countries where the state provides things such as day care and other services for families (Gauthier 1996). Other kinds of benefits for families (day care, parental leave, health care, educational subsidies) could in principle siphon resources away from family allowances. But the most recent OECD social expenditure data do not reveal a zero-sum relationship between spending on cash benefits and services for families (OECD 2004). For example, France and Denmark in 2001 both spent the equivalent of 1.5 percent of their GDP on cash benefits for families – near the OECD average of 1.4 percent. But France spent the least of any OECD country on services for families (0.004 percent of GDP), while Denmark spent the most (2.3 percent of GDP).

Family allowances are an especially good indicator of policy attention to children, because they involve direct expenditures that are politically salient. As Pampel and Adams (1992, 527) argue, family allowances are "a direct and overt expression of a nation's institutional commitment to families with children." The fact that allowances are direct cash transfers, rather than tax expenditures, makes them "politically subject to close legislative scrutiny," and thus a good "measure of the depth and effectiveness of political support for children and their parents." So while family allowances certainly are not the only kind of social welfare spending directed toward families with children, they are probably the best single indicator of the politics of support for families with children.

It may come as a surprise to those familiar with contemporary welfare state classifications that "residualist" Italy (Titmuss 1974) began the post–World War II period with one of the most generous family allowance programs in the developed world. Family allowances in Italy expanded to cover an increasing share of the total population until the mid-1970s; but aggregate and per child spending on families began to decline dramatically starting in the mid-1960s. Family spending in the Netherlands shows an opposite trend. In the decades immediately following the Second World War, spending on family allowances in the Netherlands was quite low, but in the early 1960s family allowances became a universal social insurance benefit and both aggregate and per child spending on families began to rise. The 1970s to mid-1980s marked an important expansion of family spending in the Netherlands on both a per capita and an aggregate basis, even as other programs such as unemployment insurance, disability, and old-age pensions succumbed to austerity measures (see Fig. 4.1).[1]

What drives the expansion of family allowances in the Netherlands, and their spectacular contraction in Italy, during the post–World War II period? This chapter argues that these dynamics are best understood as a product of the interaction between the structure of family allowance programs, on the one hand, and the behavior of politicians, who use these programs in order to build constituencies and win or maintain office, on the other.

---

[1] While this chapter is about family allowances, the spending in Figure 4.1 reflects other expenditures for families as well. The cross-nationally comparable OECD social expenditure data on which this figure is based do not allow us to track family allowances and other family spending separately prior to 1980.

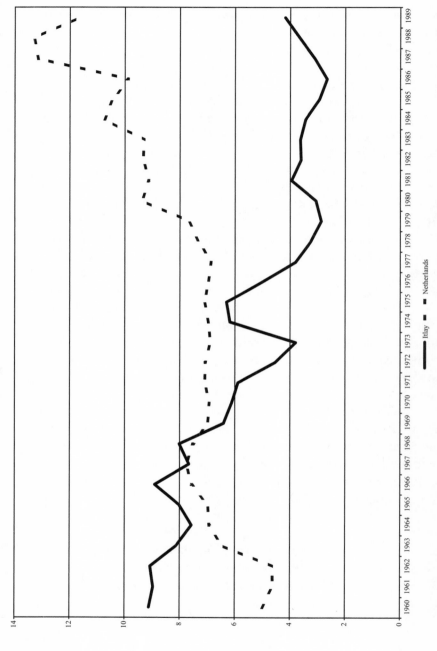

Figure 4.1 Public spending on families, per person aged 0–14, as a percentage of GDP per capita, Italy and the Netherlands. *Sources*: Expenditure data from Varley 1986; OECD 2004. GDP and demographic data from OECD 2003b. Data definitions differ between the two spending series. The figures from Varley 1986 are adjusted by the average difference between the two series for 1980–5, when both measures are available.

Itlay ■ ■ ■ Netherlands

Family Allowances

The strategic behavior of politicians both determines and is determined by the structure of family allowance programs. The structure of family allowance programs affects the behavior of politicians, but it also affects the preferences of potential constituencies, who may choose to place a higher or lower priority on family allowance benefits versus other kinds of public policies depending on the characteristics of these benefits. This intertwining of program structure, politicians' behavior, and the preferences of potential welfare state constituencies explains divergent spending on family allowances in Italy and the Netherlands. In so doing, it also helps to explain the age orientation of the social policy regimes in these two countries.

Explanations for the Level of Spending on Family Allowances

Partisan Effects on Family Allowance Spending

Scholarship on the welfare state has long recognized the importance of partisan effects on social welfare spending. These effects are hypothesized to occur either because class-based parties translate the power resources of particular classes into policy preferences or because parties are themselves carriers of ideologies and values that affect the policy preferences of legislators and government officials. It is not surprising, then, that many comparative studies of family allowance policies have posited that the strength of partisan actors, particularly Social Democratic and Christian Democratic parties and politicians, is a key determinant of policy outcomes. Evidence for this proposition is mixed, however.

Wennemo's (1994) study of cash and tax allowances for families in eighteen OECD countries during the period 1947 through 1985, for example, finds that both left and Christian Democratic power in government make a difference for the level of family benefits. Both left and Christian Democratic parties are associated with levels of spending on family allowances higher than those observed in countries where Liberal or Conservative political forces have dominated. The political effects she observes may be moderated by excluded variables, though, as Wilensky (1990) and Pampel and Adams (1992) in fact find. Demographic variables such as female labor force participation and the percentage of elderly in the population have been found to be important predictors of family policy outcomes (Wilensky 1990; Pampel and Adams 1992), as have political variables such as the influence of pressure groups including women's, family, elderly, technocratic, and employer lobbies (Wilensky 1975; Aldous, Dumon, and Johnson 1980;

Wilensky 1990; Skocpol 1992; Pedersen 1993; Pierson 1994). Still other research points to the importance of expert opinion (Gauthier 1993), party system competitiveness (van Kersbergen 1995), and institutional variables such as neo-corporatist concertation (Wilensky 1990; Pampel and Adams 1992) or the degree of government centralization (Koven and Michel 1990).

Leaving aside some of these more esoteric considerations, we can still seek independent confirmation of Wennemo's hypotheses that partisan politics and demographic constituency groups are important predictors of family allowance spending. Pampel and Adams (1992), in an eighteen-country study spanning the period 1950–80, do find some support for the notion that partisan politics matters. They do not evaluate directly the effects of Christian Democratic Party strength on family allowance spending but do find a substantial effect on the level of family allowance spending relative to other social spending produced by the percentage of the population that is Catholic. Left power resources – left party dominance of government and, more particularly, corporatist institutions – also seem to have an important impact on family allowance spending.

Van Kersbergen (1995) also considers the effect of both Christian Democratic and Social Democratic political forces on family policies. Despite his clearly articulated thesis that Christian Democratic governance results in stronger benefits for families with children, van Kersbergen's evidence for an independent effect of either Christian Democracy or Social Democracy on family allowances per se is rather weak. Net replacement rates of major income maintenance schemes for families with children versus single individuals show no systematic differences between Christian Democratic and other regimes. Van Kersbergen finds that during the 1960s the combined effects of wages and taxes do seem to result in higher disposable incomes for families with children living in Christian Democratic countries, but the results do not hold for the 1980s. Cash transfers as a percentage of the gross wage (at average production worker levels) for the (brief) period 1972–6 again offer partial support for van Kersbergen's thesis, but Sweden, New Zealand, and Norway cluster with the Christian Democratic countries on this measure. Neither do differences in post-tax, post-transfer income as a percentage of gross wages for different family types correspond to different political regimes: highly Christian Democratic Italy falls in with Japan and the United States in offering the least amount of additional support for families with children.

There is evidence that the working-class base and the egalitarian, redistributive thrust of Social Democratic political parties results in higher (and more egalitarian) welfare state spending in general. Likewise, there seems little doubt that cross-class Christian Democratic parties, with their ideological heritage of Christian social doctrine, also contribute to large but less egalitarian welfare states. However, the evidence for partisan effects on family allowance spending per se is quite mixed.

Demographic Constituency Arguments

Might focusing on demographically defined constituency groups provide a useful corrective to standard "power resources" or partisanship-based hypotheses about the sources of variation in family policies? Wennemo (1994) theorizes that while family allowance benefit levels tend to decrease over time when parties other than left or Christian Democratic are dominant, in general family allowance programs are relatively resilient to roll-back because they affect such broad constituencies. In other words, Wennemo finds that partisan politics explains the structure and level of family allowances, while an electoral argument based on the large size of the natural constituency of families with children helps to account for the fate of family allowance programs over time.

Similarly, the papers collected in Aldous et al. (1980) emphasize the importance of lobby organizations for large families for the development of family policies. While the authors of these papers find that even very numerous and well-organized family lobbies probably cannot affect policy on their own (they argue that what labor and especially employers want is far more important), family organizations do serve an important role in agenda-setting. Pedersen (1993), too, finds that employers, not the pronatalist and family lobbies in France, were ultimately responsible for the passage of generous family allowance policies. But she stresses that the fit between the ideological stances of family lobbies and pronatalist organizations, on the one hand, and the needs of employer groups, on the other, was crucial for promoting generous family allowance policies. Family lobbies cannot be held responsible for developments in family policies, but neither can they be ignored.

Perhaps more surprisingly, several studies have found support for the hypothesis that large numbers of elderly voters increase the level of spending on families with children. Wilensky (1990) explains this phenomenon with resort to the assertion that older people, having been through child-rearing themselves, understand how difficult it is and thus support public policies that make life easier for parents with children. Pampel and

Adams (1992) envision a different motivation for the "altruistic" spending effects of large numbers of elderly voters. While normal pluralist assumptions would link larger elderly populations to a stronger emphasis on pension spending, Pampel and Adams hypothesize that shrinking youth cohorts may prompt elderly voters (and policy makers) to recognize the interdependency of generations: without adequate supports for child rearing, younger cohorts will fail to produce the number of new labor market entrants that is required to maintain solvent social security systems for the elderly.

Demographically defined voting blocs and/or lobbies – groups of families with children and/or the elderly – are thus possible rivals to partisan actors in determining levels of spending on family benefits. And while, as Pierson (1994) predicts, the impact of such groups may be more pronounced during periods of attempted retrenchment, plainly there is also a case to be made that demographically based lobbies have an impact, sometimes indirect, on the construction of family allowance programs.

An Alternative View: Program Structure and Political Competition Determine Family Allowance Spending

Both partisanship-based and demographically based hypotheses about the development of family allowance policies focus their attention on forces largely exogenous to the welfare state: political parties (and their class and/or ideological bases), and political pressure groups (and the demographic trends that create them). While these external forces are surely important, one important lesson from recent literature on welfare state retrenchment is that processes endogenous to the welfare state can have an important impact on future developments.[2]

---

[2] Even during periods of welfare state construction and consolidation, such endogenous forces may limit the potential for family policies to expand. For example, developments in other policy areas with large fiscal demands (e.g., old-age pensions) may constrain the growth of family allowances. Conversely, granting family allowances to groups of beneficiaries defined by their very status within the welfare state (e.g., pensioners or people receiving unemployment benefits) could increase the potential for growth in family spending. So the development of family policies may be subject to constituency effects that arise out of the welfare state programs themselves, rather than out of any objective demographic trends. To cite another example, the family lobby, one imagines, would be far more politically important where there were family benefits to lobby for, an administrative structure to talk to, and perhaps even organizational resources to be gained from the system of family allowances itself, as in France and Belgium.

Family Allowances

One such endogenous determinant of the development of family allowance spending is the administrative structure of the programs. Universalist programs allow for a different pathway of development than do occupationally based programs. The former can be expanded only by increasing benefit levels, either across the board or by raising the income or wealth limits imposed by means tests. The latter expand in a patchwork fashion, increasing the number of beneficiaries independently of the level of benefits. These structural features of family allowance programs condition politicians' and constituencies' preferences regarding family allowance benefits. In interaction with the competitive strategies of politicians, different program structures result in very different spending patterns.

When family allowances are universal benefits, they become less useful to politicians who might wish to use them to make particularistic appeals to specific groups of voters. Thus, where political competition is particularistic rather than programmatic, family allowance programs will tend to shrink in relevance once they are universalized. Where political competition is programmatic, universal family allowances are likely to grow, particularly if family allowances have become delinked from their original meaning as wage supplements and reconceptualized as entitlements of citizenship.

At the same time, the patchwork expansion of benefits that occurs in occupational systems means that for particularistic politicians, the level of family benefits is less important than the number of new beneficiaries. So in occupational systems, the numerical expansion of family allowance beneficiaries may actually drive down both benefit levels and aggregate spending. The continuing linkage in occupational systems between wages and benefits reinforces this downward trend in the level of benefits by perpetuating the view of family allowances as a supplement to wages, rather than an independent entitlement. As long as wages are rising, most potential constituencies of family allowance programs will perceive these payments as unimportant relative to either wages or other benefits (such as pensions) that provide closer to full income replacement.

The cross-national comparative literature on family policy agrees that family allowance spending is likely to be highest when there are leftist and/or Christian Democratic parties in power (Wilensky 1990; van Kersbergen 1995) and when there is concertation between the social partners in conjunction with a high percentage of elderly people in the population (Wilensky 1990; Pampel and Adams 1992). But while both Italy and the Netherlands after World War II experienced almost uninterrupted participation of Christian Democratic parties in government and a significant policy-making role for left parties, they ultimately achieved very different levels of public support for families.

While both Italy and the Netherlands have undergone periods of intense concertation, neither growth in expenditures on family allowances nor the implementation of policies that would promote such growth coincide with the peaks in intensity of neo-corporatist policy concertation in either country. Italy has a wealth of older voters, and in the mid-1970s a minor recovery in the level of family allowance spending was in fact driven by pensioners eager to enjoy the dependent spouse allowance. But the Netherlands, which already by the early 1970s spent more on family allowances than did Italy, has one of the younger populations in Europe. Neither the partisan politics prediction nor the demographic constituency prediction accounts for the reversal of fortunes in Dutch and Italian family allowance policies over the course of the post–World War II period. A closer look at the cases is needed to account for divergent trajectories in the level of family allowance spending.

Family Allowances in the Netherlands

The first comprehensive legislation on family allowances in the Netherlands appeared in 1962, when the General Family Allowances Act (Algemene Kinderbijslagwet) guaranteed child benefits for all residents of the Netherlands starting from the third child. Family allowances were fully indexed to the cost of living in 1964. In 1980, separate legislation for the first and second children of public servants, wage earners, and low-income self-employed was merged with the laws governing family allowances for the general population. This ratified formally what had existed already in practice since 1962, a uniform family allowance benefit available to all residents of the Netherlands.

To understand why Dutch family allowances got off to a slow start relative to family allowances in Italy, it is useful to understand why the family allowances system was among the last social programs in the Netherlands to become universalized. This would be easy to understand if family allowances were, as is sometimes assumed, primarily pronatalist measures. The high postwar birth rate in the Netherlands would then explain a lack of interest in family allowances. But family allowances cannot be properly understood as pronatalist policies in the Netherlands. The brake on universalization before the early 1960s was political, rather than demographic, in nature.

Family Allowances

A combination of opposition from employers and the Protestant Reform Party (Anti-Revolutionaire Partij, or ARP) within the Labor Foundation and rather weak incentives to expand family allowances to the excluded Catholic constituency of nonpoor self-employed account for the delay in universalization. The breakthrough in 1962 came about because of a generalized trend toward a more universalistic conception of social rights in Dutch society and increased electoral competition that made expansion of family allowances to the self-employed a valuable electoral tool for both Catholic and Protestant politicians. The existence of a tax system capable of taxing the self-employed made it possible to formulate this policy expansion as a universalization of benefits.

From the Beginnings to Universalism

The history of family allowances in the Netherlands extends back to the first years of the twentieth century, and it is worth investigating the process through which the 1962 system of universal coverage emerged from the first collectively bargained agreements for textile workers and provisions for municipal workers.[3] The papal encyclical *Rerum novarum*, published in 1891, advocated a "family wage," and Dutch clergy quickly adopted the term. In 1906 the city of Amsterdam introduced a wage supplement for family heads, and confessional groups in the Netherlands shifted the focus of their social justice rhetoric from the concept of a minimum, just wage to a family wage. The year 1912 saw the introduction of the first national-level family allowances, for postal workers and teachers, and in 1918 Catholic parliamentarians passed a resolution calling for the government to consider family size in setting wages for all government workers.

During the interwar period, the national government granted family allowances to all civil servants, and family allowances were introduced for employees of some local governments. Private family allowance funds were also developing – in 1919, Catholic textile mill owners signed the first collectively bargained contract including family allowances – but by and large employers supported the idea that the state should bear most of the costs (Akkerman 1998). In 1920 the Catholic Minister of Labor announced a plan to establish a government fund for child allowances, and in 1921 the Dutch government, at the urging of Catholic trade union leaders,

[3] The historical reconstruction in this section draws largely from van Praag 1977; Damsma 1994; Rigter et al. 1995; and Akkerman 1998.

commissioned a study of the feasibility of a public family allowance system (Damsma 1994).

Socialist unions and the dominant Liberal wing of the Dutch feminist movement were opposed to the idea of a family wage, supporting instead the idea of a just minimum wage for all workers that would be high enough to support a family's needs regardless of the actual number of children present. But Catholic support for family allowances was strong, in part because it dovetailed so neatly with the Dutch Church's strong pronatalist stance during that period.[4] By the 1930s, Socialist opposition to family allowances waned as it became clear that confessional parties and unions were gaining the upper hand among both Catholic and Socialist voters as "defenders of the family."

By 1937, some 146 collectively bargained labor agreements included family allowances (van Praag 1977), and in 1938 the Family Allowances Act (Kinderbijslagswet) was passed. This act provided allowances for wage earners only, based on an insurance principle: the level of the benefit depended on the premium paid, which in turn depended on the wage level. The impetus for the 1938 bill came from Catholic legislators, but by this time the Socialist movement had accepted the idea of a general family allowance scheme covering male workers. (It is interesting to note that in the same year the Socialist Party and unions abandoned their advocacy of a state-financed old-age pension system, believing that population aging would make public pensions prohibitively expensive [van Praag 1977].) The only principled opposition to the Family Allowances Act came from Liberal parliamentarians (Akkerman 1998), who objected to state provision of any kind. Nevertheless, implementation of the act was delayed due to wartime exigencies, and it did not come into force until the Nazi occupation government's reform of the social welfare system (van der Valk 1991).

After the Second World War, legislation in 1946 expanded on the 1938 act by introducing a temporary family allowance measure to cover the first and second children of wage earners. This temporary expedient was explicitly linked to incomes policies, in that it sought to compensate employees for wage controls in the face of rising living costs. In 1948 the Pensioners' Family Allowance Act (Kinderbijslagwet Rentetrekkers) introduced child

---

[4] This strong pronatalist position may seem unwarranted, given exceptionally high population growth in the Netherlands relative to the rest of Europe (Goddijn 1975). It is important to keep in mind that pronatalism in the Netherlands during this period is essentially a result of the minority position of Dutch Catholics.

benefits for old-age and invalidity pensioners, and in 1951 another temporary family allowances act (Noodwet Kinderbijslagwet voor Kleine Zelfstandigen) introduced benefits for the first and second children of low-income self-employed families.

In 1962 separate programs for public sector workers and the self-employed were abolished and replaced by a quartet of provisions that together covered the entire population. The General Family Allowances Act (Algemene Kinderbijslagswet) of that year provided flat-rate allowances for all residents of the Netherlands from the third child, with the amount of the benefit augmented for each additional child. The Wage-Earners Family Allowances Act (Kinderbijslagswet Loontrekkers), the Self-Employed Persons Family Allowances Act (Kinderbijslagswet Zelfstanigden), and the 1963 Government Personnel Family Support Act (Kindertoeslagregeling voor Overheidspersoneel) provided additional benefits for the first two children of, respectively, employees, the self-employed with modest incomes, and public servants.

The history of Dutch family allowances up to 1962–3 shows a clear progression in the direction of citizenship-based entitlement. By the 1930s, Dutch feminists' vision of a carer's wage had been defeated, as had the Socialists' goal of a family policy defined by a minimum wage for all workers sufficient to maintain a family, plus collectively provided services for mothers. Instead, the idea of a family wage for family heads, introduced in *Rerum novarum* and favored by confessional parties and unions, prevailed.

Family allowances were introduced as part of the wage package for working men with dependent children. This type of benefit was gradually extended from a select group of civil servants and private employees to include, first, all wage earners, then social insurance pensioners and low-income self-employed persons, and finally in 1962 all residents of the Netherlands. This universalization of benefits never occurred in Italy. But why did it take so long in the Netherlands, despite the popularity of these programs and the influential report of the van Rhijn Commission, which advocated universal family allowances?

Gauthier (1993) suggests that the expansion of family allowances introduced as pronatalist policies may stall in the absence of a credible threat of population decline. Fertility rates were indeed high in the Netherlands during the immediate postwar period – so high that the Dutch government actively encouraged emigration in order to counter feared overpopulation. And it is true that Catholic concerns about their minority status and the pernicious influence of "Neo-Malthusian" birth control advocates formed a strong impetus for family allowances during the interwar period. But Dutch Catholics continued to place a high priority on reproduction even in the postwar period, a priority reflected by their extraordinarily high fertility rates (van Poppel 1985). At the same time, Catholic families were among the least likely to receive non-universal family allowances in the 1940s and 1950s, since they were concentrated in agricultural self-employment rather than in industrial or civil service jobs (Stoffelsma and Oosterhaven 1989). So despite high levels of fertility in the Dutch territory as a whole, Catholic politicians were strong advocates of expanding the family allowance system as quickly as possible – both to encourage higher birth rates among Catholic self-employed families and to capture electoral support from expansion of family allowances to this constituency.

Compared with family policies in France, Belgium, or Sweden, countries that adopted (quite different) family policies for explicitly pronatalist reasons, Dutch family allowances were considered a component of wage policies (Rigter, van den Bosch, van der Veen, and Hemerijck 1995, 222). Old-age and invalidity pensioners became eligible for family allowances in 1948, but by virtue of their status as former workers entitled to a deferred wage. Social Democratic unions continued to think of family allowances as an integral component of the wage as late as 1957. Although the Minister of Social Welfare advocated in 1955 a universal tax-financed family allowances scheme, and the Socialist trade union confederation (Nederlands Verbond de Vakverenigingen, or NVV) generally agreed with this recommendation, they made it clear that family allowances were not to be classed with other "welfare" benefits. A report from an NVV congress in October 1957 declared that tax financing of social insurance was an important goal since it would provide a means of balancing the incomes of "non- and semi-productive groups" with "a reasonable income (*including children's allowance* and after tax deduction) for the productive groups"[5] (NVV 1958). Family allowances were linked primarily to ideas about a just wage, and secondarily to ideas of poverty alleviation – not to increasing birth rates.

Still, we might reasonably presume that Catholic politicians had an objective interest in promoting expansion of benefits in order to reach their large constituency of self-employed families with numerous children. So it makes sense to ask to what extent these political actors were actually capable of and/or desirous of extending family allowances to the entire population. Catholics controlled the social welfare ministry through most

[5] Emphasis added.

of the 1950s and 1960s. And their Social Democratic coalition partners certainly had no principled objection to universal social programs, having supported universal old-age pensions in 1947. Union publications indicate that the NVV supported proposals for both universal family allowances (NVV 1955) and universal widows' and orphans' benefits (NVV 1957), though expressing a preference that such universalistic programs be financed through general revenues rather than employer and/or employee contributions. The ARP generally opposed expansionary social policy, but was not represented in government until 1952. So introducing universal family allowances should have been an easy task for Catholic politicians. What, then, accounts for the delay?

Cox (1993) assigns primary responsibility for the delay in expanding social welfare benefits in the Netherlands to the influence of confessional organizations within corporatist decision-making bodies. According to Cox, while the Catholic *Party* supported universalizing social insurance benefits, confessional employers' and labor groups opposed it and launched "counter-attacks" from within the Labor Foundation (111). In particular, the ARP's objections to universalization had an important impact on policy via the influence of Protestant representatives in the Labor Foundation. This influence stalled the expansion and universalization of social policies through the 1950s, despite the fact that a Social Democratic party was in control of government and the relevant ministries.

Many observers of Dutch social policy argue that growing secularization and depillarization of the electorate in the mid-1960s account for the explosion of new rights and social spending during this period (de Swaan 1988; Cox 1993; van Zanden 1998). According to these analysts, both Catholic and Protestant parties and organizations began a "populist campaign" (Cox 1993, 168–9) using welfare benefits as tender in a context of declining electoral margins. The ARP, which had traditionally been a party of fiscal conservatism, softened its objection to government spending under the influence of a booming economy and pressure from self-employed groups, which were threatening to exit the weakening party. Once the Social Democratic Labor Party (Partij van de Arbeid, or PvdA) began to make serious inroads into the Catholic vote in the early 1960s, Catholic politicians as well began looking for concrete benefits to offer in exchange for electoral support. Intense competition with both the PvdA and smaller left-Catholic parties increased the influence of the left current within the Catholic People's Party (Katholieke Volkspartij, or KVP), which was certainly not averse to expanding social benefits even if that meant increasing the state's role in social provision. Catholic unions were also radicalizing in response to competition from Social Democratic unions and began to support universal social benefits in response to their popularity with the public (Cox 1999).

However, the move to introduce universal family allowances in fact preceded depillarization and increasing electoral competition by some ten years (Balkenende 2000 interview; van der Veen 2000 interview). Political parties could not have changed their policy commitments quickly enough in response to depillarization to account for such a major change in the family allowance system as early as 1962 (Cuyvers 2000 interview). The growth of the welfare state in general, and of family allowances in particular, may be better understood in terms of the ideological maturation of Dutch policy makers than in terms of increasing electoral competition resulting from depillarization. In the judgment of Christian Democratic Appeal party leader Jan Peter Balkenende, "[KVP social policy makers] Veldkamp and Klompé were left by conviction, not by strategy" (Balkenende 2000 interview). Roebroek (1992), too, cites a growing consensus among confessional politicians on the desirability of state intervention as the key motivator of welfare state expansion in the 1960s, adding that of course explosive economic growth was a necessary precondition for such a consensus.

If increased electoral competitiveness in the 1960s cannot explain the drive for welfare state expansion and the adoption of universalistic welfare policies, neither did it dampen the interest of confessional parties in expanding social welfare spending. However, whether or not increasing electoral competition was the key to welfare state expansion, it still would remain to be shown why expansion of the family allowance program took the form of universalization. Here the electoral argument may be useful in augmenting the rather vague argument prevalent in the secondary literature about the ideological transformation of Dutch political culture in the 1960s.

With the breakdown of pillarization in the Netherlands, when voters' automatic ties with the traditional religious subcultures weakened, the leading parties found themselves with a new problem: how to attract voters who might decide to vote for a party other than the one affiliated with their religious denomination. For both the Protestant and Catholic parties, the most consistent source of electoral strength was also the one that was excluded from family allowances under the old occupational system. This group of voters resided in the families of the Protestant and rural Catholic self-employed. Extending family allowances to the self-employed, which in the Dutch case was accomplished by universalizing the family allowance system, covered this precise segment of crucial voters and constitutes a motive for expansion in a universalist direction.

The universalistic solution was possible because of the comprehensive Dutch tax system, which allowed citizenship-based benefits to be paid for out of general revenues. After the introduction of the income tax in 1917, there was little or no discussion of the administration of the income tax system in the Netherlands (van der Veen 2000 interview). By all accounts, it was a system that worked well and was implemented in a bureaucratically rational manner (see Ferrera 1993). The van Rhijn Commission had proposed a universal family benefit to be financed out of general revenues, but in the immediate postwar period Drees opposed the idea of extending family allowances to the self-employed on the grounds that it would be too expensive (Rigter et al. 1995, 222). By the late 1950s, however, both the Socio-Economic Council (Sociaal-Economische Raad, or SER) and a majority of parliamentarians were eager to integrate family allowances for the self-employed with legislation for wage earners. In fact, when Minister of Social Welfare van Rooy proposed in 1958 a law instituting a universal family allowance system for the third child and up, he was forced to step down because politicians in the lower house of Parliament did not find his plan generous enough. Parliamentarians argued that given the feasibility of funding the system out of general revenues, there was no reason not to extend benefits to first and second children as well (Rigter et al. 1995, 257).

The construction of a universal Dutch family allowance system based on a general tax base[6] was a key development. The strategic maneuvering of Catholic and Protestant parties to appeal to the rural self-employed created a demand for a universal benefit, and effective taxation of the self-employed made it possible for politicians to please these important constituencies as well as their urban supporters. On the one hand, politicians could offer the concrete benefit of improved family allowances to the self-employed. At the same time, the tax-financed nature of the system ensured the support of unions and employers, who in general favored universal citizenship-based social insurance but needed to be reassured that the cost of universalizing family allowances would not result in increased social insurance contributions. This compromise had, as we shall see, important consequences for the development of family allowance spending in the 1970s through

---

[6] Note however that until 1980, only benefits for the self-employed were paid out of general revenues; wage earners continued to fund their benefits via employer contributions.

1990s. It also provides a useful contrast with the Italian case, where a weak tax base prevented the implementation of a universalistic family allowance system.

From Universalism to Entitlement

Following on the universalization of the family allowance system in 1962, expenditures in the Netherlands showed a steep increase from 1963 to 1968. The mid-1960s were a phase of major growth in many areas of social policy spending, initiated by Catholic ministers Veldkamp and Klompé and strongly supported by the Catholic and Social Democratic unions. This major expansion of social welfare spending coincided with the depillarization of the Dutch electorate, beginning around 1965 and characterized by a very strong increase in competition between the major parties for lower- and middle-class voters. Between 1963 and 1972, the KVP lost half of its electorate, mostly to the Labor Party and the Radical Party (Politieke Partij Radicalen, or PPR, a left-wing offshoot of the KVP; Irving 1979, 201, 224–5). By the late 1960s, many of the Catholic Party's core voters had abandoned the KVP in order to support smaller parties like D'66, the PPR, and DS '79 (Daalder 1987). Given the intense electoral competition of the mid- to late-1960s, it is not surprising that spending on family allowances increased just as the Catholic Party found itself most in need of incentives with which to retain a key constituency: families with young children.

It is far from clear, however, that increasing electoral competition was solely responsible for the rise in family allowance spending that began in the mid-1960s. The abolition of the income ceiling for contributions (in 1963 for employees, 1964 for self-employed) and the indexation of benefits to the cost of living (1964) surely also resulted in higher spending. And even as the electoral climate became less favorable for family policy expansion in the 1970s, expenditures continued to rise.

By 1975, when the Catholic and Protestant parties began the process of merging to form the Christian Democratic Appeal (Christen Democratisch Appel, or CDA), the support base of the Christian parties was substantially older than the average voter (Bakvis 1981, 81), so an expansion of family allowances would hardly have constituted a tremendous appeal. The merger of the confessional parties effectively marginalized the left-wing elements that had pushed for higher social spending in the late 1960s (van Zanden 1998, 71), and between 1974 and 1981 CDA voters moved to the right of the political spectrum (Daalder 1987). This diminution of the core constituency of the family allowance program within the Christian Democratic parties might account for their willingness to go along with de-indexation of family allowances in 1972, a situation that continued until 1981. But even after de-indexation, family allowance spending did not decline. In fact, there was no significant decline in family allowance spending until 1984–6, when the level of family allowances was briefly frozen as part of the general austerity policies of the era.

Aggregate family allowance spending held steady through the 1970s, and from 1980 onward, the general trend was again one of strong growth in spending. Why does spending on family allowances start to rise again just when recipients are farthest from the core of the Christian Democratic electoral project, and when family allowances are less popular among voters than other kinds of welfare benefits (Palomba 1995)? While the Dutch Family Council and the Dutch Association of Housewives were active in pressing for disability benefits for housewives (Cox 1993, 164), these organizations do not seem to have been particularly concerned with family allowances (Cuyvers 2000 interview). Neither do labor unions seem to have pressed very hard for benefit increases. The combined union Urgency Program for 1973 objected to the idea of freezing benefits for the second child under the wage earner's program and called for a re-evaluation of the whole family allowance system (NVV 1973) – a call that is repeated in the Urgency Program for 1975 (NVV 1975). But it is not clear from these documents what unions wanted from a potential reorganization of the system, and van Berkel and Hindriks's (1991) survey of the relationship between unions and social insurance claimants makes no mention of the children's allowance issue.

The rise in family allowance spending in the 1980s can be attributed to three factors. First, the general climate of austerity may have led to demands for increased benefit levels. Second, the 1980 consolidation of Dutch family allowance legislation into a single law involved a change in the mode of financing the system. Whereas prior to 1980 the family allowance fund for employed workers was financed by contributions from employers and employees, after 1980 the entire system, including benefits for employees, became entirely financed out of general revenues. According to Balkenende (2000 interview), popular pressure for increases in the family allowance benefit arose immediately upon this change in financing, since payments into the system had effectively been made invisible.

Finally, and perhaps most importantly, changing the structure of the family allowance system also changed societal expectations about the function

87

that allowances should serve. Bussemaker (1998) argues that the feminist movement's drive to obtain equal rights for women under social security law in the 1970s drove up social spending in general. Individuals increasingly became entitled to benefits that were once meant to support a family head plus dependents, but the amount of benefits was not adjusted downward to account for this new trend toward "individualization" of social rights. Indeed, the public campaign to "save" family allowances in 1974–5 was spearheaded by left-wing women's groups seeking to protect benefits for single mothers (Vlek 1997; Cuyvers 2000 interview). Women's organizations pressed for increases in the level of family allowances in order to allow single mothers to continue to provide care in the home, without recourse to income from employment (Nederlandse Vrouwenbeweging 1976; Molin 1977).

The universalization of the family allowance system in 1962 thus had important consequences for expenditures in later years. The 1920s and 1930s marked a process of defining family allowances socially as a wage supplement, as we have seen. The occupational system installed in 1938 and continued in the 1940s and 1950s reinforced the notion that family allowances were primarily an antidote to wage controls and not an independent entitlement of parenthood. Once family allowances were universalized, however, they became removed from the realm of workers' benefits and came to be seen as an entitlement of citizenship. No longer linked to wages as a top-off, family allowances in the Netherlands after the 1960s came to be regarded as an entitlement that should enable a family head, male or female, employed or not, to support children.

The Dutch family allowance system got off to a slow start after World War II, relative to Italy's generous benefits in the immediate postwar period. The drive to expand the family allowance benefit in the late 1950s and early 1960s may have been a result of increasing electoral competition and a concomitant desire on the part of Catholic and Protestant parties to secure the votes of the self-employed, as many scholars argue, or it may have simply reflected a leftward shift in the ideological orientation of the Dutch polity at large. Regardless of the motive for expanding the family allowance system, it is clear that the opportunity for creating a universal, citizenship-based plan system in 1962 arose from the capacity to fund benefits for the self-employed via a system of effective taxation.

Once the family allowance system became universalized, the possibility for further use of the system to provide selective incentives to consolidate electoral gains among particular constituencies became more limited. But the growth of family allowance spending continued through the 1990s, even in the face of general austerity measures. The move from an occupational conception of family allowances to a universal, citizenship-based system changed societal expectations about the nature and function of those benefits. In the process, it created new sources of pressure to increase family benefits, which resulted in continued spending growth.

Family Allowances in Italy

Family allowance benefits in Italy have followed a path opposite to the Dutch trajectory. Italian family policy in general, and family allowances in particular, were by the 1990s widely considered to be utterly inadequate. Public debate blamed the lack of transfers and services for families for high levels of child poverty and the world's lowest fertility rates. But family allowances in Italy have not always been the "Cinderella" of social policy, as one influential tract of the late 1970s termed them (Gorrieri 1972). In the 1950s and early 1960s, family allowances were quite generous by international standards, and although they were not available to all citizens, progress toward universalization seemed well under way. Why did the expansion of Italian family allowances stall in the late 1960s? What can explain the pattern of rapid growth and then equally rapid retrenchment in the postwar period?

The strategic use of family allowances by party actors, in interaction with the occupational structure of the family allowance system, explains the developmental trajectory of family allowances in Italy. The motive for expanding the scope of family allowance benefits in Italy was the desire of politicians to reach out with selective benefits to particular groups in the electorate. Unlike in the Netherlands, however, where electoral incentives led to a universalization of family benefits, in Italy the opportunity to introduce a universal system of benefits was missing because of the underdeveloped tax system, itself a by-product of electoral clientelism. As a result, expansion of the family allowance system in Italy took place along patchwork lines, within an occupational structure that continued to feed and be fed by particularistic politics. The continuing occupationalism of the system also set a brake on the growth of family benefits by affecting the priorities of potential constituents. Family allowance funds were siphoned off to pay for other social priorities, especially pensions, in a move that the unions and the Left agreed to quite willingly. As long as family benefits remained linked conceptually to the wage system, and wages were indexed but family allowances were not, family allowances came to seem less and less important, and less and less worth defending.

General Historical Overview

Until the reforms of the mid-1980s, the basic outlines and principles of Italian family allowances all derived from developments during the Fascist period. Family allowances were first introduced in Italy during the Fascist period as a way to compensate employees with children for reduced wages resulting from reduced hours. After the Second World War, family allowances were rapidly re-established as a core feature of the welfare state and reached a peak of generosity during the mid-1950s and early 1960s. At this point, Italian family allowances, despite being available only to industrial workers and small farmers, supported a wide variety of family dependents (spouses, parents, and siblings, in addition to children and grandchildren) and were admired both within Italy and by international observers.

Family allowances were gradually extended to cover new groups of constituents, until by the mid-1970s they covered nearly 80 percent of children under eighteen in Italy. However, starting in the mid-1960s, the allowances underwent a dramatic devaluation, and by the late 1970s Italian family allowances were among the least generous in Europe. By the 1970s, surpluses in the family allowance fund were routinely diverted to pay for pensions, and family allowances dwindled to insignificance despite the favorable ratio of contributions to payouts.

The mid-1980s brought a series of reforms, including the introduction of means testing and the graduation of benefits according to family size and income. However, even after these reforms, family allowances remained restricted to needy families of dependent employees or the self-employed in agriculture, and did not become a citizenship-based form of assistance. The reforms of the 1980s, motivated by the desire to reduce spending while targeting resources more effectively to needy families, substantially decreased both the number of recipients and aggregate expenditures on family allowances. Not until the mid-1990s did there emerge an open debate on the condition of families in Italy's welfare state, a debate that has spurred in recent years a slight increase in aggregate spending on families over 1980 levels.

90

The Fascist Period

After some initial experiments during World War I that vanished with the 1920s, family allowances got their true start in Italy during the Fascist period. With economic crisis and unemployment looming, the corporatist employer association Confindustria and the Fascist labor unions signed an agreement in 1934 to reduce working hours in industry from forty-eight to forty per week, in an attempt to reduce unemployment. Workers agreed to concomitant reductions in salaries, while those workers with two or more dependent children received a family allowance to make up for some of the lost wages. The family allowances were to be funded by joint contributions from employers and employees. This interconfederal agreement, strongly advocated by Confindustria, was transformed into legislation in 1936, but without the linkage to reduced hours. By this time the Fascist pronatalist agenda was in full swing (the campaign to increase birth rates began in 1927, and in 1931 the government-sponsored Inquiry into the State of the Family came out), and government policies linked the papal encyclical *Rerum novarum*'s call for family wages to the demographic campaign.

In 1937 family allowances were extended from industry and some other sectors to agricultural employees and the self-employed with incomes under a certain threshold. Allowances for children were graduated to give greater per-child benefits to larger families. In 1940 the family allowance scheme was placed under government authority with the creation of the Single Fund for Family Allowances (Cassa Unica per Assegni Familiari, or CUAF) within the National Institute for Social Insurance (Istituto Nazionale per la Previdenza Sociale, or INPS). Allowances were extended to dependent spouses and parents in addition to children.

Three main forces drove expansion of family allowances during the Fascist period: poverty, pronatalism, and patronage. Family allowances were a way to combat poverty by supplementing the wages of low-income earners. Large families, in particular, were subject to poverty because wages were so low, and family allowances helped to prop up consumption at the lower wage levels. The demographic impulse was of obvious importance as well. Despite the fact that Italy had one of the highest birth rates in Europe at the time, the Fascist government was concerned about Italian birth rates for a variety of reasons, including the impact of the French debate over pronatalist policies, widespread emigration of men, the importance of human resources for development in a capital-scarce environment, and the influence of Church doctrine favoring high fertility (De Grazia

1992, 25). In the end, family allowances did little either to alleviate poverty or to promote more births. But they served other purposes, which ensured the survival of the system. Family allowances were a form of patronage for middle-class cadres, who formed the backbone of support for Mussolini's regime. Family allowances were much more generous for this group than for ordinary workers, despite the fact that state employees had smaller families and higher incomes than the country's working classes.

During the Second World War, family allowances lost much of their purchasing power due to declining resources and high inflation. In 1944 the child allowances returned to a flat-rate sum for each child, regardless of birth order, and the family allowances were supplemented by an additional cost of living allowance. During the war the state briefly took over financing of the allowances, but the main outlines of Italy's family allowance system had been set in place with the 1940 legislation, and after the war the old financing system returned.

The Golden Age of Italian Family Allowances: Postwar through 1964

During the immediate postwar period, family allowances rapidly regained the purchasing power they had lost to inflation, by 1951 surpassing the highest real value they had achieved during the peak of the Fascist demographic campaign. While numerous observers (see, e.g., Sabbadini 1985; Campanini 1993; Silvestrini 1994) argue that poor benefits for Italian families in the contemporary period are a result of politicians' desire to avoid any perceived continuity with hated Fascist pronatalism – a claim echoed in Valiente's (1996) work on Spain – the development of family allowances is clearly more complicated than that.

Progressive allowances for larger families, a key feature of pronatalist policies, had been removed already in 1944, and after the war progressive allowances were not reinstated. So what remained of the Fascist family allowance system after the war was simply a wage supplement that, by all accounts, was extremely popular. The system showed no sign of being dogged by the shadow of Fascism. It just kept growing and growing. From 1946 until 1955, when family allowances were automatically indexed to the cost of living, there were sixteen legislated increases to the family allowance. Contributions went up in like measure (despite the *massimale*, a ceiling on the total wage bill above which employers did not have to pay contributions, in place until 1974), so that through the 1950s and 1960s payouts rarely exceeded contributions received by the Family Allowance Fund.

Family Allowances

Family allowances arrived at this golden age in the 1950s and 1960s because they were uncontroversial. The Church liked family allowances, because while it generally opposed the idea of state intervention in the family sphere, family allowances were a cash benefit distributed to the (usually male) main earner in a household, a format relatively unthreatening to family autonomy and, within that, patriarchal authority. And after all, the family wage had been the Pope's idea to begin with. The Christian Democratic Party liked family allowances, in part because the Church liked them, and in part because the socially oriented current that was dominant within the party through the mid-1950s believed that supporting families with children, especially low-income families, was the right thing to do. Confindustria, the large employer's association, liked family allowances, because they kept wages down and because the existence of the *massimale* meant that the biggest northern employers who had the largest wage bills and who dominated Confindustria paid the least, proportionally.

Unions liked family allowances, because they were a substantial component of the wage (around 20 percent of the average industrial wage in the 1950s and 1960s), and the flat-rate format made the allowances even more helpful for low-income workers. In fact, according to Franco and Sartor (1994, 86), during this period family allowances were the social insurance program with which unions were most concerned. The Left, interested in social justice and in spurring the economic development of the south, liked family allowances because workers in the south, whose wages and living costs both tended to be lower than in the north, benefited substantially. On aggregate the family allowance system was an effective means of transferring resources from the rich, less fecund north to the poor, prolific south. Finally, Italy's family allowances were well regarded by social policy experts as an efficient system delivering tangible benefits, something in which the Italian government could take some pride (see Masini 1953; Pasi 1956). In short, there was no substantial opposition to maintaining the family allowance system as it had been laid out in the 1940s, while increasing benefits as it became necessary and/or possible.

Extending family allowances beyond the original constituency covered in the 1940 law proved trickier. Some extensions did occur during the early postwar period. In 1947 and 1948, artisans and tobacco workers came under the INPS family allowance scheme, and in 1952 all public employees came to be covered by a separate public family allowances program. In 1958 the regular family allowance scheme was extended to fishermen. Beginning in the early 1960s, there were regular proposals by Christian Democratic deputies to extend family allowances to small independent farmers, share-croppers, and tenant farmers, but this did not occur until 1967. Yet despite frequent extensions to particular economic groups, the family allowance system remained far from universal. People with weak ties to the formal labor market were excluded, as were the self-employed, and by 1960 only about half of all children under age eighteen were entitled to family allowances (Franco 1993).

Why was the family allowance program in Italy not converted into a universal, citizenship-based benefit, despite the fact that it was so popular and seemed to be on its way toward universalization in the 1950s and 1960s? Three main reasons stand out. First, family allowances were always linked conceptually to wages and were not seen as an important tool for poverty alleviation. As a result, there was little call to extend the system to cover nonworkers, however needy. Second, neither the Christian Democratic Party (Democrazia Cristiana, or DC) nor the Left was really interested in extending family allowances to either non-insured workers or the self-employed. Finally, the tax system in Italy, which did not adequately capture income from the self-employed, was not capable of supporting a major extension of the system.

Unlike in the Netherlands, there was no postwar plan to turn the old occupationally based family allowance scheme into a Beveridgean, universal program. The D'Aragona commission on social security, the direct analog to the Netherlands' van Rhijn Commission, specifically recommended a non-Beveridgean system of family allowances (Commissione per la Riforma della Previdenza Sociale 1948). The commission was explicit that family allowances were to be considered a wage supplement, not a social security benefit, and argued for a work-related benefit available to people whose main income came from dependent employment (in the form of either wages or social insurance benefits linked to employment). The self-employed were to be included in the family allowance plan, but only at a later date, once the administrative and fiscal obstacles to including them could be overcome.

The DC's lack of interest in universalizing the family allowance system sprang from the fact that their key constituencies were either already covered or derived greater benefits from *not* receiving family allowances than from receiving them. Public employees received an independent family allowance scheme in 1952, and thus did not need to be integrated into a universal benefit system. Agricultural workers and small farmers were incorporated into the wage earners' system in 1967, on quite favorable terms.

The self-employed constitute the last major constituency group of the DC that remained without entitlement to family allowances, but they derived clear benefits from remaining outside the system. In the immediate postwar years, income from self-employment was not subject to taxation, and as a matter of basic fairness, it was clear that the self-employed should not be eligible for tax-financed benefits. To incorporate the self-employed into a system of universal family allowances, it would have been necessary first to establish levies on income from self-employment, and then to enforce and collect these taxes. While income taxes on the self-employed were eventually legislated, the social insurance system (including family allowances) did not take on a universalist form to match. There was ample awareness among the public and among policy experts that the self-employed were not subject to *effective* taxation, and thus should not be included in a universal family allowance scheme.

The self-employed agreed, because in the end the DC was able to offer them a better deal even than family allowances. The self-employed remained outside the family allowance system, but in return received tacit permission to evade income taxes, as well as other kinds of protections that boosted their incomes far more than family allowances would have (for example, stiff barriers to competition from large retailers; Livi Bacci 1998 interview). There was not a greater push from the DC for universalization of the family allowance system precisely because the main group of potential DC constituents that was left out under the occupational system perceived themselves as better off without family allowances.

But policy making in Italy was not nearly as dominated by the DC as one might expect given fifty years of DC government. Especially in the area of social policy, and especially after the beginning of the center-left coalitions in 1963, Socialist Party (Partido Socialista Italiano, or PSI) and Communist Party (Partido Comunista Italiano, or PCI) politicians were closely integrated into the policy-making process. And indeed, after 1963 there was an expansion of the family allowance system to cover categories traditionally associated with the Left: unemployed workers, domestic employees, home-workers (mostly female piece-workers), part-time agricultural wage workers, and, in 1974, old-age and disability pensioners. The Left did see the expansion of family allowances as beneficial to their constituencies, and thus to their parties' fortunes. But this expansion remained tightly linked to the wage principle: family allowances were extended only to those who had a right to a supplement to their wages (or deferred wages, in the case of the unemployed and pensioners). The self-employed and those outside

95

the formal labor market did not benefit from this extension, in the former case because of the perceived impossibility of adequately taxing them, and in the latter case because as long as poverty alleviation was not the guiding principle behind family allowances, people with weak attachments to the labor market had correspondingly weak claims to entitlement.

In sum, during the 1950s and early 1960s family allowances were not universalized, but nevertheless experienced substantial growth. The level of the benefit was raised on numerous occasions, and the pool of beneficiaries expanded to cover new constituencies. Indexation between 1955 and 1961 kept the purchasing power of the allowances more or less constant, and indicates a consensus that the level was about right. So how can we understand what happens next: the quite sudden decline of family allowances through the de-indexation of benefits and the use of funds contributed to the family allowance scheme for other purposes?

1964–82: Inattention and the "Sacking" of the Family Allowance Funds

The 1961 reorganization of the family allowance scheme consolidated the numerous accounts for different sectors into three funds and reduced the variety of benefit levels to two. It also marked the beginning of the end for Italy's family allowances. The indexation of benefits to the cost of living, instituted in the legislation of 1955, ceased in 1961. This change, which would have enormous implications for the future of family allowance benefits, came about with relatively little fanfare. Confederazione Generale Italiana del Lavoro (CGIL), Confederazione Italiana Sindacati Lavoratori (CISL), and Confindustria documents for the year 1961 contain no mention of the de-indexation. Family allowances had increased along with living costs before they were indexed in 1955, so unions were probably willing to concede on the indexation issue, especially since inflation rates in the late 1950s and early 1960s were fairly low. The consolidation of schemes for different categories of workers, which meant that industrial workers ended up taking on the large deficits in the artisans' and agricultural workers' schemes, was a much more salient issue. Certainly this is what Confindustria was most concerned with, and what the Minister for Labor and Social Affairs, in his presentation to the Senate in October of 1961, spent the most breath trying to justify (Sullo 1961).

But there is another reason why de-indexing might not have seemed like an important change at the time: the *massimale* was still in place. With the *massimale* in place, employers did not have to pay contributions on their total wage bills above a certain ceiling. This meant that smaller employers, and employers in lower-wage sectors and areas, ended up paying proportionally more. In addition, since the level of the income ceiling was not indexed and had not been raised since it was instituted, contributions to the family allowance fund were not growing with the growth in the total wage bill. This was seen as putting a constraint on further expansion of the system, as expressed by Minister Sullo and (repeatedly) by the unions. The hope was that by getting rid of the *massimale*, there would be more resources to go around, and family allowances would be able to grow. The 1961 legislation agreed to abolish the *massimale* by 1964, and that was where hopes for further expansion of family allowances lay.

As it happened, after de-indexation in 1961, the real value of family allowances dropped sharply, beginning a long slide. There were two revaluations in 1964, but that year there was another significant event in the history of Italian family allowances. With surpluses in the family allowance fund growing as a result of the declining payouts, the unions and employers reached an agreement in April of 1964 to allocate the full surplus to family allowance increases. However, as the economic situation continued to worsen, other claims began to intrude on the family allowance fund's nest egg. Tripartite policy concertation, in place since 1962 and viewed by the unions as a vital contribution to keeping the new center-left government alive, resulted in agreements that weakened the financial autonomy of the family allowance fund and signaled the beginning of a new set of policy priorities. Under pressure from the government, unions agreed to delay part of the planned increase in family allowances, diverting the surplus in the Cassa Unica Assegni Familiari (CUAF) to funds for short-term unemployment benefits and the construction of workers' housing. In return, the government agreed to present a serious plan for pension reform by December of 1964. So despite a small uptick in the real value of the benefit in 1965, the agreement of 1964 marked the beginning of what key Italian observers of family policy would term the "sacrifice" (Franco and Sartor 1994, 17) or the "sacking" (Gorrieri 1979, 129–31) of family allowances in order to obtain other policy priorities.

Despite the extension of family allowances to new constituencies (short-term unemployment beneficiaries in 1964, unemployment insurance beneficiaries in 1965, the agricultural self-employed in 1967, and domestic and home workers in 1971 and 1973), aggregate spending and average benefits would suffer a real decline from 1964 onward. The only respite from this decline came in 1974–5 when the *massimale* was finally abolished and allowances were revalued to roughly 1966 levels before dropping off even more steeply again in the following year. Also in 1974 family allowances were extended to INPS disability and old-age pensioners. Because in Italy dependent spouses and parents, as well as children, are eligible for family allowances, many pensioners benefited, and this in fact marked a notable expansion of the program. After the enactment of this provision, about 55 percent of recipients of family allowances were pensioners (Sgritta and Zanatta 1993). Ironically, the only major benefit increase of the supposedly youth-oriented family allowance program after 1961 primarily benefited pensioners.

After the crucial decisions first to de-index benefits, and then to trade family allowance increases for progress on the pension front, family allowance spending underwent a precipitous decline in Italy. At a technical level, this development is explained by high inflation, which eroded the value of allowances, and the substitution of other policy priorities for ad hoc increases that might have maintained the value of the family allowance benefit. Explaining the politics of this sequence of events is somewhat more complicated.

Because of their link to the wage system, family allowances had simply ceased to be on the top of anyone's list of social policy priorities. Union documents and officials testify that the important fights on behalf of working families in the 1960s had to do with creating jobs and raising wages, not increasing family allowances (Roscani 1998 interview; Giovannini 1999 interview; Giustina 1999 interview). And as long as wages continued to rise, family allowances became less and less important relative to either wages or major social benefits such as pensions that were, unlike family allowances, meant to provide a full replacement for wages. Similarly, although family allowances might have been useful to employers because they would have helped to reduce pressure on wages, employers were loath to offer to pay more for family allowances in a period when demands for other social contributions (pensions, unemployment, sickness, etc.) were on the rise (Mariani 1999 interview). One could say that by the time anyone noticed that family allowances were being devalued out of existence, it was too late: at that point they hardly seemed worth fighting for anymore. Here again, pensioners are the exception that proves the rule. Pensioners were not only organized, vocal, and important constituents within unions and political parties; their incomes on average were also low enough that family allowances really did make a difference for them, and they exerted substantial pressure to get them in 1974–5.

Yet even as family allowance benefits declined in value, the system was expanded to include more and more people. A close examination of which new groups received benefits and how these benefits were administered in the period after devaluation suggests that family allowances were still useful to the two main parties in office, the Christian Democrats and the Socialists. Small farmers were the single most influential lobby group within the DC in the 1960s (LaPalombara 1964), and they were awarded family allowance benefits in 1967. The PSI was also able to please important constituencies with the extension of family allowance benefits to part-time agricultural workers, domestic workers, and social insurance beneficiaries. (Both the DC and the PSI probably perceived it to be in their interest to award family allowances to pensioners, a fast-growing and increasingly vocal constituency in the early 1970s.) Benefits for these new groups were administered directly by the state, rather than through employers. Politicians in the ruling coalition thus gained doubly by the expansion of the family allowance system, despite low benefit levels. The extension of benefits was targeted at their constituencies, and they had direct control over the disbursement of allowances.

Recalling the interests of clientelist politicians in the ruling coalition helps to make sense of the fact that family allowances continued to be extended while their value declined. What mattered to parties distributing patronage was not so much how big the benefit was, but how much control they had over it. Many smaller benefits were more useful for securing votes than fewer, higher ones. At the same time, unions and the political Left became increasingly disinterested in defending the level of family allowances as their value fell and they ceased to be an important part of wages.

Post-1983: Structural Reform, or Old Wine in New Bottles?

By the end of the 1970s, observers frequently bemoaned the inadequacy of family allowances in Italy. Two minor revaluations of family allowances occurred in 1980, at least partially in response to the debate sparked by Gorrieri's influential 1979 publication *The Family Budget Jungle* (La giungla dei bilanci familiari). This work launched a scathing critique of politicians and bureaucrats who had, in Gorrieri's widely shared view, misused the funds collected for family allowances to "finance a whole host of clientelist policies aimed at those who are not really in need of assistance" (Gorrieri 1979, 131). By the early 1980s, there was general agreement within the policy-making community on the need to reform the family allowance system more fundamentally.

One reason for the new attention to family allowances was a newfound concern among policy makers and politicians with poverty among families with children. The postwar Poverty Commission (1951) and Commission on Unemployment (1953) had identified families with working-age heads, especially large families, as prime candidates for poverty when adequate labor market remuneration was not forthcoming. But they had both seen boosting employment, especially in the south, as the means to alleviate this poverty. Problem cases that would not disappear as a result of more and better jobs were expected to be few, and could be taken care of by regional- and municipal-level charity programs (Camera dei Deputati 1953; Commissione Parlamentare d'Inchiesta sulla Disoccupazione 1953).

The economic boom of the 1950s and 1960s indeed did dramatically raise the standard of living of most working-age families, to the point where poverty among the elderly became the almost exclusive concern of policy makers, politicians, and union specialists interested in poverty issues. But when in the 1970s a "rediscovery" of poverty occurred in Italy, as elsewhere in Europe (see Gauthier 1993), in Italy the policy response was limited to facilitating local-level efforts to combat social exclusion and poverty among the hard-core poor such as drug addicts, the handicapped, or the homeless. The turning point came in 1982, with the publication of a European Union–sponsored report on poverty directed by Giovanni Sarpellon. Sarpellon's report echoed the results of the early postwar studies in arguing that unemployment and bad employment were among the most important causes of poverty in Italy. Sarpellon called attention in particular to the problems of large families living in the south, arguing that poverty among the elderly, while it was indeed the most prevalent form of poverty in the north, was not Italy's biggest problem (Sarpellon 1983).

Sarpellon's report came out in the context of renewed interest in Catholic circles in the issue of the family wage[7] and in the midst of the work of the government Commission on the Problems of Families (which was commissioned in 1980 and presented its final report in 1983). This commission was charged by the government with setting a coherent policy agenda for helping families, in particular the families of workers. Its final report advocated

[7] The 1981 papal encyclical *Laborem excercens* and the DC proposal for a large family allowance increase for nonworking mothers – a proposal that the PCI attacked as a cynical electoral ploy since it could not possibly be funded – were also presented at around this time.

focusing resources on poor families, given what the commission members perceived as inherent limits to the resources that could be made available for helping families. They suggested a Social Allowance (*assegno sociale*), to be given to poor families of dependent employees in order to bring them out of poverty. While the eventual goal of extending this benefit beyond employees was deemed desirable, it was argued that the fiscal system's limited capacity to collect taxes on income from self-employment made the prospect of any universal expansion difficult. The commission also suggested merging the social allowance for families with children into a more general allowance providing a basic income for the elderly poor and invalidity pensioners (Commissione Nazionale per i Problemi della Famiglia 1983). However, the commission rejected acting immediately on this last proposal, because they were concerned that its greater cost would result in money being channeled away from families with children (Franco and Sartor 1990).

In 1983, the same year as the report of the Commission on the Problems of Families, the family allowance system underwent a seemingly minor change that was the beginning of a period of substantial reform. Union-employer-government concertation in 1983 resulted in the Scotti Accord, a set of provisions designed to revive the flagging Italian economy. Under this agreement, the indexation of wages to inflation was reduced, and in compensation a new supplementary family allowance, paid out of general revenues, was adopted. However, this supplementary allowance would be available only to some families, based on their income and family size. For the first time, a means test was introduced into the Italian family allowance system, and the goal of poverty alleviation through vertical redistribution came to the forefront after decades during which the principle that family allowances should mainly aim at horizontal redistribution among wage-earners had dominated.

In 1984, cost-containment pressures led to the means-testing of regular family allowances. Meanwhile, the government's Poverty Commission, instituted in 1984, was preparing its report, which came out in 1985 (Commissione di Indagine sulla Povertá 1985). The Poverty Commission's recommendations were similar to those of the Commission on the Problem of Families, in that they supported the idea of a means-tested benefit to poor families. However, the poverty commission favored extending the benefit to the poor elderly as well as to families with children. Responding to these recommendations, in 1988 Parliament passed a government proposal to replace the family allowance system with a new program, the Allowance for the Family Unit (Assegno per il Nucleo Familiare, or ANF). It would, like family allowances after 1984, be means-tested, and benefits would be graduated by family size and income.

The concept of a "dependent" was abolished in favor of the concept of family or household "need." Benefits would be granted no longer on the basis of a person's status as a provider for dependent children or adults but on the basis of the overall level of need in the household. Allowances for children were to be given to parents, but allowances for dependent parents went directly to the elderly themselves. And single elderly persons became eligible for the ANF.

But despite the fact that family allowances had been transformed from an insurance measure into a poverty-alleviation measure for individuals of all age groups, they were still financed primarily through employer contributions. And despite the fact that the principle of need had taken over for the essentially insurance-based concept of the old family allowances, non-elderly families were eligible for benefits *only if they were headed by employees*, no matter how needy they might be. As a result, under the ANF, occupationally based contributions paid for citizenship-based assistance benefits for the elderly, but the workers financing the system could receive the benefit themselves only if they passed a means test. And poor non-elderly families had no entitlement to benefits unless they were headed by workers in the formal labor market.

This rather bizarre situation came about because of union concerns about the capacity of a tax-financed system to support adequate benefit levels. Unions withheld their objection to financing the ANF through payroll contributions because they were aware that switching to a system financed out of general revenues would imply a universalization of benefits. And if entitlement became universal, union leaders feared, the system would probably become too expensive to maintain benefits at current levels. Shifting away from payroll financing might in fact result in benefits dwindling even further. Union leaders calculated that if they could maintain a contribution-financed system, at least decent benefits would be assured for the poorest wage workers and pensioners (Saraceno 1999 interview).

What does this episode of reform tell us about the trajectory of benefits for young people in Italy? After the early 1980s key political actors recognized that families with children were not doing well and agreed that something needed to be done to combat poverty among this group. This perception continued and strengthened through the early and mid-1990s. But at the same time, policy makers believed that costs needed to be contained and that there was no room for a real expansion of family allowances (despite the fact that the family allowance fund was in surplus, paying out less than half of what it took in in contributions in the period 1980–90). The reforms of the mid-1980s responded to concerns that the old system of untargeted benefits had not worked well, and directed resources more effectively to needy families, many of which had children. On the other hand, these reforms reflected a continuing reluctance to spend even the money that was actually being collected for family allowances, let alone to take funding away from other priorities. Quite the opposite, in fact: the 1995 pension reform made official the decades-old practice of transferring funds from the family allowances account within INPS to cover part of the deficits in the pension system. The 1980s saw more attention paid to poor young families, but as was the case for the 1974–5 increase in family allowance levels, the family allowance system could be improved only on the condition that more resources also be directed to the elderly poor.

Why do family allowances in Italy follow a trajectory of declining benefit levels and patchwork expansion of family allowances to new clienteles? In the immediate postwar period, policy makers were concerned about the well-being of working families, and no one's interests were hurt by family allowances. Expansion made good political and economic sense. But family allowances were never seen as the main way of ensuring the financial stability of young families: that task was up to the labor market. Furthermore, the reliance of the Christian Democratic Party on spotty taxation of the self-employed made it undesirable for any party to push for a universal family allowance system. The de-indexing of family allowances and prioritization of other policy goals (namely, pension reform) in the mid-1960s set the stage for a rapid devaluation of family allowances. This period was marked by increasing electoral competition between Christian Democracy and parties of the Left, but all parties in government could gain electoral support simply by extending the benefit to new social groups, without regard to the benefit's declining real value. Before anyone noticed it, family allowances were so small that they had ceased to be worth fighting for, and the transfer of family allowance funds to other policy priorities, backed by a strong elderly lobby, met with little resistance.

Conclusion

This chapter has examined one program, family allowances, that constitutes an essential component of the overall age orientation of social policies in

Italy and the Netherlands. The interests of groups commonly believed to dominate welfare policy making – labor unions, employers, the Catholic Church – do not appear to determine the fate of family allowances in the post–World War II period in either Italy or the Netherlands. Political pressure from age-based interest groups – the family lobby in the Netherlands and the elderly lobby in Italy – does influence the development of spending on family allowances, but rarely decisively. The key political actors whose behavior determines spending patterns on family allowances in Italy and the Netherlands are politicians working within political parties. In some cases the demands of age-based lobbies do overlap with the strategic choices of politicians, and in these situations it is relatively straightforward to interpret policy outcomes as a result of the pressure of electorally important constituencies for specific policy goals. In other cases, however, the vote-seeking behavior of politicians affects family policy outcomes in a less direct way. Politicians' choices in other policy arenas (e.g., taxation, wage policy, pension policy) shape the potential constituencies of family allowances and the growth potential of family allowance policies, which in turn affect how attractive family allowances are as political currency for vote-seeking politicians.

If the behavior of politicians helps to create the institutional framework within which family allowances develop, it is also true that this framework, once set in place, exercises considerable influence on the behavior of politicians. In particular, the early choice of either universalist or occupationally based family allowance programs sets the boundaries within which family allowances may grow. Universalist family allowance schemes, whether means-tested or truly universal, result in welfare regimes that are relatively generous to young people. Universalism in welfare programs has been conceptualized as an indicator of the degree of cross-class solidarity achieved in welfare states (Baldwin 1990; Esping-Andersen 1990; Ferrera 1993). But if solidaristic principles underlie universalism, they do not also generate the age profile of the social policies that result from universalism. Rather, universalism and occupationalism in welfare programs condition how politicians may use these programs as tender in bargaining for votes, which is in turn responsible for their expansion or contraction.

The breakdown of pillarization in the Netherlands, with the concomitant increase in electoral competition, coincided with a major expansion of family allowance benefits. Likewise, in Italy, there was an expansion of benefits to cover key constituents of the DC and the PSI in the 1960s and 1970s, accompanied by greater government discretion in the disbursement of allowances. Both of these indicate a use of family allowance benefits for particularistic purposes, notwithstanding that the target groups in the Dutch case are far more encompassing than in the Italian case. But how politicians use programs to buy votes, and how this affects spending on family allowances, is altered by the structure (universalist or occupational) of the programs.

The Dutch family allowance program's character as a universal benefit after 1962 divorced it rhetorically from its roots as a wage supplement for workers with large families. Thus, rising wages and standards of living did not, as in Italy, make the allowances less important. Rather, as family allowances became an entitlement of parenthood, using them as the currency of electoral exchange became more costly. The only way to expand the program was to increase per child spending, and finally the family allowance, like other Dutch citizenship-based entitlements, was linked to the indexed minimum wage – even though family allowances by this time had lost their role as a wage supplement.

In Italy, by contrast, a major expansion of the *number* of family allowance beneficiaries coincided with a substantial drop in spending (both aggregate and per child) and a dramatic decline in the real value of the allowances. This decline in benefits for salaried workers occurred despite the fact that this group was the key beneficiary of the family allowance scheme as it was laid out in the pre–World War II period, and perhaps because it was a source of the Left opposition's staunchest supporters. The erosion of benefits for such a large group of voters was politically tenable, though, because just as inflation began seriously to impinge on the value of the un-indexed family allowances, wages were indexed to inflation. The smaller family allowances became as a share of take-home pay, the less interested unions were in making them a policy priority, as long as the "earned" component of wages was rising steadily and eventually became indexed to inflation. And for those groups that were not included in the original Fascist-era family allowance system or in the postwar Christian Democratic expansion to small farmers – groups such as pensioners, the unemployed, domestics, and home workers – even small family allowances were a nice bonus and sometimes a significant component of incomes that were largely unprotected from inflation.

The distinction between universalist and occupational program structures makes a difference for family allowance spending, then, for two main reasons. First, it is more expensive to expand a population-wide benefit than a piecemeal one. Second, objections to devaluation of the benefit are weaker when family allowances are viewed as a component of the wage rather than an independent entitlement. So then the important question is why family allowances were universalized in the Netherlands in 1962, but not in Italy. These program structures themselves are a result of politicians' choices about how to get the most out of public policies, in particular, tax and spending policies.

Extending family allowances to the self-employed, which in the Dutch case was accomplished by universalizing the family allowance system, was *desirable* because it granted cash benefits to a segment of the electorate that was crucial to the fortunes of both Protestant and Catholic parties during a period of electoral realignment. Universalizing the benefit was *possible* because the comprehensive Dutch tax system allowed benefits for the self-employed to be paid for out of tax revenues, rather than requiring employer and employee contributions to finance benefits for the self-employed as well.

In Italy the electoral situation was quite similar, with intense intra-DC competition for the rural self-employed electorate. But in contrast to the Dutch situation, Italy's famously unenforceable and unenforced tax system, a system whose only reliable source of revenue was automatic deductions from the pay of wage earners and salaried employees of large companies, did not permit universalization of the family allowance system. To make extending family allowances to the self-employed politically acceptable, the tax system would have had to be reformed to include small-business owners and the self-employed, as virtually every commentator on the social security system since the close of the war argued. While the DC had been able to "sell" the unfunded expansion of the family allowances system to small farmers as a necessary solidaristic gesture on behalf of industrial workers (many of whom had relatives living in the south), covering the better-off self-employed without subjecting them to contributions would have stretched that solidarity to the breaking point. But the inadequate taxation of the self-employed in Italy was in itself a valuable political resource for the DC. The family allowance system was never fully universalized because both the DC and the self-employed found it advantageous to forgo family allowances in order to maintain tax privileges. Of course, this did not preclude the piecemeal extension of inexpensive family allowances to less privileged constituencies who could be bought off for less.

In the end, it was politicians' strategic choices with regard to the tax system (non-enforcement) and the wage system (indexation of wages but not allowances) that stymied the growth of family allowances in Italy. In the Netherlands, the opposite choices made for universalization and expansion of benefits, such that by 1990 the Netherlands had the most generous cash benefits for families in the OECD. This focus on the strategic behavior of politicians in response to demand from a variety of societal groups (including labor unions, employers, family organizations, and pensioners' groups) usefully directs attention toward an under-emphasized phenomenon linked to the development of welfare states. It casts politicians as crucial actors in the design and magnitude of social programs, through vote-seeking behavior that influences both spending and features of the institutional landscape that impact social policy outcomes more indirectly.

5

Benefits for the Unemployed

YOUNG AND OLD IN THE
FORTRESS LABOR MARKET

This chapter addresses two questions: *how* and *why* do unemployment benefits in Italy treat older workers more generously than younger workers,
while in the Netherlands the opposite is true? The answer to the *how*
question is straightforward. The youth orientation of the Dutch system
of unemployment protection is due largely to two policy features: generous regular unemployment insurance benefits and universal coverage
that protects first-time job seekers. Italy's highly elderly-oriented system
of unemployment protection, on the other hand, is characterized by meager regular unemployment insurance benefits and no benefits for youth
unemployed.

The answer to the *why* question is more complicated and more interesting. Italy and the Netherlands share features that we might expect would
lead them to develop similar kinds of unemployment policies. Both display
features of what have variously been labeled Conservative-Corporatist or
Christian Democratic systems, combined with a distinct leftist presence in
policy making. The result is a male-breadwinner–centered labor market,
few active labor market policies, and low female labor force participation.
The two countries also share a history of high unemployment, numerically
rather weak labor unions, and high levels of self-employment. Yet Esping-
Andersen's (1990) characterization of the Netherlands as an almost Social
Democratic welfare state, a characterization driven largely by the generosity of Dutch unemployment benefits, highlights an important difference.
Italy and the Netherlands differ dramatically in the extent to which their
welfare states protect elderly versus non-elderly citizens from a variety of
risks, and nowhere is this difference as pronounced as in their unemployment policy regimes.

Benefits for the Unemployed

The elderly orientation of the Italian system of unemployment protection, and the relative youth orientation of the Dutch system, are a result of interactions between the structure of labor market policies that politicians and policy makers have inherited from the past and the characteristics of the competitive environments in which they find themselves. The quite different age orientations of the unemployment protection systems in the Netherlands and Italy are difficult to explain if we consider only the ideologies or power resources of political actors, but not once we include the institutional and political environment within which they act.

Standard explanations for the extreme generosity of Dutch unemployment insurance benefits, for example, attribute high replacement rates to either Christian Democratic dominance of policy making and the resulting male-breadwinner focus or, more commonly, to the societal consensus on Social Democratic ideals of universal coverage and generous benefits. Yet a closer look at the evolution of the Dutch system reveals that the policy choices that led to a relatively youth-oriented system of unemployment protection are more strongly influenced by the legacies of pre–World War I experiments with unemployment insurance and the electoral pressures associated with the breakdown of pillarization in the 1960s. Politicians eager to claim credit for a generous system of regular unemployment benefits maintained high replacement rates that dated back to 1916, and electoral pressures contributed to the creation of universalistic unemployment benefits in the mid-1960s. Once this system was in place, it generated across-the-board entitlements that grew with the pace of the rest of the welfare state until the mid-1980s. And, as we see in more detail in the following section, the combination of high replacement rates for regular unemployment insurance and universal coverage are the most important contributors to the Netherlands' youth-oriented system of unemployment protection.

In Italy, as in the Netherlands, policy legacies and the dynamics of partisan competition emerge as crucial determinants of the age orientation of the system of unemployment protection. The low level of regular unemployment benefits and the lack of coverage for youth unemployed in Italy are most often attributed to the impotence of unions and the Left in the face of employer preferences for state-subsidized short-term income replacement schemes over contribution-financed regular unemployment benefits. As in the Dutch case, however, this power resources argument begins to break down under closer scrutiny. In Italy, legacies of clientelist political competition, including a weakly enforced tax system, precluded setting replacement rates for regular unemployment insurance at a high level and scuttled plans for universal unemployment benefits. Crucially, unions and the Communist Left *altered their preferences* to account for the clientelist behavior of Christian Democratic and eventually Socialist politicians. The Left consistently concurred with policy choices that led to an elderly-oriented system of unemployment protection, often despite their stated goals of improving conditions for younger citizens. As in the Dutch case, policy legacies and the environment of political competition are important determinants of the age orientation of the Italian unemployment protection system.

This chapter begins with a comparison of unemployment benefits regimes in Italy and the Netherlands in the 1990s. The comparison goes beyond legislated replacement rates and aggregate spending to examine the consequences for different age groups of national ensembles of different types of unemployment-related programs. The second part of the chapter traces the development of the differing age profiles of unemployment policy regimes in Italy and the Netherlands, which are not a straightforward result of political pressure from groups of potential beneficiaries, employers, or trade unions. Rather, they are a long-term effect of program structures that are driven by politicians' behavior during periods of intense electoral competition.

Comparing Unemployment Benefits in Italy and the Netherlands

A comprehensive comparison of the age orientation of unemployment-related policies should begin with a global comparison of coverage and benefit levels, to determine how well an average unemployed person is protected against income loss due to joblessness. But we also want to know how younger versus older members of the work force fare within the full range of programs offering income maintenance for unemployed people. This section reviews the various kinds of unemployment benefits available in Italy and the Netherlands and the populations covered by each scheme. Next follows a closer examination of the beneficiaries of different kinds of unemployment benefits to see how older and younger workers fare under these programs.

Income Protection Programs for the Unemployed

Since 1916 in the Netherlands and 1919 in Italy, there has existed some form of state-sanctioned system for protecting workers from loss of income due to joblessness. Throughout the post–World War II period, moreover, a variety of programs supplementing traditional unemployment insurance have developed in both countries. All of the unemployment benefit programs outlined below have undergone significant changes in benefit levels, eligibility criteria, duration of benefits, and so on since their inception. The most important changes took place during two periods: from immediately after the war through the mid-1960s, when prewar systems were adapted to postwar conditions; and from the mid-1980s onward, as welfare reformers sought to adapt the postwar systems to post–oil shock realities. But the elderly orientation of the Italian system and the youth orientation of the Dutch system persisted throughout the postwar period. We can summarize the different types of income-maintenance benefits available to the unemployed in the "mature" Italian and Dutch welfare states, noting that while the systems have undergone some structural changes, especially since the mid-1980s, their relative age orientations remain distinct.

Regular Unemployment Insurance   The first national-level unemployment insurance schemes were introduced in 1916 in the Netherlands and in 1919 in Italy. The Dutch program was a voluntary scheme, financed 50 percent by the state, and paid out benefits equaling 70 percent of the prior wage for up to ten weeks. The Italian unemployment insurance law, Italy's first obligatory social insurance program of any kind, was financed by employer and employee contributions, with the state stepping in to cover deficits when necessary. The benefit was guaranteed for up to twenty weeks but, on the model that had just been adopted in Britain, offered only a "subsistence" benefit to recipients. This flat-rate benefit had three gradations according to the contribution level, but could in no case exceed 50 percent of the previous wage. For average-income earners, this amounted to a replacement rate of 36 percent of the average daily wage in industry at that time – not dramatically meaner than the unemployment provisions extant in other advanced countries at that time, but still less generous than in the Netherlands (ILO 1922).

This original divergence in replacement rates continued in the regulation of unemployment insurance benefits after World War II in Italy and the Netherlands. The Dutch introduced compulsory unemployment insurance for all employees (including agricultural employees) in 1949 with the Unemployment Insurance Act (Werkloosheidswet, or WW). This insurance provided for a (taxable) benefit equal to 80 percent of the previous salary (for heads of household), financed jointly by employers, employees, and the state, and lasting for a maximum of twenty-six weeks. (Benefits were lower for nonhousehold heads: 70 percent for singles living on their own, and 60 percent for singles living with their parents.) In 1964, the Dutch government passed a supplementary unemployment insurance act (Wijziging Wet Werkloosheidsvoorziening, or WWV) that provided benefits of 75 percent of the previous wage for people unemployed up to two years beyond the original six months covered under the WW. In 1987, as part of a major overhaul of the Dutch system of labor-market–related regulation, the benefit level was reduced to 70 percent of previous salary, still above the average replacement rate among European countries.

Italy's postwar unemployment insurance law, passed in 1949, maintained the subsistence benefit format of the old unemployment insurance system. But large increases in the cost of living during and immediately after the war meant that the new daily benefit (now a flat-rate 200 lire/day) was nowhere near subsistence level. When the law was introduced, this benefit provided for a replacement rate of only 17 percent of an average production worker's daily wage. The lack of indexation of the benefit to either wages or prices meant that the purchasing power of the benefit continued to fall, despite sporadic upward adjustments in its nominal value during the late 1950s to mid-1970s. By 1974, the regular unemployment insurance benefit had fallen to 800 lire/day, just 8.6 percent of the gross wage of an average production worker in 1974. It remained at this level until 1988 (in 1987 Italy's Constitutional Court ruled that 800 lire per day was a constitutionally inadequate benefit), when the regular unemployment insurance payment was raised to 20 percent of prior earnings. By 1999, the benefit had again been revised upward to 40 percent of prior earnings, a substantial increase, to be sure, but still much lower than in the Netherlands.

Comparing benefit replacement rates across countries can lead to inaccurate judgments about the relative generosity of different programs net of taxes and other benefits (Fawcett and Papadopoulos 1997). Unemployment insurance benefits are taxed as income in some countries and not in others, and benefits normally associated with income from work (e.g., family allowances, housing benefits, or credit for future pensions) also accrue to unemployment insurance recipients in some cases. It is useful, then, to use household income data to estimate post-tax, post-transfer benefit levels for unemployment insurance recipients. It is reassuring to note that even after taking into account taxation of unemployment benefits and the addition of family and housing benefits, the Dutch benefit remains among the most generous in the OECD, and the Italian benefit among the least generous, for a variety of model family types (Table 5.1).

Benefits for the Unemployed

Table 5.1 *Net replacement rates of unemployment insurance benefits, 1997*

	Single		Couple with two children
Ireland	31	Greece	44
Australia	33	United Kingdom	49
New Zealand	39	**Italy**	**53**
Italy	**42**	Ireland	57
United Kingdom	46	United States	57
Greece	47	Australia	62
United States	58	Belgium	64
Germany	60	Japan	64
Austria	60	New Zealand	68
Canada	62	Germany	70
Denmark	63	France	72
Belgium	64	Denmark	73
Finland	65	Spain	73
Norway	66	Norway	74
Japan	67	Austria	76
France	71	Sweden	78
Sweden	71	Portugal	79
Spain	74	Finland	83
Portugal	79	Luxembourg	87
Luxembourg	82	**Netherlands**	**89**
Netherlands	**82**	Canada	91

Note: Data reflect replacement rates of wages at average production worker earnings level after taxes and including housing and family benefits.
Source: OECD 2002.

The generosity of regular unemployment insurance benefits clearly differs markedly between Italy and the Netherlands. But regular unemployment insurance benefits in both countries are supplemented by a wide variety of other programs for unemployed workers in different sectors of the economy and with different personal characteristics. So to determine both the generosity of unemployment benefits in general and the specific orientations of these policies toward different age groups, it is necessary to look beyond the basic insurance program.

Benefits for Partial Unemployment The Netherlands provides insurance for partial loss of income due to shortened work hours or temporary layoffs, with the same benefits as for full unemployment. This benefit may also be used to cover temporary unemployment due to bad weather.

In 1979 about 24 percent of unemployment insurance payouts were for partial or short-term unemployment (CBS 1981, 360). In Italy, insurance for partial unemployment is in fact an important alternative to the ordinary unemployment insurance benefit and takes several forms: the short-time earnings replacement fund (Cassa per l'Integrazione Guadagni, or CIG), the "extraordinary" version of the same program (Cassa per l'Integrazione Guadagni Straordinaria, or CIGS), and so-called mobility allowances (*indennità di mobilità*).

The earnings replacement fund was established in 1945 to compensate industrial workers for earnings lost due to reductions in working hours. With the introduction of bans on mass layoffs after the end of the war, CIG became an important tool used by employers to manage excess productive capacity without dismissing workers outright. Throughout the 1950s and early 1960s, CIG was funded by employer contributions and was used in place of dismissals during brief periods of slack.

In 1968, however, a new, "extraordinary" form of the benefit (CIGS), funded out of general tax revenues rather than employer contributions, was introduced. During the 1970s and 1980s, CIGS became both employers' and unions' tool of choice for compensating workers during partial or full unemployment resulting from industrial restructuring, sectoral crises, cyclical downturns, and plant closures.[1] From 1975 onward, both CIG and CIGS paid out a tax-free benefit equal to 80 percent of prior gross wages – clearly a much more comprehensive form of income replacement than the ordinary unemployment insurance program.

Mobility allowances were introduced in 1991 to provide an alternative to the use of CIGS, which was coming under increasing fire. Mobility benefits are paid to workers laid off by firms in the same sectors covered under CIGS, who have been employed in the relevant firm for at least twelve months, and who are available for work in a "suitable job." The "suitable job" criteria are more generous than for regular unemployment benefits, however, and mobility beneficiaries receive special priority for job placement. The amount of the benefit is similar to CIGS. The duration of the benefit ranges from twelve to forty-eight months, depending on the unemployed person's age and the region of residence, but is longest for older workers.

---

[1] Although nominally CIGS was for temporary unemployment, in the late 1970s it became possible for redundant employees to receive CIGS benefits while working for a firm that had ceased operation.

Benefits for the Unemployed

Special Unemployment Insurance Benefits   Special unemployment benefits (*trattamenti speciali*) offer another alternative to the low regular unemployment insurance in Italy. These benefits for limited groups of workers in industry, construction, and agriculture were introduced in 1968, and pay out a benefit in most cases equal to 80 percent of prior wages. The duration of the benefit varies from scheme to scheme; in most cases the initial grant of benefit was for six months, but this can often be extended, as with CIG.

Unemployment Assistance Benefits   Protection for the long-term unemployed and first-time job seekers, which in other countries is often provided by unemployment assistance benefits, is the most conspicuous absence in the Italian arsenal against income loss due to unemployment. In the immediate aftermath of World War II, Italy introduced a special subsidy (*sussidio straordinario*) for unemployed persons, which offered a basic assistance benefit for all unemployed persons regardless of whether they held any unemployment insurance coverage. Similar assistance benefits were introduced in many European countries in order to ease the postwar transition. However, in contrast with most other European countries, Italy's national government never introduced a permanent, comprehensive unemployment assistance program.[2] As a result, there is no minimum income guarantee in Italy for unemployed people who have only scattered contribution records, who have been out of work for long periods, or who have not yet succeeded in entering the work force. Since both first-time joblessness and long-term unemployment are phenomena that disproportionately affect younger members of the work force in Italy, this lacuna biases the system of unemployment benefits in Italy against younger workers, as we discuss below.

The Netherlands does guarantee a means-tested unemployment assistance benefit to the unemployed. The level of the benefit was equal through 1995 to 100 percent of the statutory minimum wage for married heads of households; following important revisions to the social assistance law in 1995, childless beneficiaries under the age of twenty-two received only 50 percent of the minimum wage. (The minimum wage is itself linked to average earnings, such that in 1980 it was equivalent to about 80 percent of the median wage; by 2003, revisions to the system of labor market regulation and income supports had reduced the minimum wage to 52 percent

---

[2] Nor was there any other form of national-level guaranteed minimum income. A few regional governments have instituted assistance programs for the unemployed, but these benefits remain discretionary and cannot be considered a basic citizenship right even for residents of those regions.

of the median wage.) Recipients of unemployment assistance before 1995 had to be available for work, but there was no time limit on the benefit nor was any record of previous employment required. As a result of these two features, the unemployment assistance benefit was predominantly used by two groups: the long-term unemployed and first-time job seekers.

Since 1995 the Dutch unemployment assistance benefit has been limited to twenty-four months, and unemployed persons under the age of twenty-one can receive unemployment assistance only if participating in a Youth Work Guarantee (Jeugdwerkgarantiewet, or JWG) activation scheme. These changes signal a deterioration in unemployment benefits for young people relative to the quite generous years from 1964 through the late 1980s, which has occurred for reasons discussed in the final chapter of this volume. But despite the restriction of unemployment assistance benefits relative to the "golden age" of the Dutch social spending, youth unemployed in the Netherlands remain better covered by the welfare state than in Italy. Youth unemployed in the Netherlands in the last resort still have access to social assistance benefits pegged to the minimum wage, whereas Italian youth must rely for support on their families.

Unemployment Insurance Extensions for Older Workers   The prevalence of long-term unemployment among older workers in the Netherlands has prompted the government to provide extended unemployment benefits for older workers. In the Netherlands until 1999, unemployed workers over the age of fifty-seven and a half could continue to receive insurance benefits past the two-and-a-half-year cutoff point for extended unemployment insurance benefits until they reached the age of sixty-five – at which point they began receiving an old-age pension. This meant that older workers received the earnings-related benefit rather than the means-tested social minimum benefit that long-term unemployed under the age of fifty-seven and a half received after their unemployment insurance benefits ran out. In Italy, extended unemployment insurance benefits for older workers have not been available. In practice, though, older CIG beneficiaries often continue to receive benefits until they reach retirement (or early-retirement) age, and the longest duration of benefits (forty-eight months) for mobility benefits is reserved for older workers.

Early Retirement Provisions   Early retirement has been used extensively in both Italy and the Netherlands as a way of facilitating the exit from the labor market of difficult-to-employ or less-productive older workers.[3] In the Netherlands, the first experimentation with early retirement schemes began in 1976. These schemes were expanded in the late 1970s in response to high levels of youth unemployment, on the principle that facilitating the exit of older workers would make room for young entrants (OECD 1995, 88). In Dutch law, early retirement contracts (*vervroegde uittreding*, or VUT) are negotiated between employers and labor representatives within an economic sector, and then applied to all firms in that sector. By 1979, around 80 percent of all private sector employees were covered by collective agreements granting early retirement provisions (OECD 1995, 88). In most sectors the minimum retirement age under VUT is sixty or sixty-one years, although in some cases it is as low as fifty-five (OECD 1993, 71). Early retirees receive the equivalent of a full state old-age pension and supplementary occupational pension: normally, early retirement contracts require that employers make up any difference in supplementary pension benefits that would occur as a result of a shortened contribution history.

In Italy, laws regulating early retirement in specific sectors were enacted in the 1970s. Legislation in 1981 responded to the employment crisis generated in the wake of the second oil shock, expanding early retirement provisions to include workers in large firms in most sectors of the economy (Gualmini 1998, 137). Early retirement laws normally allow workers to retire with full pension benefits up to five years early – although in some cases early retirement up to ten years early may be compensated.

Disability Benefits   Both Italy and the Netherlands recorded exceedingly high rates of disability among the working-age population in the 1980s and 1990s, a peculiarity that in both countries is widely recognized as a result of the use of disability benefits as a substitute for open unemployment. In the Netherlands since the passage of the Disablement Insurance Act (Wet op de Arbeidsongschickthheidsverzekering, or WAO) in 1967, and in Italy since 1974, the criteria for disablement included not just a person's physical incapacity but the likelihood that he or she could find suitable work given local labor market conditions. The highly discretionary nature of this criterion meant that poor labor market conditions for particular population groups (southerners in Italy, older workers in the Netherlands) could be used as a reason to grant disability benefits, even in the absence of a readily identifiable disability. Aarts and de Jong (1992, 345) estimate

[3] Neither country, however, has ever had a blanket regulation permitting early retirement.

that in the 1980s between 33 and 52 percent of disability benefits in the Netherlands were really hidden unemployment benefits; Franco and Morcaldo (1990, chapter 3) estimate a similar figure for Italy. In both countries the labor market criterion for disability was revised (in Italy in 1984 and in the Netherlands in 1987 and again in 1993), due to the growing expense of carrying such a large volume of "hidden unemployment" within the disability pension system. Still, most observers remain convinced that the disability systems continue to harbor large numbers of essentially employable individuals.

Disability benefits are an appealing, and expensive, substitute for unemployment benefits in both Italy and the Netherlands because they pay more and last longer. In the Dutch case, disability benefits for employees are related to previous income – not to the social minimum, as was the case for unemployment assistance benefits. So an unemployed person on disability would continue to receive a benefit of 70 percent of prior earnings until the age of sixty-five, while someone receiving unemployment benefits would have to switch over to the social minimum two and a half years after the onset of unemployment, when unemployment insurance benefits ran out. In addition, unions and employers negotiated top-off benefits for disability in most sectors to bring the disability benefit up to 100 percent of the previous wage (de Vroom and Blomsma 1991, 104). So even for relatively short spells of unemployment, disability would still be more generous than the 75 percent extended unemployment insurance benefit. Aarts and de Jong (1992, 40) report that the after-tax replacement rate of disability benefits for a modal worker in 1980 was 87 percent.

In Italy, as in the Netherlands, disability benefits have been an appealing alternate pathway of exit from the labor market. In southern Italy, where fewer people are covered under CIGS than in the more industrialized north, and where long-term unemployment has reached epidemic levels, disability benefits work as a substitute for a regular unemployment insurance benefit pegged far below the subsistence level. Disability insurance benefits, like old-age pensions in Italy, are calculated based on formulae combining years of service and prevailing wage rates; there is no uniform benefit standard for disability claimants in different sectors. But even at the low rate pegged to the minimum pension (see chapter 6), disability benefits typically provide a higher income than regular unemployment insurance benefits, since the minimum pension is indexed to wage growth and/or inflation, while unemployment insurance is not. In 1998, the mean INPS disability benefit was 410.5 euros per month, just above the subsidized minimum pension level (data from INPS 2003).[4] At average production worker wages, this amounted to 26 percent of gross pay.

Jobs Programs   If extended unemployment insurance benefits, early retirement, and disability benefits provide supplementary forms of unemployment coverage primarily for people late in their working lives, jobs programs have been used in Italy and the Netherlands to provide both work experience and supplementary income for unemployed people. It is difficult to assess the impact of tax incentives and direct subsidies provided to private employers to stimulate employment. However, both the Italian and Dutch governments have also attempted to provide employment directly through jobs programs.

The main jobs program for unemployed workers in Italy comes in the form of socially useful jobs (*lavori socialmente utili*), which in 2000 employed approximately 200,000 long-term unemployed (Ministero del Lavoro e delle Politiche Sociali 2001, 35). These jobs, which pay a monthly allowance of 800,000 lire (Renga 1999), are reserved for workers who have exhausted other forms of unemployment coverage, especially mobility payments. There are no public jobs for first-time job seekers, although a number of subsidies are in place to encourage the hiring of youth workers, loans for setting up new businesses, and the like.

In the Netherlands, the Youth Work Guarantee Act of 1992 guaranteed a minimum-wage job for two years for unemployed people under the age of twenty-one (twenty-seven if school-leavers). In 1998, the Youth Work Guarantee was incorporated into the Job Seekers Employment Act (Wet Inschakeling Werkzoekenden, or WIW) of 1998, which required local authorities to assist in the placement of youth and long-term unemployed, in so-called WIW jobs if necessary. In 1998 a total of 42,500 formerly unemployed people were enrolled in WIW jobs and 5,000 in work-training positions; one-quarter of these were unemployed youth under the age of twenty-three. An additional 35,000 long-term unemployed were placed in jobs under the Entry-Level Jobs and Follow-Up Jobs for the Long-Term Unemployed (Ministerie van Sociale Zaken en Werkgelegenheid 1999, 33).

Summary   Table 5.2 summarizes the benefits available to unemployed people under the variety of programs discussed in this section. The clearest

---

[4] Disability benefits paid out by INPS are representative of what most employees in industry, agriculture, and commerce would receive, keeping in mind that benefits for specialized groups of workers were often higher.

Table 5.2 *Benefits for the unemployed in Italy and the Netherlands*

	Benefit	Amount	Duration	Beneficiary pool	Number of beneficiaries
Insurance-type benefits					
Italy	Regular unemployment insurance	30% of previous gross wage	6 months	Employees in most sectors	791,000
	Special unemployment benefit	80% of previous gross wage, up to a ceiling	6 months	Employees in some sectors of industry and construction	46,000
	Reduced unemployment benefits in agriculture	40%–66% of wages	3 months	Part-time workers in agriculture	383,000
	CIG/CIGS (Short-time earnings replacement schemes)	80% of previous gross wage	12 months, extendable	Employees in specified firms in industry and construction	84,000
	Mobility	80% of previous gross wage	12–48 months	Employees in specified firms in industry and construction	93,500
Netherlands	Regular unemployment insurance	70% of previous gross wage	6 months	All employees except civil servants	160,000
	Extended unemployment insurance	70% of previous gross wage	2 years after expiration of regular unemployment insurance	All employees except civil servants	
	Extended unemployment insurance for older workers	70% of previous gross wage	Until age 65	Unemployed aged 57.5 yrs or older	

Assistance benefits

Italy	Social assistance/minimum income – not available in all regions			
Netherlands	Unemployment assistance	70% of minimum wage for single person (min. wage is approx. 80% of average wage)	2 years	370,000

Other benefits with unemployment component

Italy	Disability pensions	Variable: income-related. "Minimum pension" is 26% of median net wage in industry	Indefinite	1,053,000
	Early retirement	Variable: income-related	Until retirement age	165,000 (not including transportation sector)
Netherlands	Socially useful jobs	800,000 lire/month	12 months	145,000
	Work-related disability	70% of gross prior earnings	Until age 65	275,000
	Early retirement	80%–100% of gross prior earnings	Until age 65	178,900
	Jobs schemes	Minimum wage (approx. 80% of average wage)	Varies	82,500

Note: Data are for 2000.

Sources: Ministero del Lavoro e delle Politiche Sociali 2001 and CBS 2000; 2003. Netherlands "Early retirement" figure is from CBS 2000.

differences that emerge from this comparison between Italy and the Netherlands are the striking dissimilarity in the replacement rates of regular unemployment insurance benefits in the two countries; the lack of coverage in Italy for long-term and youth unemployed; and the importance in Italy of the CIG, CIGS, and mobility programs that provide superior benefits to a restricted group of employees.

The Age Orientation of Unemployment Benefits

The comparison of benefits between a variety of more-or-less directly comparable programs – regular unemployment insurance, unemployment assistance, early retirement, disability insurance, and so on – is necessary to comprehend the basic institutional similarities and differences between the Dutch and Italian systems of unemployment protection. But the overlay of differentiated benefits makes it difficult to grasp immediately the effects of the system as a whole on specific age groups. A cross-national comparison of the age orientation of entire systems of unemployment benefits programs should take into account both the relative generosity of single programs and the extent to which these benefits are actually available to workers of different ages.

Standard unemployment benefits do not tell the whole story. In both Italy and the Netherlands, welfare state "effort" on unemployment coverage is seriously underestimated when the hidden unemployment component of disability benefits is not counted. Further, in Italy CIGS (and sometimes mobility) beneficiaries are not counted as unemployed, but many aggregate measures include CIGS and mobility payments in the unemployment expenditures category. Per capita spending measures that use registered unemployed in the denominator and include CIGS payments in the numerator overestimate the average unemployment benefit payment in Italy by 50 to 100 percent, depending on the year.

Standard unemployment insurance benefits cover widely varying percentages of the working population across countries and over time. For example, Italian unemployment insurance legislation in 1975 applied to only 51 percent of the working population, as compared with 61 percent in France, 80 percent in the United Kingdom, and 93 percent in Germany (Mittelstadt 1975, 5). In the mid-1980s, the actual percentage of unemployed persons with insurance ranged from less than 10 percent in Italy, Greece, and Portugal to over 85 percent in Belgium (Schmid and Reissert 1996, 4). Figure 5.1 shows changes over time in the percentage of registered

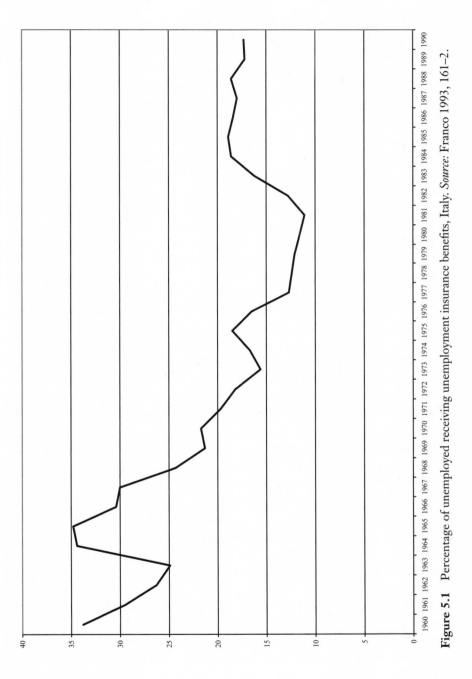

Figure 5.1 Percentage of unemployed receiving unemployment insurance benefits, Italy. *Source:* Franco 1993, 161–2.

123

unemployed receiving unemployment insurance benefits in Italy. This figure peaks in 1965 with insurance coverage for about 35 percent of Italy's
unemployed, dipping to just over 10 percent in 1981. The new definitions
introduced by Eurostat in 1992 result in even lower reported coverage
rates, hovering around 5 percent for the 1990s (Eurostat, *Labour Force Survey Results*, various years).

Despite the fact that CIG benefits in Italy provide for a higher replacement rate than unemployment insurance benefits in the Netherlands, and
despite the fact that as many people receive the generous CIG benefits as
received the meager Italian unemployment insurance benefit, the Italian
unemployment protection system taken as a whole provides remarkably
little to the modal unemployed person, who is a first-time job seeker. The
Dutch unemployment benefits system is far more generous in terms of both
benefit levels and the access that unemployed people of all age groups have
to these benefits.

Measuring aggregate spending on programs for the unemployed relative to other kinds of social spending tells us how the welfare state treats
the unemployed, in general, relative to other population groups such as
the elderly. But we have also seen that different groups of unemployed people receive widely differing amounts of income in unemployment, depending on which type of benefit program they fall under. To the extent that
different types of benefits are more likely to accrue to persons of one age
group than to another, we can also say that the unemployment system itself
may have a built-in age orientation.

The Italian unemployment system has a very clear bias toward older
members of the work force and against younger ones. In 1996, some 60 percent of all unemployed Italians were under age thirty. The rate of unemployment was 18.1 percent for twenty-five- to twenty-nine-year-olds, and only
4.8 percent for forty-five- to forty-nine-year-olds (Eurostat 1998, Table
008). Yet coverage under Italy's bewildering array of unemployment benefits
is clearly concentrated on the older age groups. By 1993, only 4 percent of
registered unemployed people under age thirty in Italy received unemployment benefits of any kind, while 20 percent of those over fifty did (Schmid
and Reissert 1996, 248). The predominance of younger people in the ranks
of the unemployed means that, overall, Italy provided unemployment
benefits for only 6 percent of the unemployed (Eurostat 1998, Table 093).

The under-thirty category in Italy overlaps with two categories of unemployed that are ineligible for insurance benefits. First-time job seekers,
who have no right to unemployment insurance benefits in Italy, made up

Benefits for the Unemployed

Table 5.3 *Age distribution of long-term unemployed population*

Age	Italy	Netherlands
Under 25	62	22
25–54	35	73
55+	3	5

Note: Data are for 1985. "Long-term unemployment" is defined as greater than one year.

Source: Calculated from Sexton 1988.

Table 5.4 *Working-age disability beneficiaries, by age*

	Netherlands	Italy
Young[a]	3	>0.5
Prime-age[b]	29	25
Older[c]	68	74

[a] Netherlands: age 15–25; Italy: age 15–29.
[b] Netherlands: age 25–45; Italy: age 30–49.
[c] Netherlands: age 45–65; Italy: age 50–59.

Sources: CBS 2003; INPS 2003.

54 percent of the unemployed in 1996 (Eurostat 1998, Table 093). The long-term unemployed, another category of unemployed persons with no right to insurance benefits under Italian law, are also concentrated in the younger age groups of the population (see Table 5.3). Even including the hidden "unemployment component" of disability benefits does not boost the coverage rates for younger workers, since the age profile of disability recipients is similarly skewed toward older workers (see Table 5.4).

The Italian unemployment system's lack of coverage for first-time job seekers and the long-term unemployed and its concentration of existing benefits on older members of the work force results in an unemployment system with two overlapping types of age bias. On the one hand, the system as a whole is limited in scope as compared with other areas of the welfare state targeted exclusively at the elderly. On the other hand, even within the limited confines of the unemployment protection system, coverage is skewed overwhelmingly toward people over the age of forty-five, and away from workers at earlier stages of family formation, skills formation, and wealth accumulation.

The Dutch unemployment system until quite recently was in this regard very different from the Italian, despite a legislative framework that is explicitly biased against younger workers in important ways. The Dutch system has since its inception graduated benefits according to the age and family status of recipients. Younger unemployed, especially those living at home, as well as single beneficiaries with no family obligations, have both lesser benefits and stricter eligibility conditions than mature household heads. In addition to this legal bias against the young, extended insurance benefits for unemployed workers close to the retirement age explicitly favors older workers. But this elderly-oriented legislative framework belies a de facto situation that is much more favorable to younger workers than in Italy.

The situation of younger unemployed workers is less dire in the Netherlands than in Italy for several reasons. First, long-terms unemployment is far less concentrated among the young in the Netherlands than in Italy (see Table 5.3), which means that more younger unemployed people in the Netherlands have access to the relatively generous but time-limited unemployment insurance benefit. But even those who are not able to claim regular unemployment benefits are better off in the Netherlands than in Italy. First-time job seekers make up half of the unemployed in Italy, versus one-quarter in the Netherlands (Eurostat 1998, Table 093). And while first-time job seekers have no benefit entitlements in Italy, through the 1970s and 1980s all first-time job seekers in the Netherlands had a right to claim unemployment assistance benefits. In the 1990s tightened eligibility standards for unemployment assistance left many more first-time job seekers to rely on the even less generous welfare (social assistance) benefit. But new investments in active labor market policies and jobs programs for young people mean that joblessness among the young remains much less common in the Netherlands, where the unemployment rate among twenty- to twenty-four-year-olds is 6 percent, than in Italy, where 33 percent of this age group are without work (Eurostat 1998, Table 008).

Rates of coverage under unemployment benefits of any kind vary much less dramatically between age groups in the Netherlands than they do in Italy: approximately 42 percent of Dutch youth under thirty, versus approximately 48 percent of Dutch workers over fifty, are covered (Schmid and Reissert 1996, Figure 8.3). This is in large part because the risks most common to young and older workers both receive some form of protection. Disability insurance, the main alternative to formal unemployment subsidies in the Netherlands, displayed a similarly flat curve of coverage rates for different age groups relative to Italy (see Table 5.4). In sum, not only does the Netherlands offer on average better protection to unemployed people than does Italy, but this protection is less skewed toward older groups in the work force.

As unemployment expanded radically beginning in the mid-1970s, existing unemployment policies took on distinctive age profiles in Italy and the Netherlands. Highly protected labor market insiders in Italy man a rapidly aging "fortress" labor market, with younger entrants lacking access to both jobs and preferred forms of unemployment coverage. In the Netherlands, as in Italy, disability benefits and early retirement buffer the early exit of older workers from the labor market. But in the Netherlands, universal unemployment assistance benefits until quite recently covered even first-time job seekers, so the youth segment of the labor market still had access to some unemployment benefits. In addition, job-creation targets linked to early exit mechanisms and subsidies are more strictly enforced in the Netherlands than in Italy, so that Dutch benefits targeted at older workers have more closely approximated the desired result of increasing employment for younger workers. This combines with the more successful Dutch vocational training system to lessen the concentration of unemployment within the youngest sectors of the labor market.

In Italy, the absence of coverage for young people, and the very low regular unemployment insurance benefits that are the only form of coverage for the noncore labor force, have combined with high rates of youth unemployment and an aging of the core work force to skew unemployment benefits toward the elderly. The combination of legislated coverage for youth unemployed and higher benefit replacement rates for regular unemployment insurance in the Netherlands has resulted in a less elderly-oriented welfare state as a whole, as well as a less elderly-oriented unemployment policy regime, as unemployment has grown since the mid-1970s. We turn next to an exploration of the origins and trajectories of these policies that have resulted in diverging age orientations of the unemployment systems in Italy and the Netherlands.

Particularism, Universalism, and the Response to Partisan Competition

As with family allowance policies, the response of politicians to partisan competition, whether a particularistic or programmatic response, has a crucial impact on the eventual age orientation of unemployment policies. How has the mode of political competition affected the development of the two

crucial policy features that result in different age orientations of unemployment benefits in Italy and the Netherlands: the replacement rate of regular
unemployment insurance benefits and coverage for youth unemployed?

Discussions of Southern European welfare states in general (see Ferrera
1996c; Gough 1996; Rhodes 1997) and Italy in particular (see Paci 1994;
Ferrera 1997) have argued that clientelist party–society linkages are responsible for the fragmentation, particularism, and inefficiency of the Italian
welfare state. Indeed, the parties most implicated in clientelist practices,
the DC and the PSI, can claim partial credit, or take partial blame, for
the unemployment policies that create such a strong elderly orientation
in Italy. The occupationalism and fragmentation of the labor market policy system, which provides crucial resources for clientelist politicians, is
itself a response to Italy's predominantly particularistic mode of political
competition.

However, the particularistic competitive strategies of center-right parties
also affected the policy preferences and behavior of left parties and labor
unions. Nowhere is this crucial, but rarely noted, consequence of clientelism
more visible than in the area of labor market policies. In an attempt to
mitigate the political effects of the DC's and PSI's clientelist capture of
the system of public administration, the PCI/(P)DS and unions in Italy
unwittingly backed policy solutions that reinforced the elderly orientation
of unemployment policies in Italy.

Of course, the Dutch system of high replacement rates and universal
youth benefits is also a result of politicians' responses to electoral pressures.
But in the Netherlands, these responses were more programmatic in nature
and resulted in a system of more generous and more universal entitlements
against the risk of unemployment for workers of all ages. A more detailed
look at the genesis of these program features will help to explicate how
politicians' responses to competition in Italy and the Netherlands structured
the age orientation of the unemployment protection systems.

Unemployment Insurance Benefits

Why did even the earliest unemployment insurance schemes in the Netherlands offer such a high (80 percent) replacement rate relative to schemes in
other countries? It may be that, as union leaders at the time feared (Kuijpers
and Schrage 1997, 91), the compulsory unemployment schemes adopted in
countries other than the Netherlands drove down benefits by taking control of the schemes out of the hands of unions. But the voluntary schemes

existing in Italy at the time received much less state "interference" than in the Netherlands, and still offered much lower benefits. A more compelling explanation for the generous benefit in the Netherlands resides in the fact that since union funds were subsidized by municipal and later state moneys (van Leeuwen 1997), they could afford to offer higher replacement rates. This program structure set the terms for the obligatory unemployment insurance program adopted after the war. By the late 1930s unions and employers had reached a consensus that a new, universal unemployment benefits scheme should cover the costs of "normal" unemployment with contributions from employers and employees, but the "costs of abnormal unemployment should be met by government," as under the old voluntary system (Kuijpers and Schrage 1997, 93).

If the 80 percent replacement rate was facilitated by rather extensive state underwriting of the costs of unemployment insurance coverage under the old voluntary system, how was this generous benefit maintained when the new obligatory system was set in place in 1949? The path of least resistance for legislators was to keep the replacement rate where it was, while universalizing coverage. Certainly, the unions and their allies in the PvdA would have been reluctant to turn over control of the voluntary system they had set up if the benefit level under the new law were reduced. But the near absence of debate in Parliament over the new rate (van Kersbergen and Becker 1988, 485) signals the eagerness of elected officials from Left, Center, and Right to accept this solution.[5] The unexpected popularity of the Drees emergency pension provisions, which provided a tremendous boost for the Labor Party in the 1946 elections, had convinced legislators of the electoral value of universal social insurance. At the same time, avoiding blame for cuts in replacement rates served politicians' interests as well as those of the unions, while the joint employee–employer management of the system in the Industrial Insurance Boards satisfied employer demands.

The low replacement rate for Italian unemployment benefits after the war also is related to the level of benefits in the prewar system. In Italy, though, the prewar system offered some of the lowest benefits in Europe (ILO 1922). Even so, Italy's unemployment insurance benefit continued to decrease in real terms after the war because benefits were not indexed to either wages or prices and were only sporadically upgraded. How can we account for this exceptional decrease in social benefits at a time when

---

[5] Only a small group of Communist Party legislators dissented, instead advocating a 100 percent replacement rate.

throughout Europe most welfare benefits were increasing? Most analysts of the Italian situation suggest that because short-time earnings replacement benefits (CIG and CIGS) provided a more generous alternative to regular unemployment insurance that was favored by both unions and employers, there was little pressure to upgrade regular unemployment insurance benefits. This argument certainly makes sense of the period after 1968, when wholly state-funded CIGS benefits were introduced. But before 1968, CIG benefits required employer contributions, and in fact Confindustria throughout the 1950s and early '60s launched repeated tirades against the "inappropriate" use of CIG benefits, caused in their opinion by the predominance of employee representatives on the provincial commissions that evaluated enterprises' requests for CIG benefits.

So if Confindustria was not wedded to the idea of using CIG benefits as an alternative for unemployment insurance in the 1950s and 1960s, and if in any case the short-term earnings replacement schemes covered only a fraction of Italy's unemployed, why did the regular unemployment benefit remain so low? Employers during this period espoused low unemployment benefits for the standard motivations related to preserving work incentives and keeping labor costs low when Italian industry was pursuing an essentially export-oriented development strategy. And through the late 1950s, Italian unions, which were by and large excluded from labor policy making, were probably too weak to counter Confindustria's efforts to keep unemployment insurance benefits low (Regalia 1984, 54). Unemployment benefits in the 1950s and early 1960s remained low primarily because employers wanted it that way.

By the middle of the 1960s, however, unions were better positioned to make demands of employers and the government. And yet raising the level of unemployment insurance benefits remained a low priority. The electoral strategy of the Left demanded, paradoxically, that unemployment benefits remain low. Agricultural employees (as opposed to the self-employed in agriculture) were a crucial constituency for the Left and a major focus of union mobilization during the years when the CGIL still acted as a "transmission belt" for the PCI. But extending unemployment benefits to this low-wage group at the flat-rate level that applied to industrial workers would have been impossible if they were to be funded solely out of contributions from the agricultural sector. At the same time the Italian unemployment insurance system received no financing from general government revenues, and could not hope to do so unless the tax system, which exempted from payments much of the ruling DC's base of self-employed voters, was reformed. A basic condition undermining the expansion of any social policies during this period (and indeed into the 1990s) was the fact that the Italian tax system was weakened by ineffective taxation of the self-employed and small businesses. But reform of the tax system was impossible because small businesses and the self-employed were ineffectively taxed as a reward for their support of the ruling Christian Democratic Party.

The only way to finance unemployment benefits was thus to subsidize them with contributions from the industrial sector, a procedure that Confindustria vigorously opposed but was powerless to prevent. Combined pressure from the Left, which favored extension of benefits to agriculture, and the Right, which opposed tax reform, maintained the cross-subsidization of agricultural unemployment benefits by the industrial sector. The result was that the unemployment insurance fund, which if it had only had to cover industrial workers could have sustained a substantial increase in benefits without raising contribution rates, ran near deficit levels. Clearly, low unemployment benefits did not worry politicians nearly as much as they worried the unemployed. As long as politicians could continually expand the *number* of beneficiaries by expanding coverage of a fragmented occupational system to new groups (which they did until 1977), unemployment benefits were useful electoral currency even at low benefit levels.

Coverage for Youth Unemployed

The electoral strategies of Christian Democrats and the Left, more than their ideologies, influenced the level of regular unemployment insurance benefits in Italy and the Netherlands. What about differences in the coverage of youth (and long-term) unemployed? In the Netherlands, this coverage fell under the Unemployment Assistance Act (Rijksgroepsregeling voor Werkloze Werknemers, RWW), a part of the General Assistance Act (Algemene Bijstandswet, ABW) of 1964. While some observers attribute high levels of social assistance benefits in the Netherlands to the Dutch culture's widely shared egalitarian beliefs, more convincing accounts argue that extensive RWW benefits were a result of partisan competition for votes in a highly volatile electorate undergoing depillarization (van Kersbergen and Becker 1988; de Swaan 1988; Cox 1993; de Rooy 1997).[6]

---

[6] Anticipated natural gas revenues also encouraged a generous mind-set.

In offering RWW assistance benefits for long-term and youth unemployed, the Dutch government brought itself into line with ILO recommendations on unemployment benefits, something that Italy never did despite being a signatory nation to the same treaty (ILO recommendation no. 44 of 1934). The problem of youth unemployment has been a difficult one for Italy for the entire postwar period. Yet the poor results are not for lack of effort. Unions, employers, left parties, and center-right parties have been painfully aware of the problem of youth unemployment, at least since demonstrations in the early days after the war pitted young unemployed protestors against Roman police and were met with emergency unemployment provisions. But permanent provisions for youth unemployed were never established because of the clientelist strategies pursued by the Christian Democrats in office and the strategic reaction of the unions and the Left to the DC's clientelism.

The Left in Italy has consistently advocated expanding active labor market policies targeted at young people, and the results are clear. When the PCI has had significant influence at the national level, if not actual cabinet representation (as from 1976 to 1979 and 1995 to 2000), and/or when unions have a strong voice during periods of corporatist policy-making arrangements (as in 1984 and from 1996 to 2001), active labor market policies aimed at employing young people have emerged. When these conditions have not been met, such policies have not emerged. Yet active labor market policies have by and large failed to reduce youth unemployment in any meaningful way. Employers have not risen to the bait of subsidies and tax relief for hiring young unemployed persons. In particular, they chafed at regulations that required them to hire youths in the order of their enrollment at the government unemployment offices, rather than hiring at will. For example, a year after the passage of a major youth employment initiative in 1977, only 6,000 of the almost 650,000 youth unemployed registered on special lists at the unemployment offices had been hired (Gualmini 1998, 129).

Why, then, given the failure of active labor market programs, has the Left not advocated a cash benefit for youth unemployed? The political Left and Italy's unions have continued to place their faith in largely ineffective active labor market policies combined with restrictive hiring procedures in order to prevent the DC from mobilizing large numbers of unemployed young people through clientelist means such as state jobs or special cash benefits. The position of the union movement in this regard is nicely summed up by then-Secretary General of the CGIL, Luciano Lama, in a statement at a 1977 union congress on the economic crisis and the problem of youth. According to Lama, "The central problem is this: work, jobs, not assistance" (Bonadonna 1977, 223). Assistance in the context of tight budgets and clientelist politics meant personalized measures that could be given out or withheld at will by the ruling parties. With constrained resources and a very large youth unemployment problem, any extension of government benefits to the youth unemployed was bound to stop short of covering everyone in need. And any partial solution would offer the opportunity for discretionary "assistentialism" that would be a rich resource for the DC.

The demands of social movements of the unemployed, perhaps because the best-articulated protests were supported by the unions and left parties, supported this policy of "refusal of assistentialism" (*rifiuto del assistenzialismo*). Leaders of the Organized Unemployed (Disoccupati Organizzati) movement in Naples in the early 1970s refused offers of state jobs and unemployment subsidies for their members, in part to dispel rumors that the movement had been infiltrated by Mafia and DC operatives seeking to co-opt desperate youth with such offers (Ramondino 1977).

The lack of comprehensive coverage for youth unemployment played into the hands of the clientelist electoral strategy of the ruling DC and their allies, who, with their deep penetration of the state apparatus, could continue to attract supporters by offering discretionary solutions to the problems of unemployed individuals. But at the same time, the Left clung to active labor market policies that employers effectively boycotted, rather than supporting unemployment benefits that they feared would be administered in a clientelist manner by the ruling parties. Thus both the Center-Right and the opposition preferred not to push for unemployment benefits for first-time job seekers.

Ideology, Strategy, and the Unemployed

The youth orientation of unemployment policies in the Netherlands is due to both the high replacement rate of regular unemployment benefits and the existence of universal coverage that includes first-time job seekers. In Italy an elderly-oriented system of unemployment benefits rests on low replacement rates for regular unemployment benefit schemes and no benefits at all for the large numbers of youth unemployed. These key policy provisions implicated in the age orientation of unemployment policies in Italy and the Netherlands are products in part of partisan competition. Yet it seems important to note that these policy outcomes are not as closely linked to the ideological positions staked out by Social Democratic and Christian Democratic parties as many scholars of the welfare state (e.g., Esping-Andersen 1985; 1990; van Kersbergen 1995) assert.

While the participation of the Social Democratic PvdA in government coalitions might explain the generous postwar unemployment provisions enacted in 1949 and 1954, it cannot account for the generosity of Dutch unemployment insurance benefits enacted by Liberal governments as far back as 1916. It is true that the Dutch assistance benefit for long-term and youth unemployed was introduced during a period of PvdA ascendance that is often described as being characterized by a widely shared progressive, egalitarian ideology. However, other explanations for the introduction of the assistance law have little to do with Social Democratic ideology per se: the changing desires of an increasingly professionalized and politically influential network of social assistance providers (Cox 1992, 1993) and the impact of intense electoral competition as a driver of benefits expansion (de Swaan 1988; Cox 1992; de Rooy 1997). In the Italian case, it was not so much the Left's inability to see an ideologically appropriate program of worker-friendly unemployment protections enacted, but rather the specific policy positions assumed by the Left in response to the ruling Center-Right's successful clientelism, that determined the age orientation of unemployment policies.

Key elements of Christian social doctrine, too, including a focus on families as the primary providers of social assistance, have been mustered to explain both very high unemployment benefits in the Netherlands and very low benefits and coverage in Italy. The Netherlands' strong male-breadwinner model may be partly responsible for the unusually high level of spending on unemployment benefits in that country, since benefits must be high enough to support an entire family (Bussemaker 1992). Yet Italy surely has just as strong a male-breadwinner orientation, and unemployment benefits remain low. The argument for Christian Democratic influence in Italy typically asserts that subsidiarity doctrine reinforces the need for and ability of cohesive (Catholic) families to care for their own, thus defusing political pressure for higher benefits or more adequate coverage for youth unemployed. Neither the Dutch story nor the Italian story about the influence of Christian Democratic ideology on unemployment policies is implausible on its face, but both cannot be true at the same time. The very indeterminacy of Christian social doctrine's policy requisites lends credence to the argument that Christian Democratic parties' competitive strategies, and not their ideologies, determine the age orientation of the unemployment policies that they promote.

The policies responsible for the diverging age orientations of Dutch and Italian unemployment protection systems result from electorally motivated decision making by politicians and policy makers. But the type of electoral competition that prevails in these two systems – programmatic in the Netherlands, particularistic in Italy – also affects the structure of unemployment benefits programs and thus ultimately their age orientation.

In the Netherlands, politicians eager to claim credit for a generous system of regular unemployment benefits maintained high replacement rates that had been instituted prior to World War II, even during periods of high unemployment. The creation of a universalistic unemployment benefits system, via extension of unemployment benefits to youth unemployed in the mid-1960s, was also achieved quite easily, coming as it did during a period of rapid economic growth, ideological consensus on universalism, and intense electoral competition.

In Italy, the absence of universal coverage and low replacement rates are also a response to electoral competition, but of a very different kind. Italian politicians, on both the Left and the Right, were loath to create a universal system of benefits because of pressures arising out of the predominant clientelist mode of political competition. In the 1950s and 1960s, the PCI and the unions would not push for higher benefits or universalistic coverage as long as financing of unemployment benefits remained squarely on the shoulders of blue- and white-collar employees. However, the Left was willing to go along with lower benefit levels if it meant bringing agricultural workers, a key potential support base, into the system. DC politicians, for their part, saw no reason to raise benefit levels as long as they could continue to expand benefits coverage to new groups of potential clients without imposing effective taxation on their key constituency of self-employed people. A similar logic dictated denying unemployment subsidies to youth unemployed beginning in the 1970s. The Left, certain that any benefit administered by a state apparatus thoroughly colonized by the DC would be used for clientelist purposes, was unwilling to advocate cash benefits for youth unemployed, and instead supported ineffective active labor market policies that went ignored by employers.

The age orientations of unemployment policies, as different as they are in Italy and the Netherlands, came about as a result of policy decisions largely unrelated to the concerns of different age groups in society. But they affected welfare reform debates and outcomes in the 1980s and

1990s in important ways, often closely linked with the question of what different age groups deserve from the state.

The extreme elderly bias of unemployment policy in Italy has not been carefully documented, but it has not gone unnoticed, either. The imbalance had become an issue in policy-making circles in Italy already by the mid-1980s. In 1980, INCA (Istituto Nazionale Confederale di Assistenza), the CGIL's social services agency, expressed frustration at the union's failure to acknowledge and correct the difficult situation of workers trying to get by on regular unemployment insurance. INCA directors, who believed that the agency's direct contact with over 150,000 unemployment claimants each year made it better able than CGIL leaders to appreciate the gravity of the situation, argued that unions should take a strong position in favor of equalizing regular unemployment benefits and CIGS benefits (Moretti and Santamaria 1990). By the mid-1980s, members of the mainstream labor union leadership had come around to INCA's position, recognizing for the first time the potential danger in pursuing policies that were alienating an entire generation of workers (Giovannini 1999 interview; Giustina 1999 interview). Unions began in this period a new emphasis on providing services for first-time job seekers, unemployed people, and youth in general.

By the early 1990s, progressive politicians, too, had begun to make overtures – for the most part unsuccessful – to Italy's younger voters, whom public opinion research had shown to have become alienated from unions and the Left. Elite Italian newspapers began carrying op-ed pieces by respected scholars and journalists and pointing out the Italian welfare system's failure to provide for Italy's younger generations.[7] Around that time, survey research in Italy also began to document public fears, increasing over time, that Italy's lopsided labor markets and welfare benefits would generate intergenerational conflict on a level not seen since 1968 (Baldissera 1996a; 1997; Boeri and Tabellini 1999b; Boeri, Börsch-Supan, and Tabellini 2001). Influential policy makers, including the director of INPS and several members of the welfare reform commission established by the government in 1998, have been outspoken advocates of reorienting Italy's welfare system toward the needs of the young.[8]

[7] *Il Sole 24 Ore*, Italy's equivalent of the *Wall Street Journal*, took the lead, publishing early articles in this vein by demographer Massimo Livi Bacci (1993), political scientist Maurizio Ferrera (1996a, 1996b), journalist Armando Massarenti (1997), and economist Giuliano Cazzola (1998a, 1998b).

[8] See, e.g., Nicola Rossi's 1997 manifesto *Meno ai padri, piu' ai figli* (Less to the parents, more to the children). Rossi was a key adviser on welfare issues to former Prime Minister D'Alema.

This new emphasis on youth has already borne fruit. The Italian system of unemployment protection has undergone important changes since the regime of the early 1980s. In addition to the switch-over in regular unemployment insurance from a minimal flat-rate benefit to a 40 percent replacement rate in the mid-1990s, in 1991 new restrictions were placed on the use of CIG and CIGS. These restrictions aimed to return the part-time earnings replacement schemes to their original function as short-term buffers for narrowly defined crisis situations. Hiring procedures in the state-run employment offices were reformed in 1987 and 1991, and a number of active labor market policies focusing on young workers were either introduced or newly incentivized beginning in 1992.

While there is certainly room in the Italian system for more thoroughgoing reform, an unmistakable new presence appeared in Italian welfare reform discussions of the 1990s. The clear disparities in treatment of different age groups generated by the labor market policies of the 1970s and 1980s have engendered a politics of conflict around the issue of age. But at the same time, this very imbalance enabled policy makers and politicians in the 1990s to mobilize public support behind a shift toward more youth-oriented labor market policies. Advocating benefits for privileged segments of the working population now plays as a throwback to the failed and reviled labor market politics of the past, a blatant pandering by politicians to powerful groups of hyper-protected insiders.

The general outlines of the "miraculous" Dutch reform of labor market and welfare policies beginning in the mid-1980s are by this time well known.[9] The implications of these policy changes for different age groups enjoy less renown. Since 1985 the minimum wage for younger workers has been reduced, social assistance benefits for young people living with their parents have been curtailed, the duration of unemployment insurance benefits has become restricted for younger workers, re-evaluations of disability benefits have forced many young claimants back to work, and in general labor market policies targeted at the young have come to include more work requirements.[10] At the same time, early retirement and long-term unemployment insurance benefits for older workers continue to be available, and reforms to the disability system have exempted most older recipients.

---

[9] See Hemerijck and van Kersbergen 1997 and Visser and Hemerijck 1997.

[10] On labor market participation policies in particular, see van Oorschot and Engelfreit 1999.

Paradoxically, the relatively even distribution of welfare spending across age groups in the Dutch system of the 1970s and 1980s has made retrenchment of youth-oriented programs easier in the Netherlands in the 1990s. Public awareness of a distributive justice "problem" between generations has not developed in the Netherlands, in marked contrast to the keen concern for the potential for intergenerational strife that surfaces in discussions about Italian welfare state reform. In Italy, the target of welfare reforms has become stereotyped as a hyper-protected insider, a resident of Italy's fortress labor market. In the Netherlands, the conflict lines in welfare reform debates have instead been drawn between the productive "actives" and the parasitic "inactives" – who, because of the generosity of the Dutch welfare system toward the young, were as likely to be young as old. The age profile of social spending has thus influenced the terms of the policy reform debate by setting standards of fairness around which reformers can mobilize new coalitions.

6

Old-Age Pensions

THE ARCHITECTURE OF
EXPENDITURE

The previous two chapters focused on the denominator of the elderly/non-elderly spending ratio, exploring the origins of different levels of spending in Italy and the Netherlands on two key social welfare programs directed at the non-elderly: family allowances and unemployment benefits. The divergent spending paths that these two countries followed in the post–World War II period, and the much greater emphasis on spending for youth and working-age adults in the Netherlands than in Italy, appeared to be a result of the interaction between the structure of social programs and the kind of competitive strategies that politicians used to gain support in the electoral arena.

This chapter focuses on the numerator of the age orientation measure: pension spending. It argues that the interaction of program structure (universal or fragmented occupational) and how politicians compete (using programmatic or particularistic appeals) shapes the development of pension expenditures in Italy and the Netherlands. In the Netherlands, public pensions have been available on a citizenship basis since immediately following World War II, and political competition has been highly programmatic. As a result, electoral pressure has not eroded the floors and ceilings that maintain benefit levels and eligibility rules at levels conducive to moderate pension expenditures, despite coverage rates of close to 100 percent. Italy, by contrast, provides subsistence-level benefits or above to only about 70 percent of the elderly. But its highly fragmented occupationalist pension system and particularistic political competition interact to create immoderate demands for pension spending on the part of both opposition and incumbents. Expenditure levels have proved extremely difficult to curb even when they are quite widely recognized as pathological for the economic system as a whole.

This chapter focuses on explaining the origins of the policy features that create divergent pension spending patterns in Italy and the Netherlands over the course of the post–World War II period. The first section of the chapter outlines pension expenditure trends in Italy and the Netherlands, highlighting the two main factors responsible for the lower aggregate spending on pensions in the Netherlands than in Italy: the level of pension benefits, particularly the most generous pensions, and the number of pension beneficiaries. The second section of the chapter presents a narrative of the development of policy features that have affected most strongly the level of benefits and the number of beneficiaries in Italy and the Netherlands: effective floors and ceilings on pension benefits, and limitations on the age at retirement. Working from this narrative, the third section of the chapter argues that spending on the elderly, far from representing a response to either the political weight of growing elderly populations or the power resources of the Left, follows a logic parallel to that observed in youth-oriented spending. The interaction between the structure of pension programs and the competitive behavior of politicians shapes the development of pension expenditures in Italy and the Netherlands, and thus the eventual age orientation of social spending more generally.

Pension Spending in Italy and the Netherlands

Since at least 1960, pension spending as a proportion of overall social spending has been significantly higher in Italy than in the Netherlands (see Fig. 6.1). In 1960, old-age and survivors' pensions registered about 55 percent of total nonhealth social expenditures in Italy and only 40 percent in the Netherlands. Spending patterns continued to diverge through the 1960s and 1970s: pensions as a share of social spending rose to almost 75 percent in Italy in 1979 and continued at very high levels through the 1990s, while in the Netherlands pension spending remained constant at about 40 percent of social expenditures through the entire period under study.[1] To account for the differing age orientation of social spending in Italy and the Netherlands, then, we need to understand why pension spending has consumed an ever-expanding portion of Italy's social budget during the post–World War II period, while in the Netherlands pension spending has never accounted for more than half of total public social expenditures.

---

[1] A slight dip in the pension share of social spending in the Netherlands can be observed during the early to mid-1980s, when spending on unemployment and disability rose dramatically.

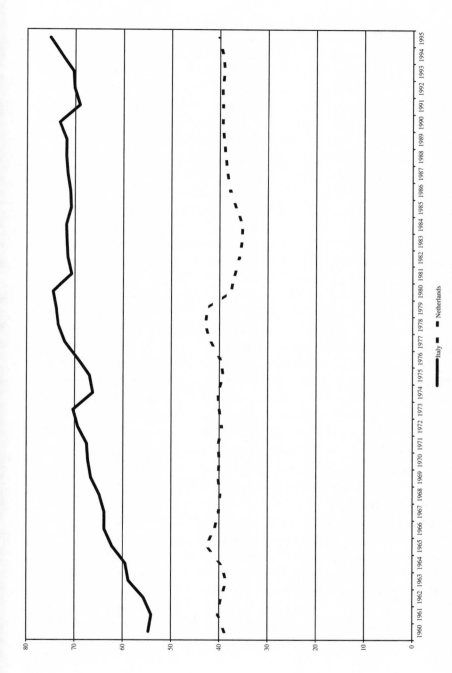

Figure 6.1 Pension spending as a percentage of total nonhealth social expenditures, Italy and the Netherlands. *Sources:* Varley 1986; OECD 2004. Data definitions differ between the two spending series. The figures from Varley 1986 are adjusted by the average difference between the two series for 1980–5, when both measures are available.

141

Italy and the Netherlands both had fragmented occupational pension systems prior to World War II (despite proposals to introduce universal citizenship-based state pensions in both countries before the war). Since 1947, however, Dutch and Italian pension systems have come to be organized quite differently. In Italy, the pension system has remained occupationally based and highly fragmented. Even after reforms in the 1990s that simplified the pension system in Italy, there remained forty-seven distinct public pension funds (Baccaro 1999, 128), each with a different set of rules and different levels of benefits. There is no citizenship right to a basic pension in Italy, and pension benefits vary dramatically depending on the sector of employment, contributory history, age at retirement, and year of retirement. The Dutch system as it evolved in the years after World War II is far less complex. In the Netherlands a basic pension (Algemene Ouderdomswet, or AOW) provides guaranteed retirement income for all residents at a modest level. For a head of household, the AOW pension is equivalent to the contracted minimum wage in industry, or about 55 percent of the median wage. In addition to the basic public pension, most Dutch residents also receive supplementary private occupational pension benefits accrued during their (or their spouses') working lives.

The two-tiered system of pension benefits in the Netherlands means that a significant portion of total pension spending in the Netherlands is not reflected in measures of public social expenditures. What effect does this private pension spending have on the age orientation of public social spending? It is unlikely that private pensions would have the same "crowding out" effect on social benefits for the non-elderly that public pension spending has. On the other hand, the availability of significant private pension benefits could *explain* lower spending on public pensions, since private benefits will reduce demand for high levels of public spending. So, a full comparison of spending in Italy and the Netherlands should take into account the existence of private supplementary pensions in the Dutch case.

Including spending on private supplementary pensions, Dutch pension spending as a proportion of total social spending is still significantly lower than in Italy. Private pension spending increases total pension spending in the Netherlands by approximately 25 percent during the period under study. The total of public plus private pension spending in the Netherlands is approximately 45 percent of total nonhealth social spending – versus Italy's 60 to 75 percent. The existence of a "second pillar" of private pensions in the Netherlands has important consequences for the development of pensions in that country. But it does not explain away the very substantial differences in spending levels between Italy and the Netherlands.

If private pension spending does not account for the dramatically lower share of social spending dedicated to pensions in the Netherlands as compared with Italy, what does? Differences in coverage rates – the percentage of elderly who receive pension benefits – cannot account for the spending differences. In fact, they make the spending differences more puzzling. The Netherlands, by virtue of its citizenship-based first pillar, provides a pension to virtually all residents over age sixty-five in the Netherlands.[2] Arriving at an analogous coverage rate in Italy is somewhat more complicated, since the various pension administration schemes count the number of pensions disbursed, not the number of recipients. Italy's national statistical agency calculated that in 1999, some 28 percent of pensioners received more than one pension (ISTAT 2000). Since 1960, the number of old-age insurance pensions disbursed per person over age sixty in Italy has risen from about 0.5 to a little over 0.6 in 1990. Social pensions, a minor, means-tested benefit available to impoverished Italians over age sixty-five since 1969, have added an additional approximately one pension for every ten persons aged over sixty-five (Franco 1993, 128–9). Assuming one pension per person, which quite seriously overestimates the coverage rate, we arrive at a maximum coverage rate of about 70 percent in the 1970s and 1980s, compared with nearly 100 percent in the Netherlands. A substantially higher proportion of elderly residents are protected against the risk of low income in the Netherlands than in Italy, yet pension spending is much higher as a percentage of social spending in Italy than in the Netherlands.

Another possible explanation for the differences in pension spending between Italy and the Netherlands concerns the average level of benefits. If pensions are substantially higher on average in Italy than in the Netherlands, that could explain why Italy devotes so much more of its social budget to pensions. At the aggregate level, this explanation is again unsatisfying. Public pension spending per person aged sixty-five and above as a percentage of GDP per capita is higher in Italy than in the Netherlands for most of the period 1960–93 (see Fig. 6.2). But the differences are not striking, and in fact during the 1970s average benefit levels were actually higher in the

---

[2] One official of the main Dutch interest group representing pensioners estimates that about 2 percent of seniors living in the Netherlands are without any pension coverage whatsoever, though they are eligible for social assistance benefits (Lokhorst 2000 interview).

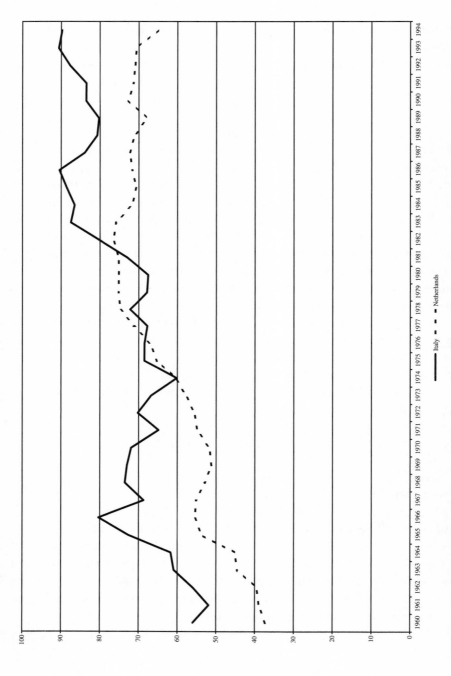

Figure 6.2 Pension spending per person aged sixty-five and over as a percentage of GDP per capita, Italy and the Netherlands.
Sources: Expenditure data from Varley 1986; OECD 2004. GDP and demographic data from OECD 2003b. Data definitions differ between the two spending series. The figures from Varley 1986 are adjusted by the average difference between the two series for 1980–5, when both measures are available.

Netherlands than in Italy. And if one were to add in the amount spent on private pensions in the Netherlands, mean benefit levels would probably be much closer throughout the entire period. The rather small difference in average generosity of public pensions is not responsible for the very large difference in the level of pension spending as a share of social expenditures in Italy and the Netherlands.

The large difference in spending levels on public pensions in Italy versus the Netherlands is due not to the existence of a private second pillar in the Netherlands, nor to differences in the percentage of the elderly population with pension entitlements, nor to differences in the average level of benefits. What does explain the difference in spending on pensions? Two factors are most important. First, while pension benefit levels at the low end are much lower in Italy than in the Netherlands, they are much higher at the high end. High replacement rates characteristic of the most generous Italian pensions are partly responsible for the very high levels of aggregate pension expenditure. Second, large numbers of people under the age of sixty-five receive old-age pensions in Italy. In the Netherlands, as in Italy, people under the age of sixty-five may receive benefits such as early retirement pensions, disability pensions, or extended unemployment benefits. But Dutch people under the age of sixty-five may not receive old-age pensions. This small difference accounts for an enormous savings on pension spending in the Netherlands relative to Italy. Let us consider each of these factors in turn.

Benefit Levels

Different levels of pension benefits for various groups of beneficiaries could account for differences in aggregate expenditures on pensions, all other things being equal. Pension spending per elderly person (as a percentage of GDP per capita) does not differ substantially *on average* between Italy and the Netherlands. But the amount that individual pensioners receive does vary widely, both within and between the two countries. Two possibilities present themselves: pension benefits that are much lower at the low end in the Netherlands, or much higher at the high end in Italy, could explain the difference in aggregate expenditure rates. The least generous pensions are significantly lower in Italy than they are in the Netherlands, a feature that accounts for persistently high rates of poverty among elderly people in Italy. But pensions at the high end are higher in Italy than in the Netherlands, even if we include the private supplementary benefits that top off most

Dutch pensions. The extreme generosity of the highest Italian pensions accounts for some of the imbalance between pension spending and other forms of social spending in Italy.

At the very lowest end of the spectrum of benefits, pensions are quite meager in both countries. In the Netherlands, the basic AOW pension is available to any resident, but receipt of the full benefit is conditional on a full fifty years of contributions (i.e., years of residency). In practice, though, the number of substandard pensions in the Netherlands is very small, since contributions are collected directly from payroll in the case of employees and as part of the income tax in the case of the self-employed. Dutch citizens living abroad may pay contributions directly for any years that they resided outside the Netherlands, thus accruing the necessary fifty years of contributions. As a result, it is only illegal immigrants and legal immigrants from outside the EU who are likely to receive AOW benefits of less than the normal level. In 1990, some 6 percent of AOW pensions were awarded for less than the full level (Sociale Verzekerings Bank data).[3]

In Italy, the lowest pension benefits are "social pensions" (*pensioni sociali*), which account for about 5 percent of public pensions disbursed. These means-tested pensions were introduced in 1969 in order to provide some income to elderly Italians who had no other means of support (primarily women). But the level of the benefit was set extremely low, equivalent to 9.4 percent of the average gross wage in 1969. Beginning in 1973, social pensions were indexed to the rate of inflation, but even so, by 1980, the benefit was equivalent to only 14.4 percent of the average wage (Ferrera 1984, 415). The level of the benefit did not improve substantially until the reforms of the late 1990s. At the very low end, then, both Italian and Dutch pensions are quite low.

Stepping one rung up the ladder, after immigrants without full public pension entitlements, the next worse-off pensioners in the Netherlands are people who are entitled to the basic AOW pension but have no private supplementary pension. AOW benefits are the sole source of pension income for about 15 percent of the current elderly (Ministerie van Sociale Zaken en Werkgelegenheid 2000).[4] The AOW pension, like other social benefits in the Netherlands, is pegged to a social minimum standard that is

[3] Of course, any resident of the Netherlands who does not have income equal to the social minimum – which is also the level of the full AOW pension – is eligible for social assistance benefits.
[4] Most of these are unmarried women with no employment history and people who worked for firms that had not established a supplementary pension plan (van Aartsen 2000 interview).

meant to allow full participation in social life. Prior to 1968, AOW benefits were indexed to a combination of prices and wages in the industrial sector. Beginning in 1964, the social minimum (and thus the AOW benefit) was set at a percentage of the statutory minimum wage, and in 1968, the social minimum was fully indexed to the growth of contracted wages in the private sector. Beginning in 1970, benefit levels were slowly upgraded relative to the minimum wage, so that by 1980, AOW pensioners were entitled to a benefit equivalent to 100 percent of the net minimum wage (in 1999, the net minimum wage was equal to 55 percent of the net average wage). The purchasing power of the AOW was eroded somewhat in the late 1980s and 1990s when the AOW benefit was temporarily delinked from growth in the minimum wage as part of a wider agreement to try to limit social spending and boost labor force participation. Still, the AOW is widely regarded as a modest but still adequate income for the elderly (de Jong, Herweijer, and de Wildt 1990; van Aartsen 2000 interview).

Italians who have a limited contributory history but are entitled to some old-age insurance benefits are the analogous second rung on the ladder of pension generosity. Such beneficiaries are entitled to "minimum pensions" (*pensioni minimi*). If the normal rules governing the relationship between contribution period and benefits levels were followed, a limited contribution period would result in a rather small pension benefit. However, since 1952, participants in the state-run pension system have been entitled after fifteen years of contributions to a minimum pension. The level of this pension is less than the full benefit that would accrue to someone in the same sector with a thirty-five- or forty-year contribution history, but substantially more than would accrue based on a fifteen-year history in the absence of the minimum pension provision. A combination of state subsidies and money drawn from the pension system's reserves makes up the shortfall.

Minimum pensions were introduced for employees in 1952, farmers in 1957, artisans in 1959, and shopkeepers in 1966. Minimum pensions make up a substantial portion of the total number of pensions disbursed. In 1980, for example, 60 percent of pensions paid out by the main state pension administrative body were minimum pensions (data from INPS 1982). The overwhelming majority of minimum pension beneficiaries are in the agricultural and self-employed sectors, and in many cases these pensions supplement other forms of income (other pensions, unreported self-employment or farm income, etc.). Still, the benefit levels are quite low – equivalent to about 25 percent of the average wage (Ferrera 1984, 416), versus the 55 percent of average wage granted to Dutch AOW beneficiaries. Once

147

again, the quite low level of the basic minimum benefit cannot explain the dramatic difference in aggregate expenditure levels between Italy and the Netherlands – especially since a much greater percentage of pensioners receives the minimum benefit (60 percent) than receives the AOW alone (15 percent).

At the upper end of the income scale for pensioners, Italy and the Netherlands reverse positions. Unsurprisingly, given the lack of private supplementary pensions in Italy, high-end public pensions in Italy tend to be higher than their counterparts in the Netherlands. But the total pension benefit including AOW and supplementary benefits does not exceed 70 percent of the average wage earned in the five years prior to retirement except in unusual circumstances. Prior to 1999, legislation surrounding the supplementary pension provision specified that "qualified" pensions could "not exceed what society considered reasonable in relation to length of service and level of salary" (Ministerie van Sociale Zaken en Werkgelegenheid 2000, 12). In practice, this meant a ceiling of 70 percent of the prior wage. This rule of thumb was formalized in legislation in 1999 that allowed for a higher ceiling on nontaxable benefits for retirees over age sixty-five with more than thirty-five years of contributions, but limited the standard benefit to 70 percent of the prior wage.

In Italy, there is no explicit limitation on the maximum pension benefit, a situation that has led to very high expenditures on pensions, despite the fact that extremely generous benefits are reserved for a relatively small portion of the elderly population. A series of measures introduced in the 1970s through 1990s aimed to reduce the inequality introduced by high replacement rates for full pensions. These measures included a system of indexation that used fixed-sum increments rather than percentage increases, resulting in greater relative increases for lower pensions, and a "solidarity tax" on high-end pensions. Replacement rates in the main state-administered schemes were capped at 80 percent of the prior wage, but this ceiling was removed in 1988 (Canziani and Demekas 1995, 3). But even at 80 percent, the Italian pension system had the highest maximum replacement rate of any European country (9). The highest pensions in Italy accrue to private sector workers with contributory histories of at least thirty-five years. The most fortunate of these are workers in specialized segments of the private sector, such as maritime workers, private sector managers, lawyers, or journalists, whose pensions are on average more than 150 percent higher than those of industrial workers with full contributory histories, and 300 percent higher than average full pensions for the self-employed (data from ISTAT 1999).

148

Old-Age Pensions

Number of Pensions

Higher replacement rates for high-end pensions in Italy account for part of the difference between Italy and the Netherlands in aggregate pension spending as a percentage of total social spending. The other factor that contributes most heavily to Italy's relatively high pension bill is the sheer number of pensions disbursed on an annual basis. Contributing to this large number of pensions are two peculiarities of the Italian system: Italians can receive more than one pension at once and are able to enjoy old-age benefits at a relatively early age. Almost 30 percent of pensioners in Italy receive more than one pension from the state (ISTAT 2000).[5] This contributes to higher per-person spending levels than would be indicated by the relatively modest average benefit in Italy. And since recipients of multiple pensions received benefits roughly 125 percent greater than recipients of single pensions (ISTAT 2000), per-person spending levels are inflated even further.

A second, and more dramatic, cause of high pension spending in Italy is the very large number of old-age pensioners under the age of sixty-five. Fully 42 percent of Italian "old-age" pensioners, some 3 million strong, are under the age of sixty-five. In contrast to the Netherlands, where the official retirement age is sixty-five for both men and women, the retirement age in Italy has been set since 1939 at sixty for men and fifty-five for women. In the 1980s and early 1990s, older members of the work force in both Italy and the Netherlands were encouraged to make way for younger job-seekers through a variety of incentives, including early retirement, extended unemployment benefits, and disability pensions. Large numbers of workers between the ages of fifty-five and sixty-five thus were effectively retired but receiving benefits other than old-age pensions in both the Netherlands and Italy. But as we saw in chapter 5, disability and long-term unemployment beneficiaries were much more likely to be older workers in Italy than in the Netherlands. Even taking into account a substantial number of early retirees in the Netherlands, the average age at pensioning is lower in Italy than in the Netherlands (OECD 1995), resulting in higher aggregate pension liabilities in Italy.

It is not just the earlier retirement age that accounts for the large number of young retirees in Italy. The feature of the Italian pension system that is most responsible for this phenomenon is the "seniority pension"

[5] This figure includes disability pensioners, but there seems little reason to suspect that disability pensioners would be more likely than old-age pensioners to have multiple pensions.

(*pensione di anzianitá*), an institution introduced in the 1960s that allows workers to retire after a set number of years of service regardless of their age. In the public sector, employees have been able to retire and begin drawing a full pension after as few as fifteen years of service; in the private sector, the standard was thirty-five years. In 1998, 2.3 million retirees (14 percent of all pensioners including disability pensioners) were seniority pensioners who had retired before the standard retirement age. Of these, one-quarter were under the age of fifty-five (ISTAT 2000). In addition to retiring earlier and thus costing more over the long run, seniority pensioners also tend to receive higher benefits than other pensioners. The mean seniority pension in 1998 was 30 percent higher than the mean standard old-age pension. The combined effects of more pensioners, longer periods of retirement, and higher benefits make seniority pensions a particularly pernicious feature of the Italian pension landscape for those concerned to cut costs, and indeed seniority pensions have been a prime target of reformers since the 1970s. Italian seniority pensions contribute to the much higher proportion of total social spending allocated to pensions in Italy as compared with the Netherlands, where no such institution exists to facilitate early retirement on a massive scale.

The responsibility for the divergence between Dutch and Italian levels of pension spending as a proportion of total social spending can be attributed, then, to a combination of policy features that create broad differences between the two countries in pension benefit levels and the number of pensioners. Benefit levels at both the low and the high ends of the income scale are affected by policy features such as the definition of an acceptable social minimum, the availability of private supplementary pensions, the level of the standard replacement rate, and the existence of specialized schemes with very high replacement rates. The number of pensions paid out, on the other hand, is determined both by the proportion of elderly who are covered and by factors such as the standard retirement age, the possibility of receiving more than one pension at a time, and the possibility of retiring with full benefits prior to the official pensionable age.

Divergent Pension System Development in Italy and the Netherlands

How can we account for the key policy features that inhibit or promote the growth of very high replacement rates for some public pensions, and those that discourage or encourage very early retirement with full pension

150

benefits? This section focuses on two constellations of policies that prove particularly important. In the Netherlands, a combination of a well-defined social minimum, a strong second pillar of private supplementary pensions, and a firm ceiling on high-end pension benefits works to hold pension benefit spending at a moderate level. In Italy, the combination of a low statutory retirement age and the extensive use of seniority pensions dramatically increases the number of pensioners.

Floors, Ceilings, and Pillars: Determining the Level of Benefits

The Netherlands The existence of a modest social minimum to which the level of the AOW benefit is pegged has contributed to keeping public pension spending in the Netherlands relatively low, while the existence of a second tier of private occupational benefits has defused pressure for an escalation of benefits for higher income earners. By contrast, the absence of a clearly defined benefit floor in Italy has not only contributed to high levels of inequality and poverty among the elderly. It has also, ironically, in combination with a limited system of private occupational pensions, resulted in a very high ceiling on public pension benefits, which in turn contributes to Italy's high levels of pension spending.

The first postwar public pension in the Netherlands, established under Red-Roman leadership in 1947 as an emergency provision, set benefits at a modest level. Large budget deficits (van Zanden 1998, 63) and the high start-up costs involved in setting up a new pension system offering benefits for all elderly citizens prohibited setting benefit levels at such a high level that they could be seen as an equivalent to the earnings they were meant to replace. Indeed, Catholic and Protestant employers' organizations strenuously resisted the idea of a universal pension set at such a high level that it would crowd out private occupational pension funds that they had set up already before the war. Instead, benefits in the new public pension system were pegged to the cost of living in different municipalities.

The new pension aimed at providing a "decent" standard of living, as foreseen by the van Rhijn Commission for Social Security Reform, which had been convened by the government in exile in London during the war and presented its report in 1947. Under Red-Roman leadership, the emergency law was replaced with a permanent pension provision in 1956, which established a more generous, uniform benefit level throughout the country, linked to a combination of price and wage levels. In 1964 all social benefits, including old-age pensions, were formally linked to a nationwide social

151

minimum, an amount that should be enough to cover minimum expenses for a "sober" lifestyle (Vrooman 2000 interview).

The Dutch system of social security, befitting its occupationalist origins, remains resolutely conceptualized by the public and by politicians as a system of work-related benefits supplemented by a safety net for those unable to work (de Jong et al. 1990, 44). However, the belief that the "safety net" aspect of the system should be based on an adequate social minimum has from a very early period enjoyed widespread support across the political spectrum and among the social partners (van der Veen 2000 interview; Vrooman 2000 interview). Socio-Economic Council recommendations on benefit levels were generally supported by a unanimous consensus of labor, employers, and government representatives on the council, and parliamentary debates surrounding the introduction of social legislation contain almost no discussion of benefit levels. The most heated arguments in both the council and the parliament focused on technical details of implementation and administration, not on the concept of benefits linked to a standard social minimum (Cox 1993; Vlek 2000 interview).

Under PvdA rule in the late 1960s and 1970s, the level of the social minimum was substantially upgraded. Not only were social benefits such as pensions linked to the minimum wage in 1964, but beginning in 1968 Social Democrats in government argued successfully that recipients of minimum wages should share more equally in the nation's growing wealth, and the level of the minimum wage itself was upgraded substantially relative to median incomes. At the same time the social minimum was upgraded numerous times, until finally, in 1980, it reached 100 percent of the net minimum wage. Why did this improvement in the level of the social minimum not result in a dramatic increase in pension spending, as occurred in Italy at around the same time?

Although the increases in the minimum wage and improvements in the indexation of benefits resulted in an improved standard of living for pension beneficiaries, both Social Democratic government officials and the director of the nonpartisan Central Planning Agency expected that linking benefits more closely to wages would actually contribute to keeping costs down (Hemerijck 1992, 325). This strategy failed to contain pressure for wage growth in the private sector, and resulted in a dramatic increase in social welfare spending, primarily in the areas of unemployment and disability benefits. But pension spending did not spiral out of control, unlike in Italy where it doubled as a share of the national income between 1960 and 1980. And despite the numerous critiques of the social welfare system that emerged beginning in the mid-1970s, the level of public pension benefits never came under attack.

Why did pension spending in the Netherlands resist the inflationary tendencies that plagued the Italian system in the 1970s and 1980s, despite linkage to an inflation-proof wage index? One possibility is that linking benefits to an adequate social minimum limits claims for large increases in benefits because benefits are already adequate. Certainly, once benefits were linked to a minimum wage that was increasing rapidly relative to average wages, arguments based on criteria of absolute need and relative social justice would have been disarmed. Even more clearly, the second pillar of private supplementary pensions played an important role in defusing pressure for higher state pension benefits. Demands for "deferred wages," or, in the parlance of Dutch industrial relations of the period, "immaterial demands," could be pushed onto the private funds quite easily, since the administration of these funds was explicitly a subject of collective bargaining. With private pensions serving as both a supplementary form of income and as a pathway for absorbing nonwage demands during collective bargaining, the public AOW could remain at a level appropriate to its original intent – a social minimum.

Perhaps more puzzling than the capacity of the AOW to resist upward pressure on benefits is the resilience of the norm, in place since the early 1960s, setting maximum replacement rates for the AOW *plus* supplementary pension at 70 percent of prior earnings. Other earnings-related benefits – unemployment and disability pensions – were set at an 80 percent replacement rate, so it seems natural that there would have been pressure for upward revision of earnings-related old-age pensions. During tight labor markets, employers were not averse to exceeding government guidelines for maximum wage increases (Hemerijck 1992), so it comes as a surprise that maximum pension benefits should have been so resistant to increases. The 70 percent norm was established as part of a tripartite agreement in the early 1960s that set the target level for pensions at 70 percent, but was never codified as a matter of public law (Westerveld 2001). The 70 percent norm was never a subject of debate, though, because if individuals wanted pension provisions higher than a 70 percent replacement rate, they were free to take out private insurance in addition to their occupational and state benefits (van Suijdam 2000 interview). Even the trade union confederations pressed for nothing higher than a 70 percent replacement rate as late as their 1971–75 Joint Programme of Action (NVV-NKV-CNV Consultative Body 1971, 34).

In the Netherlands, the early linkage of public pensions to a social minimum adequate to cover living costs for most elderly set a standard of benefits that has proven remarkably resistant to upward pressure. In particular, since the elderly are no worse off than any other social beneficiaries, and since during the 1970s the level of benefits grew faster than average earnings, it has been difficult for advocates of higher pension benefits to make a case based on either need or social justice. The presence of private schemes has also defused pressure to adjust public pensions to compensate for wage restraint. Finally, the ceiling on maximum replacement rates of 70 percent – high by European standards, but still lower than in Italy – means that even the combination of public and private benefits is not high enough to create truly exorbitant pension expenditures as in Italy.

Italy   In Italy, a configuration of policy features the reverse of those found in the Netherlands has led to extremely high public pension expenditures. The absence of an adequate social minimum, the very limited development of private supplementary pensions, and the existence of replacement rates in excess of 80 percent for selected groups of workers all contributed to Italy's runaway pension growth in the 1970s through 1990s.

Despite repeated attempts to provide pensions at a level to guarantee subsistence for the elderly, early steps toward defining an adequate social minimum did not bear fruit. As in the Netherlands, the principle of a social minimum was enshrined in Italian law quite early. Article 38 of Italy's 1947 Constitution stipulated that all citizens unable to work and without means adequate for subsistence were entitled to assistance from the state. At the same time, reform commissions called by the government to study the problem of social security in the 1940s and 1950s fell short of advocating a universal minimum pension benefit. The 1948 report of the D'Aragona Commission called in general terms for benefits that would provide "minimum economic support" (Commissione per la Riforma della Previdenza Sociale 1948, 5), but the report established that pension benefits should be tied to the level of prior earnings.

The minimum pension benefit was established in 1952 and was designed to assure minimum living standards for those individuals already covered by the occupational pension system – primarily industrial workers and public sector employees. This left out large numbers of uninsured people, including the self-employed and workers in the still-dominant agricultural sector. Even so, the main employers' association Confindustria complained that the minimum pension "contaminated" the "healthy" linkage between earnings and benefits. It objected that the 8.4 percent contribution levied on payrolls to fund the minimum pensions was too expensive and argued that the state should really cover the cost of minimum pensions out of general revenues (Confindustria 1951, 722–3).

In its final execution, the minimum pension was far from adequate for the needs of many of the insured, and as a result poverty even among the elderly with pensions remained a serious problem. A 1953 report of the parliamentary commission established to investigate the problem of poverty in Italy cited inadequate pensions as a major cause of poverty among the elderly, and recommended moving away from an insurance-based system toward a social security regime that could guarantee a minimum living standard for all (Camera dei Deputati 1953). Speakers at a conference on the problems of the elderly convened by the Christian Democratic Party in 1955 noted that the majority of old-age pensions were below the subsistence level (*Il problema delle persone anziane* 1955, 152–3). A spokesman for a Catholic-run organization devoted to pensioners stated on a radio program in 1960 that according to the Italian statistical agency's calculations from their latest household budget survey, even the basic industrial worker's pension fell short of the subsistence level (Cuzzaniti 1960).

In 1963 a special commission of experts was called by the tripartite National Council on Labor and the Economy (Consiglio Nazionele dell'Economia e del Lavoro, or CNEL) to report once again on the social security system's problems and prospects. The commission recommended implementing a two-tiered pension system consisting of a basic minimum pension for all workers adequate to meet living standards, topped off by occupational, income-linked supplements (CNEL 1963a, 26). The proposal was rejected, however, and the idea of a basic, universal pension remained outside the realm of the possible until 1969. Under pressure from unions and left parties, the major pension reform of 1968–9 contained provisions for a means-tested pension that would fulfill Italy's constitutional obligation to provide a basic income for elderly individuals with no other pension rights. Set at the very low flat rate of less than one-tenth of average wages, however, these social pensions ended up looking more like an empty gesture than like an adequate safety net for the elderly.

Even after many ad hoc improvements in benefit levels and years of indexation to inflation and/or wages, the minimum pension benefit today amounts to only one-quarter of the average wage, and the social pension less than 15 percent. As a result of the failure to establish an adequate social minimum, pressure politics surrounding pensions in Italy has been geared overwhelmingly toward the acquisition of higher benefit levels, even in cases where benefits were already well above any reasonably defined social minimum. The significant numbers of the elderly still living in poverty has, until quite recently, fed into a public perception that Italian pensions are insufficient (Baldissera 1996a; 1996b; 1997; Boeri and Tabellini 1999a). This has opened political space for demands to raise replacement rates, a practice that results in extremely generous pension provisions for small segments of the population with the most economic and/or political bargaining power.

At the same time, a low-wage strategy pursued by Italian industry through the 1960s, much as in the Netherlands, encouraged unions to pursue pension benefits as a form of deferred compensation. Unlike in the Netherlands, however, in Italy no system of private occupational pensions exists to absorb pressure for increased benefits coming out of the collective bargaining arena. In the absence of a private pension system, the strategy of using pensions as deferred compensation has led to a dramatic increase in public pension levels, especially for those sectors where workers have held the strongest bargaining positions.

What accounts for the absence of private pensions in Italy? As in the Netherlands, the assets harbored in the system of private pension funds that had been built up in the late nineteenth and early twentieth centuries were depleted by inflation and wartime destruction of real estate and industrial holdings. As in the Netherlands, the interests of both the Church and employers lay in rebuilding this private system. However, in Italy private pension funds have played an extremely limited role since World War II. The weakness of Italian capital markets, unfavorable tax treatment of private pensions, and the public system of severance payments have all discouraged private funds from developing (Franco 2000). Furthermore, according to Franco, the very generous provisions for some in the public pension system have "both reduced the demand for supplementary plans and the resources available to finance them" (10). The relationship between the generosity of public pension provisions and the development of private sector alternatives is a complex one, with causal arrows running in both directions. However, it is clear that very generous public benefits for select groups and strong private sector supplements do not coexist nearly as easily as do low public benefits and strong private supplementary funds.

If in the Netherlands strong upward pressure on pensions as a form of deferred compensation was absorbed by the system of private occupational funds, the tacit agreement to limit total pension payments to a 70 percent replacement rate kept maximum benefits within reasonable limits. In Italy, however, norms limiting the level of high-end pension benefits have been rather weaker. A government pension reform plan in 1952 proposed a rate of return on contributions that would have given a 90 percent replacement rate for average earners after forty years of contributions, and a 120 percent replacement rate for white-collar employees retiring at age sixty-five (Confindustria 1952, 720). While these generous provisions were not introduced (partly because of Confindustria's insistence that workers should not be rewarded for staying on past the age of sixty), they signal that very high replacement rates were by no means anathema to policy makers even at a time when the majority of Italians still had no pension coverage at all.

The pension reform of 1969 established a new defined-benefit system that was not linked directly to contributions, and thus a maximum replacement rate had to be specified. At this time an upper limit on pensionable earnings was also introduced. At the behest of the trade unions and over the opposition of Confindustria (Regini 1981, 137–8; Regonini 1984, 100), the maximum replacement rate was set at a rather high 80 percent of prior earnings, which served the purpose of reducing special treatments for groups such as professionals and journalists while still resulting in an increase in benefits for industrial workers. Many groups, including public sector employees and other professional groups, were exempt from this ceiling. But even for pensions subject to the 80 percent ceiling, the system of indexing pensions to wage growth meant that real replacement rates could in fact rise well above the 80 percent level as long as wages continued to rise in real value, as they did through the 1970s.[6] And the sky became the limit for all pensions after 1988 when the 80 percent ceiling was lifted. The fragmentation of the Italian pension system made it feasible to grant very high pensions to those segments of the work force who had the most bargaining

---

[6] To understand why this is the case, think of a pensioner, Antonio, who retires with a pension equal to 80 percent of his earnings in the last year of his employment. Perhaps he earned $100 a week as an employee, and thus his pension in his first year of retirement is $80 per week. Three years after his retirement, however, workers have received substantial concessions on the wage front, and wages have increased by 20 percent. So his colleague Giuseppe, who retired three years after Antonio, earns $120 a week in his last year. Half of this increase is due to inflation, so Giuseppe's real wage, relative to Antonio's ending salary, is only $110. But since Antonio's pension has been fully indexed to increases in wages, he now receives a pension equal in real, inflation-adjusted terms to 80 percent of $110, or $88. Antonio's pension three years after his retirement is now giving him a benefit equivalent to a replacement rate of 88 percent, not 80 percent. And for every year that wage growth outpaces inflation, the effective replacement rate on Antonio's pension will make similar gains.

power either contractually or because of their close relationship to the political parties in government, for example, airline pilots working for the state monopoly. The absence of strong norms (much less legislation) preventing pensions from rising above a certain level made this development almost inevitable.

The combined lack of effective floors and ceilings on pension benefits has contributed to a costly pension system in Italy, which accounts for part of the difference in the age orientation of the welfare states in Italy and the Netherlands in general. But the *level* of pension benefits is only part of the explanation. Another key to understanding the high relative cost of the Italian pension system lies in appreciating the very high *number* of pensioners in Italy and the political decisions that undergird this phenomenon.

The Effective Retirement Age: Determining the Number of Pensions

As we saw in the first section of this chapter, a fundamental difference between the Italian and Dutch pension systems that helps to explain the dramatic difference in aggregate spending levels is the age at which most people retire. Retirement occurs much earlier in Italy than in the Netherlands because of a lower statutory retirement age, and because of provisions that have made it possible for workers to retire at full pension after as few as fifteen years of service, whatever their age. What is the genesis of these differences, and how has the early average retirement age in Italy been maintained for so long despite the obvious pressure that it puts on government spending?

The Statutory Retirement Age   International Labour Office conventions in the 1930s and 1940s recommended a rather low retirement age. Signatory nations were required to provide old-age insurance for workers over the age of sixty-five, but were encouraged to set the retirement age lower than that. A 1933 ILO advisory on pensions advised that "it is recommended, as a means of relieving the labor market and of ensuring rest for the aged, that the pensionable age should be reduced to sixty, in so far as the demographic, economic and financial situation of the country permits" (ILO 1933). The 1944 convention on pensions required that "the minimum age at which old-age benefits may be claimed should be fixed at not more than sixty-five in the case of men and sixty in the case of women: Provided that a lower age may be fixed for persons who have worked for many years in arduous or unhealthy occupations" (ILO 1944).

In the Netherlands the retirement age for the 1947 emergency pensions was set at sixty-five, a limit that remained in place throughout the ten years of negotiations that led up to passage of the permanent act on public pensions in 1956. The precedent for a retirement age of sixty-five was set in pension legislation enacted prior to World War II: the 1913 Invalidity Act and the 1922 pension provisions for public servants both set the retirement age at sixty-five. Widespread youth unemployment in the immediate postwar period was addressed through an active emigration policy rather than by encouraging older workers to retire early, as per ILO recommendations. When youth employment again emerged as a problem in the late 1970s, "exit pathways" such as disability pensions, extended unemployment benefits, and private early retirement provisions provided the means for older workers to comply with societal demands to make room for younger workers (de Vroom and Blomsma 1991). As a result, there was little pressure to lower the retirement age. In union documents stretching from the early 1950s through the late 1980s, there was no mention of any demands for a lowering of the retirement age (NVV 1951–75; FNV 1977–87).

By contrast, the Italian retirement age adhered more closely to ILO guidelines. This adherence was made easy by the fact that under the Fascist government, the retirement age had been reduced from age sixty-five to age sixty for men and fifty-five for women. The rationale for this change was precisely the same as that stated in the 1933 ILO convention: to ease the shortage of jobs by encouraging older workers to exit. This of course also dovetailed neatly with the Fascist government's pronatalist agenda, which would have been impossible to maintain in the absence of jobs for workers with young children (Lapadula and Patriarca 1995, 75). The 1939 retirement age was reaffirmed in 1952 during the first comprehensive postwar overhaul of the pension system, again because of concerns about a shortage of jobs for younger workers (Confindustria 1953, 720–1).

The 1952 pension reform law did, however, make it possible for workers to retire up to five years after the retirement age, with a concomitant increase in benefits of up to 22 percent for women and up to 40 percent for men. Confindustria argued at the time that the increase in premiums necessitated by this provision constituted an unfair tax on workers (Confindustria 1952), and by 1955 it had come to the conclusion that as long as it was impossible to force workers to retire at age sixty, the retirement age should simply be raised (Confindustria 1955, 81). In 1957, the Christian Democratic Party held a second conference on the problems of the elderly, during which speakers pleaded for a consideration of the possibility of raising the retirement age by at least five years. As more than one participant remarked, this would make it possible to raise pensions by 40 to 50 percent over current levels, while maintaining contribution levels at a constant rate (*L'invecchiamento della popolazione* 1957, 29). One participant also noted that the low retirement age did not result in any increase in jobs for younger people, citing a recent survey carried out by INPS that found that 90 percent of old-age pension recipients between the ages of sixty and sixty-five continued to carry out some form of paid labor (*L'invecchiamento della popolazione* 1957, 53). Even pensioners' organizations had by 1960 come to the conclusion that raising the retirement age to sixty-five was a viable solution to the problem of low pensions (see, e.g., Cuzzaniti 1960).

In the 1960s, pressure continued to mount for an increase in the retirement age. The CNEL's 1963 report on social security also noted that Italy's low retirement age made it difficult to raise benefits to the level that the commission's members thought necessary (CNEL 1963b, 185). By 1967, the ILO had begun to soften its position on retirement ages, and in its convention on invalidity, old-age and survivors' benefits of that year in fact allowed for retirement ages higher than sixty-five "as may be fixed by the competent authority with due regard to demographic, economic and social criteria, which shall be demonstrated statistically" (ILO 1967). The government's and unions' proposals in Italy for a major pension reform in 1968 contained provisions for an increase in the retirement age, and this provision was nearly passed, before opposition from current workers who opposed an extension of their working careers scuttled the agreement (Regini and Regonini 1981, 227). Failed reform proposals in 1984, 1988, 1990, and 1991 all stipulated an increase in the pensionable age to sixty-five for both men and women, but in no case was an increase in the retirement age enacted.

Seniority Pensions   Differences in statutory retirement ages – higher in the Netherlands than in Italy – account for some of the difference in pension spending levels between the two countries. However, much of the high pension burden in Italy is accounted for not by a low statutory retirement age, but rather by a provision allowing many pensioners to retire at full pension well in advance of the statutory retirement age.

Seniority pensions were introduced for public sector workers in Italy in 1956, allowing workers to retire with full pension after twenty-five years of service (twenty years for women) regardless of whether they had reached the retirement age. In 1962, the CGIL made seniority pensions for private sector workers a key demand, citing the rationale that other groups already enjoyed this privilege (CGIL Segreteria Generale 1962, 224). A provision permitting retirement with full benefits after thirty-five years of service was introduced for private sector workers in industry, agricultural workers, and artisans in 1963, though this provision was not implemented until 1965.

In 1968 the three major union confederations initially agreed with a government proposal to eliminate seniority pensions in the private sector in return for higher pension benefits. However, the metal workers' union opposed this trade, since their workers enjoyed relatively stable employment and were thus particularly likely to actually be able to enjoy the seniority benefit (Regini and Regonini 1981, 227). Under pressure from this strong category union, the CGIL withdrew from the accord with the government and initiated a series of general strikes in 1968 and 1969. In the pension accords of 1969–70, unions were able to defend the seniority pension and win improved benefits. In a process of "leapfrogging" (Baccaro 1999, 132), in which public sector employees made up for a relative decline in their position vis-à-vis private sector workers with even stronger improvements in their own situation, a new law regulating seniority pensions in the public sector was introduced in 1973, permitting retirement at full pension after twenty years of service (fifteen for women). Another law in 1979 introduced further improvements for public sector workers.[7]

The full extent of the drain on the pension system that would be created by seniority pensions did not become clear until the second half of the 1980s, when the first generation of workers with continuous employment histories and full pension rights entered into the system. Within the main private sector pension fund, the number of seniority pensions tripled between 1980 and 1992, and by the early 1990s, seniority pensions constituted the majority of all new pensions granted by the largest state-administered pension fund (Fondo Previdenza Lavoratori Dipendenti, or FPLD; Lapadula and Patriarca 1995, 24). The failed government-sponsored pension reform proposals of the 1980s and early 1990s uniformly called for a revision of the public sector rules to bring their seniority benefit into line with the thirty-five-year period in effect for private sector workers. This goal was finally achieved in 1992 with Amato's reform, which phased in the thirty-five-year

---

[7] Law 1979/29 established that public sector workers could count seniority accrued while working in another sector, a provision that the Treasury Ministry commission predicted would result in a dramatic increase in the number of public sector seniority pensions (Ministero del Tesoro 1981, 74).

period for public sector workers. Berlusconi's 1994 reform proposal called for even more serious cuts to seniority rights. In fact, the vast majority of the savings envisioned by his plan came from curtailing the seniority benefit and imposing a 3 percent per year penalty on pensions for workers who retired before the age of sixty-five (Baccaro 1999, 142). But Berlusconi's reform plan failed, and it was not until the Dini reform of 1995 that the seniority pension was finally dismantled – and even then, over a long phase-in period.

What accounts for the resilience of Italy's very low effective retirement age? Criticism of seniority pensions has been loud and sustained, at least since the 1980s. A 1981 report of a study commission convened by the Treasury Ministry report deemed Italy's early retirement age "anomalous" and argued that it was "absolutely necessary" that the retirement age be raised and that the discrepancy between the retirement age for men and women be eliminated. It went on to call for an "urgent" reform of the public sector seniority pension system, bringing it in line with rules in the private sector (Ministero del Tesoro 1981, 71–5). With regard to the situation in the private sector, INPS president Giacinto Militello declared at a 1987 conference on "The Future of the Italian Pension System" that "the progressive raising of the retirement age appears to be a necessary instrument for keeping predictable increases in pension spending under control" (Militello 1987, 10). A 1988 conference on social insurance convened by INPS also recommended raising the retirement age as soon as possible (Alvaro and Carloni 1989, 281), as well as harmonizing rules between the public and private sectors. And Italy's main union confederations have demonstrated a willingness to support raising the retirement age and eliminating most seniority provisions, as evidenced by their support of reform proposals in 1968, 1992, and 1995. So why has the low effective retirement age not been raised?

Some analysts argue that structural features of the Italian economy have played an important role in preventing the introduction of a higher retirement age and more stringent early retirement rules. INPS (1989, 279) summarizes the debate over raising the retirement age as a tension between two conflicting goals: reducing expenditures and responding to an inadequate supply of employment opportunities. Lapadula and Patriarca (1995) essentially agree, arguing that the "backwardness" of the Italian economy and its business enterprises are at the root of the "delicate" problem of reforming seniority pensions. In this view, Italian firms have used seniority pensions as part of a system of "permanent restructuring" based on restricting labor supply rather than finding ways to retrain and use labor more effectively. The fiscal crisis of the 1980s and 1990s introduced pressure to eliminate seniority pensions. But the prospect of radically reducing access to seniority pensions is a frightening one given the continuing shortage of jobs, and political opposition to cuts has been fierce. This structural explanation for the resilience of seniority pensions in Italy's private sector does not, however, explain extremely generous provisions for public sector workers, who would presumably be protected from market pressures in any case.

Public opinion surely plays a role in maintaining the low retirement age and seniority pension benefits. In a 1994 nationwide poll, 71 percent of Italians opposed raising the retirement age (Baldissera 1997). As Regonini (1990, 359–60) remarks, issues such as raising the retirement age and harmonizing the rules governing early retirement between public and private sector workers are particularly unlikely to be passed by legislators, because the groups that would be affected are so large and cross over party lines. So political pressure from the electorate at large has made it difficult to raise the effective retirement age in Italy, even when officials at the Ministry of Labor, the Ministry of Finance, the governing board of INPS, and the confederal level of the main unions agreed that it would be desirable.

Explaining Differences in Pension Spending: Competing Hypotheses

The preceding section outlined the political and institutional dynamics underlying several key policy features that determine the level of pension expenditures in Italy and the Netherlands. What do these dynamics tell us about how social policies become oriented toward different age groups in the population? And how do they reflect on existing claims about the sources of pension spending in particular?

This section makes the case that aggregate levels of pension spending are influenced by a combination of how pension systems are structured and how political competition either reinforces or works to undermine those structures. Citizenship-based pension programs will lead to lower aggregate pension spending because uniform benefits for all citizens make it easy to calculate future costs and difficult for politicians to use increased pension benefits as a currency of political exchange. Fragmented occupational pension programs, by contrast, provide both a smokescreen to hide behind and the currency with which politicians may bargain should they wish to contract private deals with small segments of the electorate. Particularistic political competition can thus be expected to undermine attempts to introduce universal citizenship-based benefits and maintain pension policy structures that are conducive to very high expenditure levels.

But the cautious reader will surely wonder whether this argument is unnecessarily complex. After all, a large and growing literature in comparative political economy points to the role of power resources in determining levels of (or changes in) pension spending. Variations in the power resources of labor and the Left, on the one hand, or the elderly, on the other hand, are said to determine how much governments spend on old-age pensions. It is worth addressing these arguments carefully, since they have such intuitive force.

The left power resources argument holds that pensions are more generous and more widespread where representatives of working-class groups are politically powerful. This political power may come about as a result of strong and centralized labor unions, neo-corporatist labor relations institutions that include labor in policy making, left parties that command a large share of the vote, or control over key governmental positions. Whatever the avenue by which the working class arrives at its strength, the outcome is expected to be broad, encompassing, and generous pension provisions.

On its face, the claim that left power resources could be responsible for higher pension spending in Italy than in the Netherlands is problematic. Esping-Andersen (1990) and others characterize the Netherlands as an "almost Social Democratic" country, while no one would mistake Italy as anything other than a stronghold of Christian Democracy. The Dutch PvdA has been a partner in government for much of the postwar period, while in Italy the main leftist party, PCI (which changed its name in 1989 to the Democratic Party of the Left, or PDS), was shut out of government until 1994. (The Socialist Party of Italy, or PSI, cannot properly be considered a leftist party, since during the postwar period it has followed a centrist policy agenda when it has followed one at all.)

Dutch unions, too, have been much more closely involved in policy making than have Italian unions, by virtue of the multiple corporatist institutions in which they participate and in which many key policy decisions are made. The most important of these institutions, the SER, is a tripartite body that the government was obliged until the mid-1990s to consult before submitting any social policy legislation to Parliament for consideration. Even after this obligation was removed, governments have continued to honor it in practice, voluntarily submitting policy proposals to the SER for review. By most definitions, then, the Left has had more power in the Netherlands than in Italy for most of the postwar period, yet pension spending is lower in the Netherlands than in Italy. The prediction that left power resources will lead to higher social welfare spending, including pensions, is not borne out by a broad characterization of these two cases.

But this broad portrait of Social Democracy in the two countries misses much. The Left is not as strong in the Netherlands, nor as weak in Italy, as one might suspect. Despite the presence of Red-Roman political coalitions in the Netherlands throughout much of the period from 1950 to 1970, the Ministry of Social Affairs remained controlled by Catholic politicians for most of the period. Developments in the public pension system following Drees's initial emergency provision in 1947 have come largely under the watch of Christian Democracy, not Social Democracy. As for Italy, despite its characterization as a Christian Democratic single-party-dominant system (Barnes 1990), the Left has not been uninvolved in the area of pension policy. Communist legislators in Italy have been closely involved in pension policy making through their positions on the parliamentary committees responsible for social policy and on the board of directors of the state pension agency. And as Cazzola (1995, 26–7) remarks, somewhat ruefully, most social legislation in the 1970s and 1980s was passed in Parliament with almost unanimous approval of both government and opposition legislators). Finally, Italian unions, like their Dutch counterparts, have been closely involved in the pension policy-making process during both periods of neo-corporatist concertation and episodes of more conflicting labor relations. And while Golden Age Dutch corporatism was primarily a system for wage control (Hemerijck 1992, chapter 7), in Italy concertation has often occurred explicitly around the issue of social policy.

So resolving the question of how much impact Social Democracy has on pension spending is a bit more complicated than it first appears. Lower pension spending is clearly associated with a more Social Democratically oriented polity in the Netherlands, and higher pension spending with Christian Democratic dominance in Italy. Setting aside these broad characterizations, could it still be the case that the variable political power of the Left is responsible for higher pension spending in Italy and for lower expenditures in the Netherlands?

Even taking a more nuanced view of the strength of Social Democratic actors and institutions in these two countries, our conclusion still must be that the strength or weakness of the Left is not the key to explaining different patterns of aggregate pension spending. In neither Italy nor the Netherlands does the level of left power resources bear primary responsibility for the policy features that most affect the level of benefits and the number of beneficiaries, and thus create large differences in pension spending between the two countries.

The concept of an adequate social minimum, which I argue was crucial for containing the level of high-end benefits in the Netherlands, seems to have been supported by a very widespread societal consensus. All political parties, and employers and crown members as well as labor representatives on the Socio-Economic Council, agreed on the desirability of a pension benefit linked to an adequate social minimum, even while they disagreed quite strongly on key features of how the pension system should be administered. The establishment of benefit levels based on a social minimum adequate to meet living costs cannot, then, be attributed to a "weakness" of Social Democracy, the more so since the Labor Party was an active participant in government and particularly in social affairs, and corporatist institutions were at their strongest, during the period when the social minimum was established.

The failure of the PvdA to completely dominate government and neo-corporatist policy-making bodies in the Netherlands immediately following World War II could conceivably explain why a viable system of private supplementary pensions remained in place, though it must be noted that unions were supportive of a private system even if the Social Democratic Party was not. While PvdA politicians would have preferred to replace the private system entirely with a public universal benefit early in the postwar period, unions were eager to maintain an important role for private supplementary benefits on the condition that they be allowed to share in their administration. The supplementary pension system was also desirable to unions because it gave them something other than wages to bargain over in a period of stringent wage controls.

Neither the PvdA nor labor unions in the Netherlands have played an important role in limiting the number of pension beneficiaries, either. Social Democrats do not appear to have requested at any point a lowering of the statutory retirement age, but neither do they seem to have been responsible for setting the retirement age at sixty-five to begin with. Again, this appears to have been a matter of rather broad societal consensus dating from the prewar period. Social Democratic actors have pushed for the maintenance of avenues of early exit from the work force – for example, disability pensions, early retirement, and extended unemployment provisions – but employers have been equally adamant supporters of such measures. It does not appear, then, that the variable strength of Social Democracy over the years in the

Netherlands has been responsible for either setting in place or maintaining the policies that we have seen lead to low pension spending relative to Italy.

Nor is the Left in Italy the primary architect of policies encouraging higher pension spending. In the period prior to 1969, left parties and unions both advocated a universal pension system with a fixed social minimum, and their pressure tactics were aimed primarily at improving low-end pensions. Neither is there any evidence that the Left or labor unions in any way stymied the growth of private pensions. High benefit levels for high-end pensions have certainly been supported by some professional associations, but the confederal unions have pushed for a ceiling on pensionable income, and there is a clear relationship between left partisanship and sponsorship of pension bills aimed at the most encompassing and lowest-income groups (Maestri 1987). Category unions such as those representing metal workers did press for higher benefits for their own sectors, and sometimes won. But once the confederal unions gained control of the administration of INPS in 1971, unions increasingly stood in favor of reducing high-end benefits (Regini and Regonini 1981, 240). Ultimate responsibility for very high high-end pensions in Italy lies with politicians, primarily politicians of the DC and the PSI, whose generosity toward key sectors (public employees, managers, and professionals) resulted in a constant ratcheting up of expectations.

The most important provisions determining the number of pension beneficiaries in Italy – the early retirement age and access to seniority pensions – were put into place during periods when neither unions nor left parties had any input into social policy formation (the Fascist period in the case of the retirement age, and the mid-1950s in the case of seniority pensions for public sector workers). Can they be held responsible for the failure to reform these system features? Unions, at least at the confederal level, supported proposals to raise the retirement age and cut seniority privileges at least as often as they opposed such measures. Left parties have played a more ambiguous role. While the rhetoric of left politicians has emphasized reducing the privileges of public sector workers, PCI/(P)DS politicians have tended to vote in much the same way as other politicians on major pension legislation (Regonini 1987, 103; Maestri 1994). It does seem to be the case that when unions are incorporated into the process of reform, reforms tend to go more smoothly and parties are less tempted to reach out to their militant base to gain consensus (Regini and Regonini 1981; Baccaro 2000). However, there is little evidence to suggest a distinctive Social Democratic partisan impact on pension reform that would allow us to attribute Italy's high pension spending to the power resources of the Left.

If left power resources do not explain differences in pension spending between Italy and the Netherlands, what about the power of the elderly? Perhaps pensioners, who stand to benefit most directly from high pension benefits, are responsible for pushing for the growth of public pension spending and for opposing any attempts to curtail benefits. To the extent that the elderly constitute an overwhelming bloc of voters or are organized into pressure groups that can effectively lobby for pro-elderly legislation, they may be responsible for the shape and size of a nation's pension system. Of course, other constituencies besides the elderly stand to gain from generous pensions: one need only think of adult children of the elderly, who benefit by having the burden of care for their parents taken over by the state, or of current workers, for whom generous pensions constitute a promise of payment in the future. Nevertheless, there is good reason to suspect that a politically mobilized and powerful elderly lobby can have an important impact on pension spending.

The gray power hypothesis predicts that more elderly voters, and stronger organizations of the elderly, should result in higher pension spending. Italy has a substantially older population now than does the Netherlands, and pensioners in Italy are organized into powerful pensioners' unions of their own within the national confederations, while Dutch pensioners have had limited success organizing within the union movement. So one could conclude that higher pension spending in Italy occurs because the elderly are more powerful political actors there than they are in the Netherlands.

But as with the characterization of the Netherlands as "almost Social Democratic" and Italy as purely Christian Democratic, this image is not entirely correct. Until rather recently, both Italy and the Netherlands had quite young populations by European standards. It is only since the late 1970s that the Italian population has begun to age dramatically. And the elderly have played an important role in Dutch political life, just as they have in Italy. Since the immediate postwar period, the elderly have been an important constituency for Dutch political parties, especially the PvdA, which still enjoys favor among seniors as the party of Drees and the first universal pension. The elderly in the Netherlands have been represented since the 1950s by interest groups that work as equivalents to the unions in Italy. These groups became quite active in the 1980s and 1990s and are regularly consulted on policy matters relating to the elderly. Furthermore, the early 1990s saw the emergence and entry into Parliament of several pensioners' parties in the Netherlands. These parties were not large, and they did not maintain their parliamentary seats for long. But they did succeed in drawing enough voters away from the Christian Democratic Party to force that party to back off from proposals to cut pensions (Balkenende 2000 interview; Green-Pedersen 2002).

Not only is the difference in the level of political influence of the elderly in Italy and the Netherlands not as great as one might initially assume. In both countries, key policies that set the stage for future expenditure levels were already in place well before the elderly became a powerful political lobby. In the Netherlands, seniors strongly supported the universal pension introduced by Drees in 1947, but had no involvement in the preservation of the private occupational pillar. And the establishment of a social minimum and the retirement age of sixty-five seem not to have been issues of public debate. In Italy pensioners' organizations lobbied for better low-end benefits and a universal pension system, but had little success. And they were involved neither in the establishment of public sector seniority pensions nor in the setting of the low statutory retirement age. The gray power hypothesis then cannot account for the establishment of the program features most responsible for high pension spending in Italy and lower spending in the Netherlands.

It might still be the case, however, that the elderly have played a more important role in maintaining program features that might otherwise have gone by the wayside. This would accord with Pierson's (1994) argument that beneficiaries of the welfare state come into their own as important political actors primarily during periods of attempted retrenchment. There is some support for this argument on the Dutch side. The elderly in the Netherlands in the 1980s and 1990s have tended to mobilize reactively around proposed cuts to their benefits, not proactively to counter such proposals as has been the case with other groups such as single mothers or the disabled (Vlek 2000 interview). Dutch elderly organizations have spoken out against effective cuts in AOW pension benefits resulting from de-indexation (in the 1980s and early 1990s) and the imposition of taxes on AOW benefits (in the mid-1990s). However, it was not until pensioners' parties posed a serious threat to the Christian Democratic Party in the late 1990s that these protests began to see any results. Protests by elderly organizations successfully derailed an attempt to introduce social security taxes on AOW benefits in 2000 and have effectively brought to the agenda the issue of pensioners' representation on the boards of private pension funds.

Paradoxically, the record shows that Italy's very strong pensioners' unions have actually taken quite moderate stands on the issue of pension reform, contrary to the presumption of many commentators that they would oppose any reforms. Pensioners' unions were formed after World War II to advance the interests of former workers, and through the mid-1970s their demands were focused almost entirely on improving pension provisions and health care for the elderly. As the pensioners' unions gained experience and independence, their leadership gradually became a source of expertise for the union confederations in the area of social policy as a whole. And rather than using their new role to push solely for policies in the short-term self-interest of current pensioners, the pensioners' unions began increasingly to adopt a broader view of their role as defenders of the welfare state. For example, in 1976, well before the union confederations or political parties had taken up the call for pension reform, the CISL pensioners' affiliate (Federazione Nazionale Pensionati, or FNP) argued that unless the pension system were reformed substantially, there was a danger of collapse in the long term (FNP 1992, 12).

Pensioners' unions supported the failed pension reforms of 1978–9 and the successful ones of 1992, 1995, and 1996. The yearly unified policy documents put forth by the three largest pensioners' unions in the 1990s express consistent support for proposals to introduce more equity into the pension system by limiting seniority pensions and raises for the highest public old-age pensions. In 1992, the assistant secretary general of the FNP stated, "We know that the current public pension system is characterized by injustice, corporativism, waste, and unfair distribution, especially between public and private sectors; pension spending is ungovernable. . . . The reform of public pensions can no longer be delayed. It is necessary to rationalize, reorganize, and overcome imbalances and unfair inequalities" (Noseda 1992, 89).

In 1995, pensioners' union members voted an overwhelming 91 percent in favor of the proposed pension reform in the union referendum called by the confederations to solicit the opinion of the membership (Baccaro 1999, 150). One could argue that the pensioners' unions supported these reforms because they placed most of the cost of reform on future pensioners. Indeed, the end result of the negotiated reforms placed the heaviest burdens on current workers with less than eighteen years of accumulated contributions. However, many provisions did affect current pensioners, most notably minimum pension recipients and public servants about to retire on seniority pensions. Contrary to the expectations of the gray power hypothesis, strong pensioners' groups in Italy have in many instances advocated reforms that would reduce pension spending, whereas in the Netherlands rather weaker pensioners' parties have nevertheless successfully acted to protect pension benefit levels even when other kinds of social benefits were subject to cuts.

Political Competition and Program Structure

The level of the standard replacement rate and the existence of specialized schemes with very high replacement rates are the key policy features that account for differences in benefit levels between Italy and the Netherlands. We've seen that neither differences in the strength of Social Democratic actors nor the relative power of elderly lobbies can explain these policy differences. But the structure of the welfare state and the nature of political competition do affect these policies in important ways.

In the Netherlands a comprehensively enforced tax system that included the self-employed as well as employees provided a firm fiscal basis for a universal pension system, just as it allowed the development of universal family allowance and unemployment policies. The Left and the Right were able to agree on a pension system that covered both employees and the self-employed, because employees and the self-employed both contributed: employees through payroll deductions, the self-employed via the tax system (Ferrera 1993, 169). And as we have seen, the universalistic nature of the pension system impeded the growth of pension expenditures by establishing a basic social minimum that prevented claims for benefits expansion based on criteria of need.

The primarily programmatic mode of political competition in the Netherlands, combined with the removal of much negotiation over pensions to the private second pillar, has provided little incentive to attempt to upgrade benefits for small constituencies. This in turn has allowed the Netherlands to avoid the phenomenon of leapfrogging benefits for different groups that contributed to ever-increasing expenditures in the Italian case. At the same time, the universal pension system provides few footholds for those politicians who might wish to use it to pursue a more particularistic mode of interest aggregation in the Netherlands. Finally, the flat-rate structure of the AOW means that projecting pension outlays is a simple matter.[8]

---

[8] The legacy of expertise in economic forecasting left by Jan Tinbergen, the first Nobel Prize winner in economics and director of the Dutch Central Planning Bureau during the immediate postwar period, also added to the ease of pension forecasting in the Netherlands. Comparable expertise did not exist in Italian economics departments at the time.

Thus it has always been obvious, even to actors who might have advocated higher pension benefits, what would be the consequences for other social programs of raising pension benefits. So the universalistic structure of the Dutch pension system and the programmatic nature of political competition have reinforced each other and help to explain why the system established immediately after World War II did not take on more particularistic features.

The opposite configuration, a tight bundling of particularistic political competition and fragmented occupational program structure, is clearly visible in the case of Italian pensions, where the highly complex and differentiated public pension scheme and a clientelist mode of political competition reinforced each other in several ways. First, as with family allowances and unemployment benefits, Christian Democratic politicians' particularistic use of the tax code made it impossible to introduce universal pension benefits at a guaranteed social minimum level, which could have helped to contain costs. Second, the eagerness of politicians, particularly of the DC and the PSI, to provide benefits for key political supporters contributed to the proliferation of special treatment for public sector employees, which we have seen increased both the level of benefits and the number of beneficiaries in the pension system as a whole. Finally, the fragmentation of the pension system impeded reform, by setting the stage for competition between different sectoral groups and by hampering the ability of pension administrators and other experts to formulate accurate projections. Let us address each of these points in turn.

Particularism, Taxation and the Failure of Universalism The main obstacle in Italy to implementing the universalistic pension proposals of the early postwar period was the tax system. The reports of the D'Aragona Commission (Commissione per la Riforma della Previdenza Sociale 1948) and the CNEL reform commission (CNEL 1963a; 1963b) both cite the impossibility of adequately assessing and collecting pension contributions, especially among the self-employed, as reasons to continue providing pension benefits on an occupational basis. Labor unions, too, which professed support for the idea of universal coverage, feared that any universalization of the system would be paid for out of increased payroll taxes on employees, and so repeatedly called for fiscal reform as a prerequisite of pension reform (see CISL Consiglio Generale 1950, 13; 1956, 150; 1958, 178; CGIL Segreteria Generale 1962, 226; CGIL-CISL-UIL Segreteria Interconfederale 1970, 201).

By the early 1960s, Italy's pension system was categorized by two types of funds: those running a surplus, primarily the FPLD and the special funds for small groups, such as journalists; and those running large deficits, primarily the funds for agricultural workers, artisans, and shopkeepers. The latter funds had been set up in the late 1950s and early 1960s by DC governments in order to benefit clienteles that were particularly important to the DC (Regonini 1996, 90). These funds ran large deficits because contribution rates were very low and access to benefits was available even for people with very limited contributory histories. While the state subsidized these pensions out of general revenues to some degree, in large part it was the employees' funds that were asked to make up for shortfalls in a form of "enforced solidarity" (Ferrera 1993, 262). By the late 1960s, both Confindustria and the unions were complaining about the increased payroll taxes that had become necessary to support this burden, and union support for universalizing the pension system waned.

The implementation of the social pension provision between 1965 and 1970 was the final nail in the coffin of the Left's hope for a universal pension system with an adequate social minimum. A tripartite agreement in 1964 established this new benefit for persons over sixty-five without other means of support, and it was agreed that benefits should be financed out of state revenues deposited in a new Social Fund. It was also agreed that the level of the benefit would be sufficient to provide for a "decent" standard of living, as stipulated in Article 38 of the 1947 Constitution. By 1968, however, both Confindustria and the labor unions had lodged complaints that state contributions to the Social Fund were inadequate to cover its costs, and the fund was instead drawing resources from the FPLD. At this point it had become clear that social pensions , which constituted the benefits floor in the Italian system, would have to be paid out of employees' pockets if they were to be paid at all, and union support for upgrading the level of the benefit to an adequate social minimum faded (Ferrera 1993, 262). As a result of the state's inability to finance a universal social minimum out of general revenues, the safety net that was implemented for retirees in Italy remained at a level so low as to constitute a meaningless support. This absence of a social minimum and the continued fragmented, occupational nature of the Italian pension system contributed, as we have seen, to Italy's very high pension expenditures in the 1980s and 1990s.

The reluctance of successive administrations to execute the tax laws continued even after the definitive defeat of proposals to establish a universal pension system with an adequate social minimum. Evasion of pension contributions for employees continued to be an important issue from the late 1970s onward. In 1978 the CGIL and the PCI began to complain quite insistently about the failure of employers to make contributions on behalf of their employees. This practice contributed to the deficits that had begun to plague even the stronger funds administered by INPS. A 1978 union proposal to make evasion of payments a criminal offense was defeated by the DC government – in part because it would have meant absorbing the system of occupational injury compensation into INPS, which was controlled by the unions, and thus would make unavailable a key source of patronage for the government (Regini and Regonini 1981, 233). A 1980 study commissioned by the Labor Inspectorate, INPS, and unions revealed that in the 10,074 firms studied, there was evasion of payment for 42 percent of employees (Regonini 1984, 106). A report by an independent watchdog group noted that evasion of contributions was facilitated by the very small proportion of the work force of either the Labor Inspectorate or INPS devoted to enforcement (CENSIS 1983, 237). "Administrative incentives" for evasion that emanated from the government bureaucracy fostered a lack of compliance with the tax code (Regonini 1984, 106).

Both the tax laws (failure to adequately tax key clienteles of the DC) and their implementation (failure to enforce those laws that were in place) sprang from the particularistic mode of political competition pursued by politicians of Italy's leading political parties during the postwar period. The inability to collect revenues from key economic sectors in turn made it impossible to universalize the pension system and provide an adequate social minimum without placing an excessive burden on employees. This constellation of problems radically altered the Italian Left's preferences with regard to universalization and benefit levels. And, most importantly for the future of pension expenditures in Italy, the continued fragmentation characteristic of Italy's occupationalist pension regime led to a system in which reform became nearly impossible for a period of almost thirty years.

The Pension System as a By-product of Clientelism If particularistic political practices prevented the implementation of a tax system capable of sustaining a political coalition for universal pensions, clientelism also had more direct effects on the pension system. In particular, the extreme generosity of pension provisions for public sector workers, which as we have seen contributed both to high benefit levels (via the absence of a ceiling on benefits) and large numbers of pensioners (via generous seniority provisions), can be seen as a direct outgrowth of the competitive strategies of the DC, PSI, and PCI.

To most observers, Italy's proliferation of pension provisions, each with its own benefit formula, contribution rate, degree of state subsidy, rules governing retirement age, years of service required to enter into the plan, and so on, constitute proof positive that the pension system has been used as a way to attract support from particular groups in the population (Regini 1981; Regini and Regonini 1981; Ferrera 1984; Paci 1984; Maestri 1994). So does the practice of staffing pension agencies with party supporters and of deciding pension claims based on an applicant's party affiliation (Regonini 1996, 90–1). This perception is not limited to the scholarly community, of course. Even the undersecretary of labor, in the midst of the 1982 pension debate, dispatched a telegram accusing two representatives of the majority coalition of "rampant particularism for pernicious electoral reasons" (quoted in Regonini 1984, 108).

Christian Democratic politicians advocated extending pension benefits to the self-employed on very generous terms during the 1950s and 1960s as part of a strategy to purchase loyalty from these groups. But during the postwar period, state employees have been the most important target of clientelist pension legislation, for obvious reasons. As the staff of public and quasi-public organizations came to be dominated by supporters of the governing parties, public sector pension benefits took on special cachet with politicians associated with these parties. Special provisions for public sector employees reach back into the Fascist period (Cherubini 1977; Paci 1984). During the postwar era, however, special provisions for public sector workers were defended and extended by parties in government, as a fundamental aspect of their electoral strategy. Not only have public sector employees been the recipients of the largest volume of pension legislation during the period 1948–83, but attention to this sector has come predominantly from DC and PSI lawmakers (parliamentarians and government officials; Maestri 1994). The extremely generous pension provisions enjoyed by public sector employees, provisions that have contributed in no small way to the development of high pension expenditures in Italy, can be quite directly attributed to the particularistic competitive strategies employed by politicians of the ruling parties in Italy during the postwar period.

What is perhaps less widely appreciated is the extent to which the clientelist behavior of the DC (and later PSI) drew parties of the opposition into a mode of pension policy making that has exacerbated the expenditure problem. In the 1950s and 1960s, the Left was opposed to the DC's practice of extending pension rights to new groups without making these new groups responsible for financing them. However, the Left was too weak to block this practice (Regini 1981, 122). But even after 1969, when they had more control over pension legislation, unions opposed moves to universalize the pension system in part because they feared that a state-run system would bring their constituencies into the clientelist orbit of the DC, as had happened earlier with agricultural employees (127). Instead, they followed a strategy of attempting to upgrade benefits for their constituencies to the level enjoyed by public sector employees (Baccaro 1999). In the words of Ferrera (1993, 267), "The biggest novelty of [the reform of] 1969 in a political sense was . . . the enlargement of the spoils system to include the PCI and unions, opening the way to that 'assistential grand coalition' responsible for the profound imbalances that characterized the Italian welfare state in the years to come." The Left and the unions tried to match every gain made by public sector workers (and other privileged clients of the ruling parties), and to the extent that they succeeded, in turn the privileged clients demanded more privileges. This led to an upward spiral of benefit levels, and a downward spiral of contributory requirements, in the 1970s and 1980s. These developments are attributable in the first instance to the particularistic mode of competition engaged in by the DC and the PSI. But the strategy of the opposition parties and of labor unions has been conditioned by this mode of competition among the dominant parties, such that the Left ultimately shares responsibility for the expansion of the pension sector at the expense of other social spending.

Fragmentation and the Difficulty of Reform   The ratcheting up of benefits and privileges in the Italian pension system is a by-product of particularistic political competition, but also of pension system fragmentation. This dynamic is much less likely to occur in the absence of multiple different regimes for different occupational categories, since it would require an audacious first-mover to break the status quo of benefits equality. But the high degree of fragmentation in Italy's pension system has made it difficult to achieve reform for other reasons, as well.

First, the pre-existing occupational system contributed to the demise of universalistic reform proposals in the 1940s–60s. In principle the Italian Left, particularly the Center-Left, supported a universalistic pension scheme. But in a context of particularistic behavior by the ruling DC, unions had a strong incentive to maintain the pre-existing occupational funds, over which they had some modicum of control, rather than giving everything over to a central, DC-run universal scheme (Ferrera 1993). Once again the interplay of clientelism and fragmentation affects the Left's preferences and behavior, with the opposition parties and unions coming to support particularistic fragmentation under the threat of an even more damaging particularistic universalism.

Fragmentation further impinges on prospects for reform because it makes forecasting expenditures more difficult. In one of the earlier projections of pension expenditures in Italy, the 1963 CNEL report predicted that pension spending would reach 56 percent of total social spending by 1980, an amount that the commission considered to be too high. But this projection failed to take into account the potential for explosive growth of the pension sector inherent in the existing, segmented regime (Franco 2000, 18–19). Even apart from the political dynamics of reform that a highly fragmented system generates, it has proved remarkably difficult to arrive at any agreement about future pension liabilities based solely on economic considerations. At a 2000 conference convened by the research arm of INPS, one employee of INPS reported that the complexity of the pension system in Italy was such that the bureaucracy lacked the econometric tools necessary to forecast pension expenditures accurately. In fact, the first long-term forecasts of pension expenditures in Italy date from the late 1970s (Franco 2000, 12). Competing studies from the 1980s (Franco and Morcaldo 1986; Alvaro, Pedullá, and Ricci 1987; Ministero del Tesoro 1988; INPS 1989) resulted in widely varying forecasts, with the most optimistic scenarios suggesting little need for reform. Under such circumstances of uncertainty, it is not surprising that it has been difficult to make a strong case for reform. The high levels of fragmentation and differentiation in the Italian pension system, a feature closely allied to the particularistic nature of political competition in that country, have made it difficult to see who benefits and who loses from the current system, and thus to generate a viable coalition for reform.

Conclusion

This chapter has argued that differences in pension spending, an important determinant of the age orientation of social spending in Italy and the Netherlands, are a product of differences in both the structure of pension programs and the type of political appeals that politicians make to the electorate in these two countries. Contrary to the standard literature on comparative social policy, I find that the level of spending on pensions in Italy and the Netherlands is not reducible to differences in the power resources of either organized labor and the Left or the elderly lobby.

A number of specific policy choices have contributed to high pension spending in Italy and lower expenditures in the Netherlands. The establishment of an adequate social minimum, the presence of a second pillar of private occupational pensions, limits on maximum pension benefits, and a relatively high retirement age have contained pension costs in the Netherlands. At the same time, weak income guarantees for the poorest elderly, unlimited pension benefits at the high end, and a very low retirement age have contributed to extremely high pension expenditures in Italy. Analysis of the role of left-leaning and pro-elderly actors in the formation of these policies reveals that neither the power resources of the Left nor so-called gray power can explain divergent spending patterns in Italy and the Netherlands. Rather, these developments provide support for the political-institutional argument developed in chapter 3.

If a universalistic pension program and programmatic political competition in the Netherlands serve as a kind of null hypothesis, the development of pension spending in Italy provides a clear illustration of how the interaction of particularistic political competition and occupationalist program structure leads to high levels of spending on the elderly. The citizenship-based pension program in the Netherlands, a program built on the base of a comprehensive tax system and a politics of programmatic appeals, keeps spending down because uniform benefits for all citizens make it easy to calculate the future costs of raising pensions. This universal system also discourages politicians from using pension benefits as a currency of political exchange, since it is impossible to raise pensions for one segment of the electorate alone. This in turn prevents the ratcheting up of pension benefits for different sectors that proved so expensive in the Italian case. Italy's fragmented occupational pension system, by contrast, provides crucial resources for clientelist politicians, whose opposition to reforming such a system in turn provides occupationalism with a means of self-propagation. In addition, the combination of fragmented occupationalism and political particularism also alters the incentives and behavior even of political actors whose normal mode of operation might be more programmatic, such that eventually they, too, come to support the fragmented pension system status quo. Both the universalism-programmatic politics dyad and the occupationalism-particularistic politics dyad are resilient and self-reinforcing, properties that explain the ability of these political-institutional characteristics of welfare states to shape the flow of benefits to different constituencies over long periods of time.

7

Conclusion

This book has sought to elucidate how and why social policies in the rich democracies vary in the way that they treat older and younger members of society. Yet in the course of devising a strategy for measuring the age orientation of social policies, testing alternative theories, and elaborating mechanisms through the use of case studies, less attention has been paid to the question of why, after all, the "age" of welfare matters. This final chapter, then, explores the implications of the book's findings about the age orientation of welfare states for the well-being of different age groups and for scholarship about the welfare state.

Age Orientation, Poverty, and Inequality

How does the age orientation of welfare states contribute to the well-being of different groups in the population? We might think first of the welfare state's capacity to reduce the incidence of poverty among children, working-age adults, or the elderly. It seems reasonable to assume that, other things being equal, elderly-oriented welfare states would do a better job at reducing poverty among the elderly than among non-elderly adults and children. On the other hand, in relatively youth-oriented welfare states, which in fact merely spend roughly equally on the old and the young, the poverty reduction due to taxes and transfers should be more equal across age groups.

This proposition is in theory testable using cross-nationally comparable household-level data on income from the market and from social programs. Such data are available from the Luxembourg Income Study (LIS) project. Unfortunately, in practice we can do little more than speculate with these data. Measuring the amount of poverty reduction that a welfare state carries out depends on having reliable household-level data on income both before and after taxes and transfers are taken into account. But recall that opaque administration of tax systems is a prime resource for clientelist politicians, who are concentrated in the elderly-oriented welfare states. As a result, many countries characterized by particularistic political competition either do not participate in LIS (e.g., Japan, Greece, Portugal) or do not provide LIS with pretax income data (e.g., Italy, Belgium), making it impossible to estimate the poverty reduction carried out by the welfare states in these countries. It is of course telling that the problems in the data reflect the causal mechanism hypothesized to underlie the very outcomes that interest us.

Eliminating many of the most elderly-oriented countries from consideration due to a lack of data also makes it harder to examine the effects of age orientation on poverty even in those countries for which pretax income data *are* available, by reducing the already small number of cases. Poverty and poverty reduction are complex phenomena, and the weight of any one potential cause (e.g., age orientation) must be considered in light of other attributes of welfare states and labor markets that may also affect income distribution and poverty. The amount of poverty reduction carried out by a welfare state is likely to be related to the amount of poverty before taxes and transfers, as well as to the size of the welfare state and the level of inequality generated by the labor market, not to mention the political, societal, and economic variables that are the root causes of the intermediate-level phenomena. Without these controls it is impossible to estimate the impact of age orientation per se. But once we remove Italy, Belgium, and other countries for which there is no pretax data from the analysis, we have LIS data to work with for only eleven (mostly youth-oriented) countries – not enough to allow for any statistical control.

What we can say, then, about how age orientation affects the ability of welfare states to reduce poverty in different age groups is limited to what the raw data tell us from those countries where information is available. A very low level of aggregate spending seems to limit the quality of outcomes for the very young regardless of how much or how little is spent on other age groups. None of the smallest welfare states (the United States, Australia, Ireland, Canada) is able to substantially reduce poverty levels in families with children (Fig. 7.1). At the same time, there is a great deal of variation in how much even these small welfare states reduce poverty

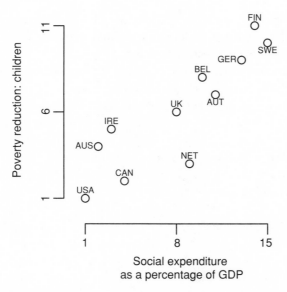

Figure 7.1 Welfare state spending and poverty reduction: children. *Note:* Poverty reduction is percentage change in poverty rates pre- and post-taxes and transfers. Poverty rate is percentage of children aged 18 and under and not household heads living in households with income of less than 50% of size-adjusted median. *Sources:* Spending: OECD 2004; poverty: author's calculations from LIS (Wave IV data).

among elderly and non-elderly adults (Figs. 7.2 and 7.3). Relatively youth-oriented Ireland does much better for non-elderly adults than any of the other residualist welfare states, and Australia and Canada do better than the quite elderly-oriented United States. Size matters – but at the margin, so does age orientation.

The age orientation of welfare states may also affect the degree of inequality among different age groups. Clearly, elderly-oriented welfare states are not likely to reduce inequality much in *any* age group, despite relatively generous spending on the elderly. (The occupational programs that generate high aggregate spending on the elderly are designed to preserve status differentials, so they tend to reproduce labor market inequalities.) But we lack the pretax income data that would allow us to see whether most elderly-oriented welfare states differ systematically (and net of other factors) from more youth-oriented ones in the way that they mitigate market inequalities among different age groups. Another revealing and still more data-intensive test of the effects of age orientation on inequality would come from examining inequality within cohorts over time. Does a

Conclusion

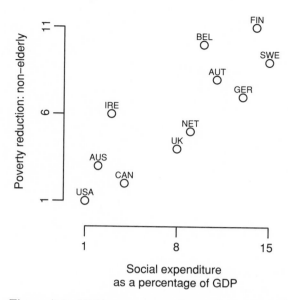

Figure 7.2 Welfare state spending and poverty reduction: non-elderly adults. *Note:* Poverty reduction is percentage change in poverty rates pre- and post-taxes and transfers. Poverty rate is percentage of adults aged 18–64 living in households with income of less than 50% of size-adjusted median. *Sources:* Spending: OECD 2004; poverty: author's calculations from LIS (Wave IV data).

youth-oriented welfare state reduce inequality over time? If so, does all youth-oriented spending have this effect, or only some? Is the cost over a cohort's lifetime greater or less than if the same degree of reduction in inequality were achieved through transfers to older age groups alone? These answers are surely worth knowing, as welfare states in the industrialized countries shift their budget allocations across different age groups and different types of policies (e.g., active vs. passive labor market policies, services vs. transfers).

The results of elderly-oriented social spending for the capacity of welfare states to perform arguably their most important function – protecting vulnerable outsiders – are pernicious. In the account presented here, the quality of political life emerges as a key determinant of the quality of social benefits and ultimately social welfare, echoing Marshall's (1950) linkage of political and social citizenship. Where programmatic party competition prevails, new social programs can come forward to meet the emerging social needs of adults and children struggling to balance work and caring responsibilities in a changing labor market, and can constrain the otherwise powerful

183

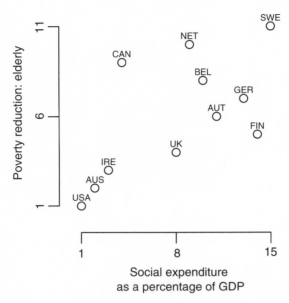

Figure 7.3 Welfare state spending and poverty reduction: elderly adults. *Notes:* Poverty reduction is percentage change in poverty rates pre- and post-taxes and transfers. Poverty rate is percentage of adults aged 65 and older living in households with income of less than 50% of size-adjusted median. *Sources:* Spending: OECD 2004; poverty: author's calculations from LIS (Wave IV data).

budgetary expansionism of social benefits for protected core workers and pensioners. In settings where particularism prevails, however, benefits are concentrated on a relatively small group of privileged, aging insiders, while the growing mass of outsiders is left to fend for itself. Let us review how and why this comes to pass.

Program Structure, Political Competition, and the "Age" of Welfare

This book has argued that the age orientation of welfare is a largely unintended consequence of the structure of social programs and the mode of political competition in which politicians engage. Early choices about the structure of social programs are reinforced by the way that politicians use these programs to compete for votes, and give rise to welfare states that treat the old and the young quite differently. The causes normally adduced to explain differences among welfare states – the economic circumstances facing welfare states, the political power of Social Democrats or Christian

Democrats, the influence of welfare state constituencies such as senior citizens – tell us rather little about why some countries spend more on their elderly or their children than others do.

Welfare state programs organized in different ways and put in place during a first critical juncture in the early twentieth century mature into welfare states that privilege different age groups. But in order for welfare state structures selected at this first critical juncture to "stick" for long enough to affect the age orientation of welfare spending in the 1990s, initial choices about the structure of social programs must be continually reinforced. The competitive environment within which politicians operated during a second critical period after World War II supplies just such a mechanism of reinforcement.

The countries that in the 1980s and 1990s had the most elderly-oriented social spending – Greece, Japan, Italy, the United States, Spain, and Austria – were welfare states that entered World War II with occupational social programs and never, or only recently, added a significant layer of citizenship-based benefits. Other countries that had occupational welfare states after World War II – the Netherlands, Germany, and France – were able to develop more youth-oriented citizenship-based programs, to "switch tracks," as I termed it in chapter 3. What accounts for the different pathways pursued by these two groups of countries following the second critical juncture? I argue that above all the path to highly elderly-oriented social policies versus a more moderate age orientation is determined by the way in which politicians use social benefits and other policies, such as taxation and labor market policies, to compete with one another.

In countries where politicians competed in an environment of particularistic politics and clientelism, fragmented occupational program structures provided critical resources for politicians, and were thus never abolished. At the same time, the attachment of clientelist politicians to particularistic administration of taxes, social security, and labor market regulation made universalistic social programs unpalatable even for leftist politicians, who were, in most countries, less inclined to compete along particularistic lines for reasons of ideology. In countries where political competition occurred along primarily programmatic lines, it was easier to introduce citizenship-based programs because politicians were less tempted to undermine tax systems in order to reward self-employed voters. They were also less tempted to tailor existing fragmented occupational social programs to appeal to micro-clienteles, and thus less devoted to the preservation of occupational program structures.

The original choice to organize social programs along either citizenship-based or occupational lines had a lasting influence on the age orientation of social policies in a wide range of industrialized countries. But this choice was not necessarily a permanent one. At key moments such institutional choices need to be reaffirmed. In the welfare states of Europe, North America, and the Pacific, the predominant mode of political competition in the period following World War II served as the backdrop against which institutional structures were either reaffirmed or renegotiated. The mode of political competition, programmatic or particularistic, thus has important consequences for the age orientation of social spending, channeling as it does the choices politicians make about how to structure and distribute social welfare benefits.

The development of family allowance policies, unemployment-related benefits, and old-age pensions in Italy and the Netherlands illustrates how the structure of social programs and the competitive behavior of politicians interacted to produce an elderly-oriented welfare state in Italy and more youth-oriented spending in the Netherlands. Italy's elderly-oriented welfare state is characterized by fragmented occupational social programs that do very little for children and working-age adults. At the same time, Italian pension spending is lavish (even if the distribution of this spending means that many elderly are left without adequate resources). The relatively youth-oriented Dutch welfare state has universal citizenship-based benefits that are quite generous for children and working-age adults, and moderate public pension spending that is supplemented by an equally moderate private occupational pension system. These very different constellations of policy outcomes can be explained by the mutually reinforcing dynamics of social program development and political competition in the two countries.

Britain's victory in World War II ensured that the Beveridgean model of social protection would become the archetype of the modern welfare state. Universal citizenship-based programs such as those in the Netherlands became the stock-in-trade of programmatically oriented politicians seeking to make their mark by providing public goods, rather than private benefits. Programmatically inspired political competition in the Netherlands in the postwar period thus spurred the development of universal social programs to complement or replace pre-existing occupational ones. Politicians in Italy also sought to use the programs of the welfare state to generate electoral support. Much as in the Netherlands, Italy's moderate Communist Party hoped to consolidate its working- and middle-class base by offering a vision of a new, universal, citizenship-based system. But Italian Christian Democratic (and later Socialist) politicians' strategic use of the welfare state, tax system, and public employment service soon made the goal of universalism seem less possible, and less desirable, to the mainstream Communist Left.

When politicians in the Netherlands used the welfare state to "buy" votes during periods of intense electoral competition, the universalization of benefits such as family allowances and pensions was one result. But in Italy, when social programs became the currency of electoral competition, occupational programs became more fragmented and more entrenched. The presence of a large group of powerful politicians competing in a clientelistic mode explains the persistence of fragmented occupational family allowances, unemployment benefits, and pensions in Italy during a period when many other countries of Europe were moving toward a more universalistic conception of the welfare state.

The earliest traces of clientelism followed in this book are to be found not in the welfare state itself but in the tax systems that underlie social programs. Clientelist domination of the legislature and the public administration in Italy in the early postwar years impinged on the development of a well-functioning tax system. Politicians and tax collectors looked the other way as valuable electoral constituencies such as the self-employed failed to report income or pay taxes on the income they did report. A fragmented and highly complex tax system eventually reified many of the special privileges granted in practice to valuable friends and allies of the Christian Democratic Party. The result was a tax system in Italy that could not support, either financially or politically, the weight of citizenship-based social programs.

Political coalitions advocating universal family allowances, unemployment benefits, and old-age pensions unraveled in Italy by the 1970s as it became clear that universalizing social insurance would mean adding benefits for the self-employed that would be financed by taxing industrial workers. Clientelist use of the tax system had made universal social programs impossible in Italy. In the Netherlands, quite the opposite occurred: there, a capable fiscal administration was the precondition for agreements that extended occupational family allowances, unemployment benefits, and old-age pensions into a full-fledged safety net entitling the self-employed and non-employed to the same benefits as employees.

Clientelist use of the tax system ensured that occupational social programs in Italy could not be replaced. But these programs, which provided different levels and types of benefits for different groups of workers, were also a gold mine for politicians who used particularistic strategies to compete for votes and win elections. Multiple, differentiated benefit categories within a single program – such as Italy's scores of separate public pension funds or multiple different programs providing cash benefits for the unemployed – are not just ex post facto evidence that politicians used the welfare state to target benefits to small groups of voters. The existence of such fragmentation also made it easier to justify new forms of discretionary targeting of benefits like a better replacement rate here, or a shorter reference income period there. As the fragmentation of the Italian welfare state increased, the very complexity and opacity of what Italian commentators have come to call "micro-corporativism" in turn protected the politicians who engaged in it. A thicket of highly specialized provisions has made it difficult for the public (and sometimes even for policy makers) to know when changes have occurred, and even harder for them to understand what the consequences of such changes might be for the public interest. For all of these reasons, politicians who compete using clientelism have been loath to see occupational fragmentation overturned, or even reformed.

Occupationalism stuck in Italy for two main reasons. First, clientelist political competition made it difficult to develop the neutral state capacities, like strong tax systems or functioning labor exchanges, that are necessary to make universal social programs politically and financially viable. Second, occupational welfare programs themselves provided valuable resources for clientelist politicians. In the Netherlands, on the other hand, neutral state capacities provided strong foundations for universal, citizenship-based programs. These programs, in their transparency and lack of differentiated benefits, both reflected and encouraged programmatic political competition.

The distinction between occupational and citizenship-based social programs also affected the *demand side* of social policy making in important, if less obvious, ways. Prior to the 1960s, benefits for children and working-age adults were, in Continental Europe, typically cast as wage supplements. Family allowances were put in place to make up for wage restraint or reduced hours; unemployment benefits were extended to those excluded from the labor market on a long-term basis only in cases of emergency or restructuring. When such benefits become a part of the apparatus of a citizenship-based welfare system, though, as they did in the Netherlands in the 1960s, they take on a different meaning. No longer simply wage supplements, in the Netherlands family allowances and long-term unemployment benefits grew into full-fledged entitlements, with accompanying

Conclusion

expectations about the appropriate level of the benefit.[1] In Italy, however, where family allowances and benefits for the unemployed remained occupational in nature, benefit levels were allowed to drift downward as wages and standards of living grew. Non-indexation of unemployment benefits and of family allowances in Italy doubly doomed those programs: as long as wages were rising, few people noticed that the benefit levels were falling, and once the benefit had shrunk to insignificance, very few people cared to spend political capital defending them.

Universal programs for the non-elderly grew quite rapidly in the Netherlands because, once divorced from wages, these benefits turned into expensive individual entitlements. At the same time, their undifferentiated structure meant that if politicians used these programs in an attempt to capture the votes of any group interested in the program, benefit levels would increase across the board. A raise for one is a raise for all in a citizenship-based social program. Occupational programs in Italy, on the other hand, could remain modest and yet still provide valuable currency to politicians. Even cash rewards too small to be much more than symbolic could be used to secure votes, as long as there were people who were not getting anything at all. This was an important reason why the Left came to oppose modest cash benefits for the youth unemployed in Italy.

If even small youth-oriented benefits can be useful for clientelist politicians in an unsaturated marketplace, large and highly salient benefits such as old-age pensions take on a life of their own. Differently situated constituencies press for ever better benefits, and the lack of transparency inherent to fragmented occupational regimes makes it possible for politicians to provide without invoking the public's wrath. This situation has made Italy's pension system extraordinarily resistant to change – more resistant, I would argue, than a policy feedback model based simply on blame-avoiding politicians would suggest.

In universal, citizenship-based pension systems such as the Netherlands', on the other hand, private or supplementary occupational pensions often act as a release valve for pressures to increase pensions. This safeguard is necessary since the budgetary consequences of increasing benefit levels in a universal program that provides even a modest income for retirement are so visible. Universal benefits that by their nature are relatively large – that

[1] Bussemaker (1992) has usefully discussed this transformation with reference to the "individualization" – extension to women as an independent entitlement – of benefits previously reserved for male breadwinners.

189

is, provide more than temporary or partial income support for large groups of people – thus are more resistant to expansionary politicking than either fragmented occupational benefits or smaller citizenship-based benefits such as family allowances or unemployment benefits.

Clientelist political competition in Italy locked into place pre-existing occupational programs, resulting in declining benefits for the non-elderly and an explosion of pension spending. In the Netherlands, citizenship-based programs grew on a base of neutral state capacities provided by programmatic political competition, and in turn reinforced the tendency in that system to compete along programmatic lines. The development of social spending in different areas (strong growth in the area of new entitlements of the non-elderly, and more cautious growth in the larger old-age pension program) resulted in a relatively youth-oriented welfare state.

Implications for the Study of Welfare State Politics

The argument presented in this book highlights two features of welfare states that have until now received very little attention in the literature on comparative social policy: (1) how the structure of welfare state programs interacts over time with demographic and labor market shifts and (2) the use that politicians make of such programs in their competitive battles with one another. But the explanation for why welfare states differ in their age orientation is perhaps most surprising because it has so little to do with age. The political power of age-based political actors and the beliefs they are presumed to carry with them about what is a just distribution across the life course play far less of a role in determining the "age" of welfare than one might expect.

At the margins, pressure groups representing both elderly and non-elderly constituencies (pensioners, families with children, and the unemployed) have certainly had an impact on social policies. And there is no question that the age orientation of social policies has become a subject of political contention for demographically defined pressure groups. But the age orientation of social policies should not be mistaken for a *result* of these constituency demands. Rather, policy drift (see Hacker 2004) resulting from sticky institutions in a changing environment is responsible for the outcomes we observe. It creates policies that benefit particular groups and for which these groups now fight, but which are actually the result of long-term processes having little to do with the demands of welfare state clienteles.

190

Conclusion

The interpretation of welfare state age orientations as a product of Christian Democracy falters on similar ground. Not only is the relationship between Christian Democratic strength and age orientation inconsistent (Italy, the Netherlands, Germany, and Ireland all have strong Christian Democratic political actors, but their age orientations range across the spectrum from rather youth-oriented to very elderly-oriented). Perhaps more important, welfare state structures such as status-preserving occupational social insurance programs and family policies that reinforce patriarchal authority – which accord with Catholic social doctrine and are often assumed to be a result of the power of actors motivated by it – are not necessarily the result of Christian Democratic power. The thoroughness with which Christian Democracy dominated the state in Italy makes that country a hard case among the Christian Democratic welfare states for this argument. But even in Italy, these classically "Christian Democratic" welfare state structures appear more as spandrels (see Gould and Lewontin 1979), by-products of some other set of evolutionary processes, than as true outcomes of Christian Democratic actors pursuing ideologically motivated policy goals.

The power of Social Democracy proves to be an equally poor predictor of the age orientation of welfare states. The egalitarian ideologies of working-class actors do not necessarily favor age-neutral social spending. The Left may defend either an aging core work force or younger labor market outsiders, depending on dynamics internal to the organized labor movement, on which policy solutions seem possible, and on the tactics of the opposition. In our cases, we saw the Left's social policy preferences change depending on the competitive strategies of the Center-Right. It would be impossible to pin variation in the age orientation of social spending to the strength of working-class ideologies and actors without knowing much more about the political and institutional environment within which they operate.

As with Christian Democracy and Social Democracy, the preferences of employers are unlikely to be homogeneous enough across space and time to account for variation in the age orientation of welfare states. Still, we might expect employers in small, open economies to create and defend universalistic social policies, on the theory that these would lower employers' direct nonwage labor costs. This could, over the long run, have the unintended consequence of creating more youth-oriented social policies in countries whose economies are highly exposed to international markets. But not all small, open economies opted for citizenship-based welfare states at our first critical juncture around the turn of the century (the Netherlands and Ireland did not), and even after the second critical juncture, some small, open economies (e.g., Belgium and Austria) maintained their occupational welfare states. The presumed preferences of employers within this relatively homogenous set of countries do not then account for the divergences in welfare state structures that produce varying age orientations.

As this brief summary makes clear, the argument presented in this book differs in some fundamental ways from traditional studies of comparative social policy. In the first place, my argument focuses more on the supply side of welfare politics than do explanations that appeal to the logic of constituency demand. While welfare state beneficiaries certainly have a role to play in requesting or acquiescing to certain policy solutions, both politicians and existing institutions are critical in shaping these demands. Welfare states cannot be read simply as the revealed or congealed preferences of powerful constituency groups. But neither can the supply of social policies be read simply as an expression of politicians' power to enact ideologically motivated or interest-based programmatic goals. What political representatives of employers and the working class want, and what they can get, affects the choice for universalism versus occupationalism at our first critical juncture. But we have seen that the competitive environment in which politicians of all ideological stripes find themselves determines crucially the kinds of social policies that they will support.

In this view, (some) institutions are the result of purposive action, but not necessarily of rational choice in the sense of action that pursues optimal policies given a certain set of ideologies or a certain demographic base. Because (other) institutions constrain the preferences of political actors, it is not possible to read their policy choices from their ideologies, their constituencies, or their place in the productive structure. This is not simply to say that political actors seek office or votes but not policies. Politicians *are* policy seekers, but the policies they seek are not necessarily the ones that inductive logic tells us they should prefer, in part because pre-existing institutions constrain their choices and make some options seem more appealing than others.

Still, the unintended consequences of institutional design may look very much like results of the ideologically motivated policy choices of powerful political actors. Elderly-oriented welfare states look like the outcome of successful lobbying by powerful senior interest groups. Age-neutral social spending looks like a victory for the egalitarian principles of working-class-based parties. But an important conclusion of this book is that such appearances can be misleading. While political actors do come to have a stake in these social policy institutions, they did not invent them. The age orientation of welfare states is a result of formal policy institutions, kept rigid by their bundling with informal political institutions and failing to adjust to long-term processes of demographic and social change.

Deep structural configurations such as these can coincide with and/or conceal what scholars and lay observers alike more often view as the short- to medium-term preferences of parties, politicians, or interest groups. This capacity for masquerade is probably part of what gives some institutions their resiliency. But if welfare state outcomes are marked by the unintended consequences of institutional design, then it makes little sense to think about the development of welfare states over the relatively *longue durée* of the postwar period purely in terms of purposive action guided by partisan goals and ideologies. In fact, observing the process by which both institutions and interests develop over the entire postwar period, rather than focusing on the correlation between interests and institutions in recent years, highlights a less actor-centered alternative set of causes of welfare state consequences (see Pierson 2004).

The unintended consequences of institutional rigidities undoubtedly play a larger role in structuring welfare state outcomes than much of the previous literature has allowed. Policy drift allows old institutions and struc- tures to generate new outcomes as the context within which they operate changes. The age orientation of welfare states is an outgrowth of early choices about welfare state structures, choices that were made without con- cern for the shape of the labor market, public finance, family structures, or demographic trends one hundred years hence. Yet as the societal substrate within which institutions are embedded changed, so too did the effects of these institutions. It seems likely that other attributes of welfare states that are also affected by the institutional form of social policies – attributes such as aggregate social spending or the extent to which welfare states decommodify workers – may also rely more than has often been recog- nized on policy drift and the unintended consequences of earlier policy decisions.

If this is true, then neither the age orientation of welfare states nor some of these other characteristics of welfare states that interest scholars should be interpreted purely as offshoots of the standard configurations of ideolog- ical or power resource variables. To focus on pre-existing institutions and on the prevailing political rules of the game forces us to consider the resources that specific contexts of competition confer on (or deny to) politicians, as well as these actors' ideologies and goals. Even when politicians are ideologically committed to particular policy goals, they may eventually press for other, sub-optimal policy solutions, as is vividly illustrated in the studies of Italian policy development in chapters 4 to 6. Left-leaning political actors in Italy repeatedly chose not to pursue the generous universal social benefits that they had once advocated because the political strategies of center and right politicians made other, second-best solutions preferable. This is not to deny the importance of power resources or of purposive action on the part of politicians and other policy makers, both of which have undeniably contributed to the shape of welfare states as we know them today. But all politicians must do their work within specific contexts, only some of which permit them to choose policies that are optimal from the standpoint of their ideological or organizational commitments.

This finding illuminates an important but often overlooked characteristic of the roughly one-half of polities in the advanced industrialized countries where programmatic political competition is not the norm. Particularistic political competition, even when it is the preferred style of a minority of politicians, sends out ripples that affect the entire political system. This is because clientelist behavior on the part of ruling politicians is infectious: it informs not only the strategies of the clientelists, but also the strategies and eventually policy preferences of opposition politicians. The clearest example from this work is the way in which particularistic manipulation of the tax system in Italy contributed to left politicians' and union leaders' decision to abandon the project of building a universalistic welfare state.

When even a small set of powerful politicians begins to shape institutions in a way that optimizes their particularistic competitive strategies, it forces other politicians to change their strategies and preferences as well. This gives a first-mover advantage to politicians who build institutions, because these institutions reinforce particular competitive strategies. And it accounts for the persistent bundling of the mode of political competition and the structure of welfare state programs. Sets of institutions become path-dependent because of the increasing returns that each generates for the other.

Possibilities for Institutional Change

The persistence of social policy institutions set in place in the late nineteenth century and reinforced by different types of political competition creates, unintentionally, patterns of social spending that generate inequalities in well-being among different age groups in the late twentieth century. But are these outcomes set in stone for all time? How does the "stickiness" of these institutions affect the development of welfare states during the current period, when policy makers have become more aware of how current demographic and labor market conditions combine with welfare state institutions to produce sometimes undesirable spending patterns? What circumstances might we expect to contribute to changing the long-established age orientations of welfare states?

A new critical juncture could occur, signaling a dramatic shift in age orientations, if some external force were to generate a change in either the competitive behavior of politicians or the way social programs are organized. This would effectively decouple the two, allowing one to change without requiring that the other give way at the same time. A few candidates present themselves, especially in Europe, where the collapse of Communism in the East in 1989, the globalization of trade, and European monetary union in 1992 have had far-reaching effects on social, economic, and political institutions. So far, though, none of these exogenous shocks seems to have generated enough momentum to shift the age orientation of social spending meaningfully.

The fall of the Berlin Wall contributed to the overthrow of clientelist political regimes in Italy and Austria in the early 1990s, as electorates that had once tightly held their noses and voted for stability against the Communist threat began to consider other options. But while clientelist politicians have passed out of office (temporarily, in many cases), it will take more time to undo the effects of fifty years of particularistic public administration. Left governments in Italy in the 1990s – the first in the postwar period – were finally able to reform the tax system and lay the groundwork for tax financing of a variety of new citizenship-based social programs. But whether these changes will weather alternation with a right that is still largely particularistic in orientation, and whether they will be enough to turn the ocean liner that is the Italian pension system and free up resources for a more age-balanced repertoire of social spending, remain to be seen.

The internationalization of trade might also generate pressure for a shift in the age orientation of social spending. Growing international competition has increased employers' sensitivity to nonwage labor costs, resulting in a push from some Continental European employers to convert payroll-financed occupational benefits to citizenship-based programs paid for out of general revenues. (Rising health care costs and private pension fund insolvency have led some large employers in the United States to call for more

195

public welfare solutions, as well.) However, at the same time, governments (particularly subnational governments) are looking for ways to shift costs onto the social partners (see, e.g., Campbell and Morgan 2005), so the net effect of these counterpressures may be no movement at all.

A third potential source of pressure for change in domestic institutions, European monetary union, is probably the most likely candidate to generate a critical juncture signaling a new path toward substantial changes in the age orientation of social spending. In particular, the criterion that government budget deficits not exceed 3 percent of GDP generates pressure both for tax reform and for spending cuts. Tax reform, as we have seen, is a necessary (but not sufficient) condition for financing citizenship-based social programs that would be more youth-oriented in nature. More immediately, the Maastricht criteria demand fiscal restraint even where the public, unions, or employers might not be sensitive to the costs of social spending. When the possibility of deficit financing of social welfare disappears, spending begins to look more like a finite pie. Under these new circumstances welfare state politics are more likely to focus on the allocation of total social spending among different competing groups, including different age groups. Indeed, in Italy the reframing of the "crisis of the welfare state" as a crisis of intergenerational allocation coincided with that country's drive to join the monetary union.

In theory, there is no reason that a shift in age orientation must await a cataclysmic change or a new critical juncture (Streeck and Thelen 2005). If the age orientations observed in the 1990s are largely a result of how social policy institutions "fit" with a society's demography and labor market, new demographic and economic changes could cause a change in age orientation as well. But societal changes of a magnitude capable of generating a new age orientation without concomitant institutional changes seem unlikely to occur in the near future. Even with loosened immigration controls and more generous family policies, populations in the rich democracies will continue to age. And while the fortress labor markets of Continental Europe are becoming increasingly open to younger and female workers, these former labor market outsiders are often integrated on a part-time or flexible basis without access to the same social rights as the aging core work force. So social policies are not likely to "drift" their way toward new age orientations.

Another potential source of change is a breakdown in the tight coupling between the mode of political competition and the structure of social programs. If dynamics internal to the welfare state – some kind of policy

Conclusion

feedback – were to break down the supportive relationship between clientelism and occupationalism, or between programmatic competition and universal social benefits, so that they no longer generated increasing returns for one another, we might observe a shift in the age orientation of a welfare state.

Pierson (1994) and Campbell (2003) posit a type of policy feedback in which welfare state programs create and define over time beneficiary groups with the potential to act politically to preserve their benefits when they are threatened. This constituency-based feedback model leads us to expect that in youth-oriented welfare states, all other things being equal, we would see movements of single mothers, youth unemployed, families on assistance benefits, and so on, springing up to protect from retrenchment the programs that benefit them.[2] In elderly-oriented welfare regimes, on the other hand, the absence of meaningful social spending programs geared toward working-age adults and children should discourage the growth of policy feedbacks in which groups of relatively youthful beneficiaries coalesce to defend "their" programs from cuts. In fact, though, movements of and/or for the elderly (pensioners' parties, pensioners' unions, elderly advocacy groups) exist in all advanced industrialized countries. And while the elderly are not responsible for the age orientation of social spending as it has emerged in the twentieth century, there is good evidence to suggest that organized gray power may actually help to limit spending on the elderly in certain contexts (Campbell and Lynch 2000; Anderson and Lynch 2003).

The reform trajectories of welfare states with varying age orientations do not appear to follow a pure constituency feedback model. It is true that some of the most youth-oriented countries (Finland and Denmark) have become even more youth-oriented since 1990, while some of the most elderly-oriented (Japan and the United States) have moved even further in that direction. The recent enactment of a prescription drug benefit for the elderly in the United States while over forty million working-age adults and children go without any health insurance, for example, pushes that country toward an even more pronounced elderly orientation. However, the Dutch and Italian case studies suggest that the age orientation of social spending

[2] Of course, all other things are not equal, and the likelihood of such groups emerging probably depends not only on a variety of program characteristics independent of expenditures (the degree of stigma associated with benefits, the method of financing, the locus of administration, etc. – see Ingram and Schneider 1993; Schneider and Ingram 1993; Soss 1999; Mettler 2002) – but also on characteristics of the broader political, economic, and social environment.

may instead generate a different kind of policy feedback – one based on norms rather than voting blocs – that impacts the politics of welfare state reform in different ways.

The numerical and organizational strength of the elderly has been important in the politics of welfare reform in the last decade in elderly-oriented Italy, as a constituency-based feedback model would lead us to expect. The elderly in Italy have indeed exercised a powerful constraining role in pension system reform debates. But it is worth noting that since the mid-1970s this role has been played predominantly by pensioners as voters, and not by the pensioners' parties (insignificant and ephemeral) or pensioners' unions (large and significant, but surprisingly moderate in their demands; Campbell and Lynch 2000; Anderson and Lynch 2003). Furthermore, we saw in chapter 6 that Italian politicians have developed their own distinctive interests in maintaining expensive pension provisions, quite apart from demands arising independently from the elderly. Constituency-based feedback models do not help us to distinguish in this case between the possibly contradictory demands of organized interest groups as opposed to voters, and they discount the importance of politicians' independent interest in particular programs.

From the point of view of the policy feedback literature, it is more surprising that the elderly in the relatively youth-oriented Dutch welfare state have also proven to be a powerful political lobby. In 1994, elderly organizations reacted to the Christian Democratic leadership's threat to cut pensions by forming two new pensioners' parties and placing seven members in Parliament. As a result of this political strength, the elderly have been able to contain cuts to their programs, including exempting pensions from freezes at a time when other social benefits were subject to austerity measures. In the field of labor market policies, similarly, older workers have been much less affected by retrenchments than have younger ones. At the same time, sustained mobilization of younger welfare state beneficiaries was notably absent in the 1990s, with the exception of some important protests against disability insurance reform. How are we to understand this paradox?

Policy feedbacks in Italy and the Netherlands do not appear to depend just on the nature of social programs, and hence on the size and shape of the constituency groups that these programs create. Rather, the age profile of social spending seems to set the parameters for emerging debates over intergenerational equity. In a pathway that echoes Levy's (1999) vice-into-virtue framework more closely than Weaver's (1986) and Pierson's (1994) blame-avoidance scenario, reforms in the Netherlands and Italy are taking place in the areas where they are arguably most needed, and not simply in the areas where groups of welfare state beneficiaries are weakest.

In Italy since the mid-1990s, the educated elite have increasingly come to blame the welfare state's maladies on the "hyper-protected" elderly and on the groups that in reality or in perception work on their behalf (the splinter Communist party Rifondazione Comunista, which has assumed the musty mantle of defender of the existing pension system, and the pensioners' unions). These are the new villains in a country that many have come to see as, in the words of former Prime Minister Massimo D'Alema, "a society organized against the young" (Di Caro 1997). As a result, some politically vulnerable categories of pensioners, especially women, have seen cutbacks that affect them immediately, and benefits for future pensioners have been scaled back. At the same time, efforts to increase protections for the young and for working-age adults in Italy have seen real results, even at a time of fiscal contraction. By contrast, the young in the Netherlands are the ones cast in the role of the villain. Successful welfare state cuts in the 1990s targeted "inactive," "parasitic" working-aged adults, especially young adults, while pensioners came out ahead.

The age orientation of social policies then seems to create a kind of ideational policy feedback among elites, structuring how they perceive the welfare state to administer intergenerational justice, and thus setting new parameters for discussions about welfare retrenchment and reform. Under what circumstances ideational feedbacks (a kind of backlash against the existing age orientation of the welfare state) can take root among mass publics is a question for further research. But there is reason to think that ideational feedbacks may be particularly important in shaping political struggles over the age orientation of a welfare state, where, to borrow strong words from Albert Hirschman (1977), questions of justice and fairness may move the passions nearly as much as interest does.

References

Selected Interviews

Italy

Bondanini, Giampiero (Confindustria), Rome, June 24, 1999.
Cox, Robert (political scientist, University of Oklahoma), Florence, March 29, 1999.
Franco, Daniele (Bank of Italy), Rome, June 3, 1999.
Giovannini, Elio (CGIL-Metalmeccanici, retired), Rome, June 3, 1999.
Giustina, Vittorio (Centro Studi CISL), Florence, February 17, 1999.
Grammicia, Giorgio (legal consultant), Rome, June 24, 1999.
Livi Bacci, Massimo (demographer, University of Florence), Florence, September 25, 1998.
Mariani, Isidoro (Confindustria, retired), Rome, June 24, 1999.
Roscani, Bruno (CGIL-Pensionati), Rome, November 12, 1998.
Saraceno, Chiara (sociologist, University of Turin and member, National Commission on the Problems of Families), Turin, March 8, 1999.
Settimi, Pino (pensions consultant), Rome, September 28, 1998.

Netherlands

van Aartsen, Wim (Dutch Senior Party [ASP]), Weert, June 19, 2000.
Balkenende, Jan Peter (Prime Minister, CDA party leader), The Hague, June 7, 2000.
Cuyvers, Peter (Netherlands Family Council), The Hague, May 22, 2000.
de Jong, Henk (CNV-Senioren), Utrecht, May 18, 2000.
Lokhorst, Bert (Dutch League for 50+ers [ANBO]), Utrecht, June 2000.
Quispel, Yvonne (National Office against Age Discrimination), Utrecht, June 23, 2000.
van Suijdam, Danielle (CNV), Utrecht, May 18, 2000.
van der Veen, Romke (historian, University of Twente), Enschede, June 6, 2000.

Vlek, Ruud (political scientist, University of Amsterdam), Amsterdam, June 2, 2000.
Vrooman, Cok (Socio-Cultural Planning Bureau), The Hague, June 7, 2000.

Other Sources

Aarts, Leo, and Philip de Jong. 1992. *Economic Aspects of Disability Behavior.* Amsterdam: North-Holland.

Addis, Elisabetta. 1998. Gender in the Italian Welfare State Reforms. Seminar Paper WS/1, European Forum, European University Institute, Florence.

Adema, William, Mark Pearson, Marcel Einerhard, Bengt Eklind, and Joergen Lotz. 1997. Net Public Social Expenditure. Labour Market and Social Policy Occasional Papers 19. Paris: OECD.

Akkerman, Tjitske. 1998. Political Participation and Social Rights: The Triumph of the Breadwinner in the Netherlands. In *Gender, Participation and Citizenship in the Netherlands*, ed. J. Bussemaker and R. Voet. Brookfield, Vt.: Ashgate.

Aldous, Joan, Wilfried Dumon, and Katrina Johnson. 1980. *The Politics and Programs of Family Policy: United States and European Perspectives.* Notre Dame, Ind., and Leuven, Belgium: Center for the Study of Man, University of Notre Dame, and Leuven University Press.

Alvaro, Giuseppe, and Dante Carloni. 1989. Le ipotesi di riforma: Vecchi schemi e nuovi scenari. In *Novant'anni di previdenza in Italia: Culture, politiche, strutture. Atti del Convegno. Roma, 9/20 novembre 1989* (Supplement to Issue 1 of *Previdenza Sociale*), pp. 263–99.

Alvaro, Giuseppe, Giovanni Pedullá, and Lelia Ricci. 1987. Sull'evoluzione del sistema economico italiano e dei trattamenti pensionistici agli inizi del 2000. In *Il futuro del sistema pensionistico italiano*, ed. INPS. Rome: INPS.

Anderson, Karen, and Julia Lynch. 2003. Solidarity Forever? Unions, Pensioners and Welfare State Reform in Europe. Paper prepared for presentation at the annual meeting of the American Political Science Association, Philadelphia, August 26, 2003.

Arnold, Douglas. 1990. *The Logic of Congressional Action.* New Haven: Yale University Press.

Baccaro, Lucio. 1999. The Organizational Consequences of Democracy: Labor Unions and Economic Reforms in Contemporary Italy. Ph.D. diss., Sloan School of Management and Department of Political Science, Massachusetts Institute of Technology.

Baccaro, Lucio. 2000. Negotiating Pension Reform with the Unions: The Italian Experience in European Perspective. Paper presented at Twelfth International Conference of Europeanists, Chicago, March 30–April 2, 2000.

Bakvis, Herman. 1981. *Catholic Power in the Netherlands.* Montreal: McGill-Queen's University Press.

Balchin, Paul, ed. 1996. *Housing Policy in Europe.* London: Routledge.

Baldissera, Alberto. 1996a. Conservare o cambiare il sistema pensionistico italiano? *ISPO Political Trend* 12: 30–43.

References

Baldissera, Alberto. 1996b. La rivolta dei capelli grigi: Il caso italiano e francese. In *Il paese dei paradossi. Le basi sociali della politica in Italia*, ed. N. Negri and L. Sciolla. Rome: Nuova Italia Scientifica.

Baldissera, Alberto. 1997. Eppur si muove. *ISPO Political Trend* 20: 39–49.

Baldwin, Peter. 1990. *The Politics of Social Solidarity: Class Bases in the European Welfare State, 1875–1975*. Cambridge: Cambridge University Press.

Barnes, Samuel. 1990. Maintaining Hegemony in Italy: "The Softer They Rise, the Slower They Fall!" In *Uncommon Democracies: The One-Party Dominant Regimes*, ed. T. J. Pempel. Ithaca, N.Y.: Cornell University Press.

Baumgartner, Frank, and Bryan Jones. 1993. *Agendas and Instability in American Politics*. Chicago: University of Chicago Press.

van Berkel, H. H. A., and H. T. Hindriks. 1991. *Uitkeringsgerechtigden en vakbeweging: Over de modernisering van het arbeidstelsel*. Utrecht: Rijksuniversiteit te Utrecht.

Birchfield, Vicki, and Markus Crepaz. 1998. The Impact of Constitutional Structures and Collective and Competitive Veto Points on Income Inequality in Industrialized Democracies. *European Journal of Political Research* 34: 175–200.

Blondel, Jean, and Maurizio Cotta. 2000. The Nature of Party Government. New York: Palgrave.

Boeri, Tito, and Guido Tabellini. 1999a. Ora si puó riformare il Welfare. *Il Sole 24 Ore* (January 19).

Boeri, Tito, and Guido Tabellini. 1999b. Un problema di rappresentanza piú che di maggioranze. In *Il muro delle pensioni*, ed. Tito Boeri and Andrea Brugiavini. Milan: Il Sol 24 Ore.

Boeri, Tito, Axel Börsch-Supan, and Guido Tabellini. 2001. Welfare State Reform: A Survey of What Europeans Want. *Economic Policy* 16 (32): 9–50.

Boleat, Mark. 1985. *National Housing Finance Systems*. London: CroomHelm.

Bonadonna, Salvatore, ed. 1977. *Sindacato e questione giovanile*. Bari: DiDonato.

Bradley, David, Evelyne Huber, Stephanie Moller, François Nielsen, and John Stephens. 2001. Distribution and Redistribution in Post-Industrial Democracies. Paper prepared for the annual meeting of the American Political Science Association, San Francisco, August 30–September 2.

Bussemaker, Jet. 1992. Feminism and the Welfare State: On Gender and Individualism in the Netherlands. *History of European Ideas* 15 (4–6): 655–61.

Bussemaker, Jet. 1998. Rationales of Care in Contemporary Welfare States: The Case of Childcare in the Netherlands. *Social Politics* 5 (1): 70–96.

Camera dei Deputati. 1953. *Atti della commissione parlamentare di inchiesta sulla miseria in Italia e sui mezzi per combatterla*. In *Relazione generale*, vol. 1. Milan: Istituto Editoriale Italiano.

Cameron, David. 1984. Social Democracy, Corporatism, Labor Quiescence and the Representation of Economic Interests in Advanced Capitalist Society. In *Order and Conflict in Contemporary Capitalism*, ed. J. H. Goldthorpe. Oxford: Oxford University Press.

Campanini, G. 1993. Le ragioni culturali di una politica familiare non adeguata: risorse e percorsi per una nuova stagione politica. Conference paper, Seminario di Studio: Diritto di cittadinanza della famiglia: Una proposta di politica sociale ed economica, Forum delle Associazioni Familiari, Rome, November 5–6, 1993.

Campbell, Andrea L. 2003. *How Policies Make Citizens: Senior Political Activism and the American Welfare State*. Princeton: Princeton University Press.

Campbell, Andrea, and Julia Lynch. 2000. Whose "Gray Power"? Elderly Voters, Elderly Lobbies, and Welfare Reform in Italy and the United States. *Italian Politics and Society* 53 (summer 2000): 11–39.

Campbell, Andrea, and Kimberly Morgan. 2005. Federalism and the Politics of Old-Age Care in Germany and the United States. *Comparative Political Studies* (38): 887–914.

Canziani, Patrizia, and Dmitri Demekas. 1995. The Italian Public Pension System: Current Prospects and Reform Options. Working paper, International Monetary Fund, Washington, D.C.

Castles, Francis, and Maurizio Ferrera. 1996. Home Ownership and the Welfare State: Is Southern Europe Different? *South European Society and Politics* 1 (2): 163–85.

Cazorla, José. 1992. Del clientelismo tradicional al clientelismo de partido: Evolución y características. Working Paper 55, Institut de Ciencies Politiques i Socials, Barcelona.

Cazzola, Giuliano. 1995. *Le nuove pensioni degli italiani*. Bologna: Il Mulino.

Cazzola, Giuliano. 1998a. Pensioni d'anzianitá: Iniquo peso contro i giovani. *Il Sole 24 Ore*, September 3, p. 1.

Cazzola, Giuliano. 1998b. Per reiquilibrare i rapporti tra generazioni occorrerebbe una severitá che finora il governo non ha dimostrato; welfare tutte sulle spalle dei giovani. *Il Sole 24 Ore*, April 3, p. 4.

CBS. 1981. *The Year in Figures*. Amsterdam: Centraal Bureau voor de Statistiek.

CBS. 2000. *The Year in Figures*. Amsterdam: Centraal Bureau voor de Statistiek.

CBS. 2003. *StatLine* 2003. Http://statline.cbs.nl/StatWeb/start.asp?LA=en&DM= SLEN&lp=Search/Search, accessed December 2003.

CENSIS. 1983. *Spesa pubblica e politica sociale: Libro bianco sulla crisi dello stato assistenziale*. Milan: Angeli.

CGIL Segreteria Generale. 1962. Sui miglioramenti ai pensionati e la riforma generale dell'assicurazione pensioni. In *La CGIL dal V al VI congresso: Atti e documenti*, ed. CGIL. Rome: Editrice Sindacale Italiana.

CGIL-CISL-UIL Segreteria Interconfederale. 1970. CGIL-CISL-UIL a rumor sulla politica economica e sociale. In *La CGIL dal VII all' VIII Congresso* 1 (1973): 199–201. Rome: Editrice Sindacale Italiana.

Cherubini, Arnaldo. 1977. *Storia della previdenza sociale in Italia (1869–1960)*. Rome: Riuniti.

CISL Consiglio Generale. 1950. Mozione sulle linee d'indirizzo e sugli obiettivi dell'azione sindacale. In *Documenti ufficiali dal 1950 al 1958: Appendice alla Relazione della Segreteria confederale al III° Congresso nazionale* (1959), ed. Ufficio Studi della CISL, 13–18. Rome: CISL.

References

CISL Consiglio Generale. 1956. Mozione relative all'attuazione del Piano Vanoni per lo sviluppo del reddito e dell'occupazione. In *Documenti ufficiali dal 1950 al 1958: Appendice alla Relazione della Segreteria confederale al III° Congresso nazionale* (1959), ed. Ufficio Studi della CISL, 149–53. Rome: CISL.

CISL Consiglio Generale. 1958. Raccomandazione della CISL ai partiti nella imminenza delle elezioni politiche. In *Documenti ufficiali dal 1950 al 1958: Appendice alla Relazione della Segreteria confederale al III° Congresso nazionale* (1959), ed. Ufficio Studi della CISL, 177–180. Rome: CISL.

CNEL. 1963a. *Osservazioni e proposte sulla riforma della previdenza sociale.* Rome: CNEL.

CNEL. 1963b. *Relazione preliminare sulla riforma della previdenza sociale.* Rome: CNEL.

Commissione di Indagine sulla Povertá. 1985. *La povertá in Italia: Rapporto conclusivo della Commissione di studio istituita presso la Presidenza del Consiglio dei ministri.* Rome: Istituto Poligrafico e Zecca dello Stato.

Commissione Nazionale per i Problemi della Famiglia. 1983. *Famiglia e reddito. La redistribuzione monetaria del reddito in funzione della situazione familiare.* Rome: Ministero del Lavoro e della Previdenza Sociale, Istituto Poligrafico e Zecca dello Stato.

Commissione Parlamentare d'Inchiesta sulla Disoccupazione. 1953. Gli atti della commissione parlamentare d'inchiesta sulla disoccupazione. *Rassegna di statistiche del lavoro* 5 (2): 124–70.

Commissione per la Riforma della Previdenza Sociale. 1948. *Relazione sui lavori della Commissione, 4 luglio 1947–29 febbraio 1948.* Rome: Ministero del Lavoro e della Previdenza Sociale.

Confindustria. 1951. *Annuario.* Rome: Confindustria.

Confindustria. 1952. *Annuario.* Rome: Confindustria.

Confindustria. 1953. *Annuario.* Rome: Confindustria.

Confindustria. 1955. *Annuario.* Rome: Confindustria.

Converse, Philip. 1964. The Nature of Belief Systems in Mass Publics. In *Ideology and Discontent*, ed. D. Apter. London: Free Press of Glencoe.

Cotta, Maurizo. 2000. Conclusion: From the Simple World of Party Government to a More Complex View of Party-Government Relationships. In Blondel and Cotta 2000, pp. 196–222.

Cox, Robert. 1992. After Corporatism: A Comparison of the Role of Medical Professionals and Social Workers in the Dutch Welfare State. *Comparative Political Studies* 24 (4): 532–52.

Cox, Robert. 1993. *The Development of the Dutch Welfare State: From Workers' Insurance to Universal Entitlement.* Pittsburgh: University of Pittsburgh Press.

Crepaz, Markus. 1998. Inclusion versus Exclusion: Political Institutions and Welfare Expenditures. *Comparative Politics* (October): 61–80.

Crouch, Colin. 1985. Conditions for Trade Union Wage Restraint. In *The Politics of Inflation and Economic Stagnation: Theoretical Approaches and International Case Studies*, ed. L. Lindberg, C. Maier, and B. Barry. Washington, D.C.: Brookings Institution.

Cuzzaniti, Roberto. 1960. *Basta la pensione per l'assistenza? Conversazione tenuta alla RAI-TV il 6 novembre 1960, ore 19.15 sul Terzo Programma, per i ciclo "Il problema degli Anziani in Italia."* Rome: RAI-TV.

Daalder, Hans. 1987. The Dutch Party System: From Segmentation to Polarization – And Then? In *Party Systems in Denmark, Austria, Switzerland, the Netherlands, and Belgium*, ed. H. Daalder. London: Frances Pinter.

Damsma, Dirk. 1994. Family Wages or Family Allowances? Debates in the Dutch Labour Movement, 1890–1920. In *Economic and Social History in the Netherlands. Family Strategies and Changing Labour Relations*. Amsterdam: Netherlands Economic History Archives.

Daniels, Norman. 1988. *Am I My Parents' Keeper? An Essay on Justice between the Young and the Old*. Oxford: Oxford University Press.

De Grazia, Victoria. 1992. *How Fascism Ruled Women*. Berkeley: University of California Press.

Di Caro, Paola. 1997. "D'Alema sfida sindacato e Rifondazione. Schiaffo al leader della Cgil: per lo Stato sociale ci vuole il coraggio di cambiare." *Corriere della Sera* February 23, p. 3.

Dumon, Wilfried. 1992. *National Family Policies in EC-Countries*, vol. 1. Brussels: European Observatory of National Family Policies.

Esping-Andersen, Gøsta. 1985. *Politics against Markets*. Princeton: Princeton University Press.

Esping-Andersen, Gøsta. 1990. *The Three Worlds of Welfare Capitalism*. Princeton: Princeton University Press.

Esping-Andersen, Gøsta. 1996. Welfare States without Work: The Impasse of Labour Shedding and Familialism in Continental European Social Policy. In *Welfare States in Transition*, ed. G. Esping-Andersen. London: Sage.

Esping-Andersen, Gøsta. 1997. Welfare States at the End of the Century: The Impact of Labour Market, Family and Demographic Change. In *Family, Market and Community: Equity and Efficiency in Social Policy*, ed. P. Hennessy and M. Pearson. Paris: OECD.

Estevez-Abe, Margarita, Torben Iversen, and David Soskice. 2001. Social Protection and the Formation of Skills: A Reinterpretation of the Welfare State. In *Varieties of Capitalism: The Institutional Foundations of Comparative Advantage*, ed. Peter A. Hall and David Soskice. New York: Oxford University Press.

Eurostat. Various years. *Labour Force Survey Results*. Luxembourg: Office for Official Publications of the European Communities.

Fawcett, Helen, and Theodoros Papadopoulos. 1997. Social Exclusion, Social Citizenship and Decommodification: An Evaluation of the Adequacy of Support for the Unemployed in the European Union. *West European Politics* 20 (3): 1–30.

Ferrera, Maurizio. 1984. *Il welfare state in Italia: Sviluppo e crisi in prospettiva comparata*. Bologna: Il Mulino.

Ferrera, Maurizio. 1993. *Modelli di solidarietá: Politica e riforme sociali nelle democrazie*. Bologna: Il Mulino.

Ferrera, Maurizio. 1996a. Le pensioni a scapito della famiglia. *Il Sole 24 Ore*, July 12, p. 7.

References

Ferrera, Maurizio. 1996b. Queste pensioni sono la minaccia dei giovani. *Il Sole 24 Ore*, June 28, p. 7.

Ferrera, Maurizio. 1996c. The "Southern Model" of Welfare in Social Europe. *Journal of European Social Policy* 6 (1): 17–37.

Ferrera, Maurizio. 1997. The Uncertain Future of the Italian Welfare State. *West European Politics* 20 (1): 231–49.

Flora, Peter. 1986. *Growth to Limits: The Western European Welfare States since World War II*. Berlin and New York: DeGruyter.

Flora, Peter, and Jens Alber. 1981. Modernization, Democratization, and the Development of Welfare States in Western Europe. In *The Development of Welfare States in Europe and America*, ed. P. Flora and A. Heidenheimer. New Brunswick, N.J.: Transaction Books.

Flora, Peter, and Jens Alber. 1983. *State, Economy and Society in Western Europe, 1815–1975: A Data Handbook in Two Volumes*. Frankfurt am Main and Chicago: Campus Verlag and St. James Press.

Flora, Peter, and Arnold Heidenheimer. 1981. *The Development of Welfare States in Europe and America*. New Brunswick, N.J.: Transaction Books.

FNP. 1992. *Breve storia della FNP: Corsi di formazione di base*. Rome: FNP-CISL.

FNV. 1977–87. *FNV News*. Vols. 2–25.

Franco, Daniele. 1993. *L'espansione della spesa pubblica in Italia*. Bologna: Il Mulino.

Franco, Daniele. 2000. Italy: A Never-Ending Pension Reform. Paper presented at the NBER-Kiel Institute Conference: Coping with the Pension Crisis – Where Does Europe Stand?, Kiel, March 6.

Franco, Daniele, and Giancarlo Morcaldo. 1986. *Un modello di previsione degli squilibri del sistema previdenziale*. Rome: Istituto Poligrafico e Zecca dello Stato.

Franco, Daniele, and Giancarlo Morcaldo. 1990. *La spesa per la tutela degli invalidi in Italia*. Milan: FrancoAngeli.

Franco, Daniele, and Nicola Sartor. 1990. *Stato e famiglia: Obiettivi e strumenti del sostegno pubblico dei carichi familiari*. Milan: FrancoAngeli.

Franco, Daniele, and Nicola Sartor. 1994. Il sostegno pubblico alla famiglia fra nuove povertá e declino demografico. *Economia e Lavoro* 28 (1): 15–32.

García, Soledad, and Neovi Karakatsanis. 2001. Social Policy, Democracy, and Citizenship in Southern Europe. In *Parties, Politics and Democracy in the New Southern Europe*, ed. R. Gunther and N. Diamondouros. Baltimore: Johns Hopkins University Press.

Gauthiér, Anne. 1993. Towards Renewed Fears of Population and Family Decline. *European Journal of Population* (9): 143–67.

Gauthiér, Anne. 1996. *The State and the Family: A Comparative Analysis of Family Policies in Industrialized Countries*. New York: Oxford University Press.

Gerber, Elisabeth, and John Jackson. 1993. Endogenous Preferences and the Study of Institutions. *American Political Science Review* 87 (3): 639–56.

Gilens, Martin. 1999. *Why Americans Hate Welfare: Race, Media, and the Politics of Antipoverty Policy*. Chicago: University of Chicago Press.

Goddijn, Walter. 1975. *The Deferred Revolution: A Social Experiment in Church Innovation in Holland, 1960–1970*. Amsterdam: Elsevier.

References

Gorrieri, Ermanno. 1972. *La giungla retributiva*. Bologna: Il Mulino.

Gorrieri, Ermanno. 1979. *La giungla dei bilanci familiari*. Bologna: Mulino.

Gough, Ian. 1996. Social Assistance in Southern Europe. *South European Society and Politics* 1 (1): 1–23.

Gould, Stephen Jay, and Richard Lewontin. 1979. The Spandrels of San Marco and the Panglossian Paradigm: A Critique of the Adaptationist Programme. *Proceedings of the Royal Society of London B* 205: 581–98.

Green-Pedersen, Christoffer. 2002. *The Politics of Justification: Party Competition and Welfare-State Retrenchment in Denmark and the Netherlands from 1982 to 1998*. Amsterdam: Amsterdam University Press.

Gualmini, Elisabetta. 1998. *La politica del lavoro*. Bologna: Il Mulino.

Hacker, Jacob. 2004. Privatizing Risk without Privatizing the Welfare State: The Hidden Politics of Social Policy Retrenchment in the United States. *American Political Science Review* 98 (2): 243–60.

Hemerijck, Anton. 1992. The Historical Contingencies of Dutch Corporatism. Ph.D. diss., Oxford University.

Hemerijck, Anton, and Kees van Kersbergen. 1997. A Miraculous Model? Explaining the New Politics of the Welfare State in the Netherlands. *Acta Politica* 32 (3): 258–80.

Heston, Alan, Robert Summers, and Bettina Aten. 2002. Penn World Table Version 6.1. Center for International Comparisons at the University of Pennsylvania (CICUP). Http://pwt.econ.upenn.edu/php_site, accessed October 2002.

Hicks, Alexander, and Joya Misra. 1993. Political Resources and the Growth of Welfare in Affluent Democracies, 1960–1982. *American Journal of Sociology* 99 (3): 668–710.

Hicks, Alexander, and Duane Swank. 1992. Politics, Institutions, and Welfare Spending in Industrialized Democracies, 1960–82. *American Political Science Review* 86 (3): 658–74.

Hirschman, Albert. 1977. *The Passions and the Interests: Political Arguments for Capitalism before Its Triumph*. Princeton: Princeton University Press.

Hopkin, Jonathan. 2001. A "Southern Model" of Electoral Mobilisation? Clientelism and Electoral Politics in Spain. *West European Politics* 24 (1): 115–36.

Howard, Christopher. 1997. *The Hidden Welfare State: Tax Expenditures and Social Policy in the United States*. Princeton: Princeton University Press.

Huber, Evelyene, Charles Ragin, and John Stephens. 1993. Social Democracy, Christian Democracy, Constitutional Structure, and the Welfare State. *American Journal of Sociology* 99 (3): 711–74.

ILO. 1922. *Remedies for Unemployment*. Geneva: ILO.

ILO. 1933. Recommendation Concerning the General Principles of Invalidity, Old-Age and Widows' and Orphans' Insurance (Recommendation R043). Http://www.ilo.org/ilolex/english/recdisp1.htm, accessed November 2005.

ILO. 1934. Recommendation concerning Unemployment Provisions (Recommendation R044). Http://www.ilo.org/ilolex/english/recdispl.htm, accessed November 2005.

References

ILO. 1944. Recommendation Concerning Income Security (Recommendation R067). Http://www.ilo.org/ilolex/english/recdisp1.htm, accessed November 2005.

ILO. 1967. Convention Concerning Invalidity, Old-Age and Survivors' Benefits (Convention C128). Http://www.ilo.org/ilolex/english/recdisp1.htm, accessed November 2005.

Imergut, Ellen. 1992. *Health Politics: Interests and Institutions in Western Europe.* Princeton: Princeton University Press.

Ingram, Helen, and Anne Schneider. 1993. Constructing Citizenship: The Subtle Messages of Policy Design. In *Public Policy for Democracy*, ed. H. Ingram and S. R. Smith. Washington, D.C.: Brookings Institution.

INPS. 1982. *Notizie statistiche.* Rome: INPS.

INPS. 1989. Il modello INPS e le prime proiezioni al 2010. *Previdenza Sociale* (supplement to no. 3).

INPS. 2003. *Banche dati statistiche on-line* 2003. Http://www.banchedatistatistiche.inps.it/sas_stat/pensioni/tab2.html, accessed December 2003.

L'invecchiamento della popolazione in Italia: Atti del secondo convegno di studio sui problemi dell'assistenza alle persone anziane. 1957. Rome: Edizioni 5 Lune.

Irving, R. E. M. 1979. *The Christian Democratic Parties of Western Europe.* London: Allen & Unwin.

ISTAT. 1999. I beneficiari delle pensioni di anzianitá anno 1998. *Statistiche in breve* (December 28).

ISTAT. 2000. Le prestazioni pensionistiche al 31 dicembre 1999. *Statistiche in breve* (June 6).

Jencks, Christopher, and Barbara Boyle Torrey. 1988. Beyond Income and Poverty: Trends in Social Welfare among Children and the Elderly since 1960. In *The Vulnerable*, ed. J. L. Palmer, T. Smeeding, and B. B. Torrey. Washington, D.C.: Urban Institute.

Johnson, Paul, Christopher Conrad, and David Thomson, eds. 1989. *Workers versus Pensioners: Intergenerational Justice in an Ageing World.* Manchester: Manchester University Press.

de Jong, Philip, Michiel Herweijer, and Jaap de Wildt. 1990. *Form and Reform of the Dutch Social Security System.* Deventer: Kluwer Law and Taxation Publishers.

Jurado, Teresa. 2002. *Youth in Transition: Housing, Employment, Social Policies and Families in France and Spain.* Aldershot, England, and Burlington, Vt.: Ashgate.

Jurado, Teresa, and Manuela Naldini. 1996. Is the South So Different? Italian and Spanish Families in Comparative Perspective. *South European Society and Politics* 1 (3): 42–66.

Kangas, Ollie. In press. Labor Markets against Politics: The Development of Finnish Pension Policies. In *Oxford Handbook of West European Pension Politics*, ed. Karen M. Anderson, Ellen M. Immergut, and Isabelle Schulze. Oxford: Oxford University Press.

Katzenstein, Peter. 1985. *Small States in World Markets: Industrial Policy in Europe.* Ithaca, N.Y.: Cornell University Press.

Kaufmann, Daniel, Aart Kraay, and Massimo Mastruzzi. 2003. Governance Matters III: Governance Indicators for 1996–2002. World Bank Policy Research Working Paper 3106. Washington, D.C.: World Bank.

Kemeny, Jim. 1980. The Political Economy of Housing. In *Essays in the Comparative Political Economy of Australian Capitalism*, ed. E. L. Wheelwright and K. Buckley. Sydney: Australia and New Zealand Book Company.

Kemeny, Jim. 1981. *The Myth of Home Ownership*. London: Routledge and Kegan Paul.

van Kersbergen, Kees. 1995. *Social Capitalism: A Study of Christian Democracy and the Welfare State*. London: Routledge.

van Kersbergen, Kees, and Uwe Becker. 1988. The Netherlands: A Passive Social Democratic Welfare State in a Christian Democratic Ruled Society. *Journal of Social Policy* 17: 477–99.

Kitschelt, Herbert. 2000. Linkages between Citizens and Politicians in Democratic Polities. *Comparative Political Studies* 33 (6/7): 845–79.

Korpi, Walter. 1983. *The Democratic Class Struggle*. London: Routledge and Kegan Paul.

Kotlikoff, Laurence, and Willi Liebfritz. 1998. An International Comparison of Generational Accounts. NBER Working Paper 6447. Cambridge, Mass.: National Bureau of Economic Research.

Koven, Seth, and Sonya Michel. 1990. Womanly Duties: Maternalist Politics and the Origins of Welfare States in France, Great Britain, and the United States, 1880–1920. *American Historical Review* 95 (4): 1076–108.

Kuijpers, Ivo, and Peter Schrage. 1997. Squaring the Circle: Unemployment Insurance in the Netherlands from Wage Bargaining Instrument to Compulsory Legislation, 1861–1949. In *Labour, Social Policy, and the Welfare State. Papers Presented to the Ninth British-Dutch Conference on Labour History, Bergen 1994*, ed. A. Knotter, B. Altena, and D. Damsma. Amsterdam: Stichting beheer IISG.

Lapadula, Beniamino, and Stefano Patriarca. 1995. *La rivoluzione delle pensioni*. Rome: Ediesse.

LaPalombara, Joseph. 1964. *Interest Groups in Italian Politics*. Princeton: Princeton University Press.

Laslett, Peter, and James Fishkin, eds. 1992. *Justice between Age Groups and Generations*. New Haven: Yale University Press.

van Leeuwen, Marco. 1997. Collective Agreements, Unions and Welfare in the Netherlands, c. 1910–1960. In *Labour, Social Policy, and the Welfare State. Papers Presented to the Ninth British-Dutch Conference on Labour History, Bergen 1994*, ed. A. Knotter, B. Altena, and D. Damsma. Amsterdam: Stichting beheer IISG.

Lehmbruch, Gerhard. 1984. Concertation and the Structure of Corporatist Networks. In *Order and Conflict in Contemporary Capitalism*, ed. J. Goldthorpe. Oxford: Oxford University Press.

Leibfried, Stephan. 1992. Toward a European Welfare State: On Integrating Poverty Regimes in the European Community. In *Social Policy in a Changing Europe*, ed. Z. Ferge and J. E. Kolberg. Frankfurt: Campus Verlag.

References

Leo XIII, Pope. 1891. *Rerum novarum.* Http://www.vatican.va/holy_father/leo_xiii/encyclicals/documents/hf_l-xiii_enc_15051891_rerum-novarum_en.html, accessed November 2005.

Levy, Jonah. 1999. Vice into Virtue? Progressive Politics and Welfare Reform in Continental Europe. *Politics and Society* 27 (2): 239–73.

Lijphart, Arend, and Don Aitkin. 1994. *Electoral Systems and Party Systems: A Study of Twenty-seven Democracies, 1945–1990.* Oxford: Oxford University Press.

Livi Bacci, Massimo. 1993. Stato sociale in crisi: E tra le generazioni è giá conflitto. *Il Sole 24 Ore,* October 13, p. 17.

Longman, Phillip. 1987. *Born to Pay: The New Politics of Aging in America.* Boston: Houghton Mifflin.

Lynch, Julia. 2001. The Age-Orientation of Social Policy Regimes in OECD Countries. *Journal of Social Policy* 30 (3): 411–36.

Lyrintzis, Christos. 1984. Political Parties in Post-Junta Greece: A Case of "Bureaucratic Clientelism"? *West European Politics* 7 (2): 99–118.

Maestri, Giovanni Ezio. 1987. La regolazione dei conflitti redistributivi in Italia: Il caso della politica pensionistica. *Stato e Mercato* 20: 249–79.

Maestri, Giovanni Ezio. 1994. *Rappresentanza degli interessi, partiti e consenso: Giungla pensionistica, clientelismo e competizione politica in Italia.* Milan: FrancoAngeli.

Manow, Philip. 1997. Cross-Class Alliances in Welfare Reform: A Theoretical Framework. Paper prepared for the workshop "The New Politics of Welfare," Center for European Studies, Harvard University, Cambridge, Mass., December 5–7.

Mares, Isabela. 2001. Firms and the Welfare State: When, Why and How Does Social Policy Matter to Employers? In *Varieties of Capitalism: The Institutional Foundations of Comparative Advantage,* ed. P. Hall and D. Soskice. Oxford: Oxford University Press.

Mares, Isabela. 2003. *The Politics of Social Risk: Business and Welfare State Development.* New York: Cambridge University Press.

Marshall, T. H. 1950. Citizenship and Social Class. In *Citizenship and Social Class and Other Essays,* ed. T. H. Marshall. Cambridge: Cambridge University Press.

Masini, Carlo Alberto. 1953. Gli assegni familiari e le altre prestazioni familiari nel sistema italiano. In *Atti delle giornate internazionali di studi sulle prestazioni familiari,* ed. INPS. Rome: INPS.

Massarenti, Armando. 1997. Il welfare delle categorie privilegiate danneggia le prospettive delle generazioni future; troppo garantiti contro poco protetti. *Il Sole 24 Ore,* December 6, p. 4.

Mettler, Suzanne. 2002. Bringing the State Back in to Civic Engagement: Policy Feedback Effects of the G.I. Bill for World War II Veterans. *American Political Science Review* 96: 351–65.

Meyer, Jack, and Marilyn Moon. 1988. Health Care Spending on Children and the Elderly. In *The Vulnerable,* ed. J. L. Palmer, T. Smeeding, and B. B. Torrey. Washington, D.C.: Urban Institute.

Militello, Giacinto. 1987. Il futuro del sistema pensionistico italiano. In *Il futuro del sistema pensionistico italiano,* ed. INPS. Rome: INPS.

Millar, Jane, and Jane Warman. 1996. *Family Obligations in Europe*. London: Family Policy Studies Centre.

Ministerie van Sociale Zaken en Werkgelegenheid. [1999]. *Efforts to Reintegrate the Unemployed: An Overview*. The Hague: Ministerie van Sociale Zaken en Werkgelegenheid.

Ministerie van Sociale Zaken en Werkgelegenheid. 2000. *The Old Age Pension System in the Netherlands: A Brief Outline*. The Hague: Ministerie van Sociale Zaken en Werkgelegenheid.

Ministero del Lavoro e delle Politiche Sociali. 2001. *Rapporto di Monitoraggio Politiche del Lavoro*. Rome: Istituto Poligrafico e Zecca dello Stato.

Ministero del Tesoro. 1981. *Relazione della commissione di studio istituita dal Ministero del Tesoro*. Rome: Istituto Poligrafico e Zecca dello Stato.

Ministero del Tesoro. 1988. *Metodi per la previsione a lungo termine degli squilibri previdenziali*. Rome: Istituto Poligrafico e Zecca dello Stato.

MISSOC. 1995. *Social Protection in the Member States of the Union*. Brussels: Commission of the European Communities.

Mittelstadt, Axel. 1975. Unemployment Benefits and Related Payments in Seven Major Countries. *OECD Economic Outlook Occasional Studies* (July): 3–22.

Molin, Hanna. 1977. Nogmaals de Kinderbijslag. *Vrouwen* 30 (6): 14.

Moretti, Sante, and Domenico Santamaria. 1990. Avviare una vertenza sui trattamenti di disoccupazione. *Assistenza Sociale* 34 (1): 16–21.

Myles, John. 1989. *Old Age in the Welfare State: The Political Economy of Public Pensions*, 2nd ed. Boston: Little, Brown.

Naldini, Manuela. 2003. *The Family in the Mediterranean Welfare State*. London: Frank Cass.

Natali, David, and Martin Rhodes. 2004. Reforming Pensions in Italy and France: Policy Trade-offs and Redistributive Effects. Paper presented at the ESPAnet Conference on "European Social Policy: Meeting the Needs of a New Europe," St. Anthony's College, Oxford, September 9–11.

Nederlandse Vrouwenbeweging. 1976. N.V.B. Schrijft aan de Kamer: Handen af van de Kinderbijslag en de Kinderaftrek. *Vrouwen* 30 (1): 3–4.

Noseda, Antonio. 1992. Costo del lavoro, oneri sociali e questioni previdenziali. *Oggidomani anziani* 5 (1): 83–91.

NVV. 1951–75. *Information Bulletin of the Netherlands Federation of Trade Unions* 13–104.

NVV. 1955. Definitive Children's Allowance Regulation. *Information Bulletin of the Netherlands Federation of Trade Unions* 34 (November): 18.

NVV. 1957. Invalidity and Widows' and Orphans' Insurance Scheme in the Netherlands. *Information Bulletin of the Netherlands Federation of Trade Unions* 42 (April): 7–8.

NVV. 1958. Extraordinary Congress of the NVV. *Information Bulletin of the Netherlands Federation of Trade Unions* 47 (April): 1–30.

NVV. 1973. Urgency Program of the Consultative Body NVV, NKV, CNV for the Government Policy in 1973. *Information Bulletin of the Netherlands Federation of Trade Unions* 105 (August): 3–9.

References

NVV. 1975. Urgency Programme 1975 of NVV, NKV and CNV. *Information Bulletin of the Netherlands Federation of Trade Unions* 106 (January): 1–14.

NVV-NKV-CNV Consultative Body. 1971. Programme of Action for 1971 to 1975. *Information Bulletin of the Netherlands Federation of Trade Unions* 101 (July): 2–42.

OECD. 1993. *The Labour Market in the Netherlands.* Paris: OECD.

OECD. 1995. *The Transition from Work to Retirement.* Paris: OECD.

OECD. 1996. Tax Expenditures: Recent Experiences. Report prepared by the Working Party on Tax Policy Analysis and Tax Statistics, Committee on Fiscal Affairs, OECD, Paris.

OECD. 1998. *OECD Health Expenditures Database 1998.* CD-ROM. Paris: OECD.

OECD. 2002. *Benefits and Wages: OECD Indicators.* Paris: OECD Publications Service.

OECD. 2003a. *OECD Education Database.* OECD, September 30. Http://80-www1.oecd.org.ezp1.harvard.edu/scripts/cde/members/EDU_UOEAuthenticate.asp, accessed November 2003.

OECD. 2003b. *OECD Health Data 2003.* CD-ROM. Paris: OECD.

OECD. 2004. *OECD Social Expenditures Database (SOCX).* OECD 2004. Http://www.sourceoecd.org, accessed November 2005.

OECD. Various years. *Economic Outlook.* Paris: OECD.

OECD. Various years. *Labour Force Statistics.* Paris: OECD.

Offe, Claus. 1981. The Attribution of Status to Interest Groups: Observations on the West German Case. In *Organizing Interests in Western Europe: Pluralism, Corporatism, and the Transformation of Politics*, ed. S. Berger. Cambridge: Cambridge University Press.

O'Higgins, Michael. 1988. The Allocation of Public Resources to Children and the Elderly in OECD Countries. In *The Vulnerable*, ed. J. L. Palmer, T. Smeeding, and B. B. Torrey. Washington, D.C.: Urban Institute.

Olson, Mancur. 1982. *The Rise and Decline of Nations: Economic Growth, Stagflation, and Social Rigidities.* New Haven: Yale University Press.

van Oorschot, Wim, and Richard Engelfreit. 1999. Work, Work, Work. Labour Market Participation Policies in the Netherlands (1970–2000). Paper presented at the conference "The Modernisation of Social Protection and Employment," European University Institute, Florence, Italy, April 15 and 16.

Orloff, Ann. 1993. *The Politics of Pensions: A Comparative Analysis of Britain, Canada, and the United States, 1880–1940.* Madison: University of Wisconsin Press.

Paci, Massimo. 1984. Il sistema di welfare italiano tra tradizione clientelare e prospettive di riforma. In *Welfare state all'italiana*, ed. U. Ascoli. Rome: La Terza.

Paci, Massimo. 1994. Stato sociale italiano. Quel che resta dopo le ultime elezioni. *Politica ed Economia* 4 (August): 18–22.

Palme, Joakim. 1990. *Pension Rights in Welfare Capitalism: The Development of Old-Age Pensions in 18 OECD Countries, 1930–1985.* Stockholm: Swedish Institute for Social Research.

Palomba, Rossella. 1995. Italy: The Invisible Change. In *Population, Family, and Welfare: A Comparative Survey of European Attitudes*, ed. H. Moors and R. Palomba. Oxford: Oxford University Press.

Pampel, Fred. 1994. Population Aging, Class Context, and Age Inequality in Public Spending. *American Journal of Sociology* 100 (1): 153–95.

Pampel, Fred, and Paul Adams. 1992. The Effects of Demographic Change and Political Structure on Family Allowance Expenditures. *Social Service Review* (December): 524–46.

Pampel, Fred, and John Williamson. 1989. *Age, Class, Politics, and the Welfare State*. Cambridge: Cambridge University Press.

Pasi, Luigi. 1956. Gli assegni familiari. *Rassegna del Lavoro Quaderno* 1963 (3): 7–26.

Pedersen, Susan. 1993. *Family, Dependence, and the Origins of the Welfare State: Britain and France, 1914–1945*. Cambridge: Cambridge University Press.

Piattoni, Simona. 2001. Clientelism in Comparative and Historical Perspective. In *Clientelism, Interests, and Democratic Representation: The European Experience in Comparative Perspective*, ed. S. Piattoni. Cambridge: Cambridge University Press.

Pierson, Paul. 1994. *Dismantling the Welfare State? Reagan, Thatcher, and the Politics of Retrenchment*. Cambridge: Cambridge University Press.

Pierson, Paul. 2000. Increasing Returns, Path Dependence, and the Study of Politics. *American Political Science Review* 94 (2): 251–67.

Pierson, Paul. 2004. *Politics in Time: History, Institutions, and Social Analysis*. Princeton: Princeton University Press.

Pius XI, Pope. 1931. *Quadragesimo anno*. Http://www.vatican.va/holy_father/pius_xi/encyclicals/documents/hf_p-xi_enc_19310515_quadragesimo-anno_en.html, accessed November 2005.

van Poppel, Frans. 1985. Late Fertility Decline in the Netherlands: The Influence of Religious Denomination, Socio-Economic Group and Region. *European Journal of Population* 1985 (1): 347–73.

van Praag, Philip. 1977. Views and Concepts Relating to Population Problems in the Netherlands, 1918–1939. *Population Studies* 31 (2): 251–65.

Il problema delle persone anziane nello società italiana: Atti del primo convegno di studio sui problemi dell'assistenza alle persone anziane. 1955. Rome: Edizioni 5 Lune.

Ramondino, Fabrizia, ed. 1977. *Napoli, i disoccupati organizzati: I protagonisti raccontano*. Milan: Feltrinelli Economica.

Regalia, Ida. 1984. Le politiche del lavoro. In *Welfare state all'italiana*, ed. U. Ascoli. Rome: Laterza.

Regini, Marino. 1981. *I dilemmi del sindacato*. Bologna: Il Mulino.

Regini, Marino, and Gloria Regonini. 1981. La politica delle pensioni in Italia: Il ruolo del movimento sindacale. *Giornale di diritto del lavoro e di relazioni industriali* 10: 217–42.

Regonini, Gloria. 1984. Il sistema pensionistico: Risorse e vincoli. In *Welfare state all'italiana*, ed. U. Ascoli. Rome: La Terza.

Regonini, Gloria. 1987. La formazione della politica pensionistica tra governo e parlamento. *Rivista trimestrale di scienza dell'amministrazione* 34 (3): 99–129.

Regonini, Gloria. 1990. La politica delle pensioni. In *Le politiche pubbliche in Italia*, ed. B. Dente. Bologna: Il Mulino.

Regonini, Gloria. 1996. Partiti e pensioni: Legami mancanti. In *Il gigante dai piedi di argilla: La crisi del regime partitocratico in Italia*, ed. M. Cotta and P. Isernia. Bologna: Il Mulino.

References

Renga, Simonetta. 1999. The Evolution of the Italian Social Security System for the Unemployed. Working Paper WS/74. Florence: EUI.

Rhodes, Martin. 1997. Southern European Welfare States: Identity, Problems, and Prospects for Reform. In *Southern European Welfare States*, ed. M. Rhodes. Portland, Ore.: Frank Cass.

Rigter, D. P., E. A. M. van den Bosch, R. J. van der Veen, and A. C. Hemerijck. 1995. *Tussen sociale wil en werkelijkheid: Een geschiedenis van het beleid van het ministerie van Sociale Zaken*. 's-Gravenhage: Ministerie van Sociale Zaken en Werkgelegenheid.

Ritter, Gerhard. 1983. *Social Welfare in Germany and Britain*. New York: Berg.

Roebroek, Joop. 1992. *The Imprisoned State*. Tilburg: Katholieke Universiteit Brabant.

de Rooy, P. 1997. Great Men and a Single Woman: Politics and Social Security in the Netherlands. In *Labour, Social Policy, and the Welfare State. Papers Presented to the Ninth British-Dutch Conference on Labour History, Bergen 1994*, ed. A. Knotter, B. Altena, and D. Damsma. Amsterdam: Stichting beheer IISG.

Rossi, Nicola. 1997. *Meno ai padri, più ai figli*. Bologna: Il Mulino.

Sabbadini, Linda Laura. 1985. Opinioni e ateggiamenti degli italiani sulle tendenze demografiche. Rapporto su: C'è spazio per una politica demografica in tema di natalitá in Italia? Working Paper 04/85. Rome: Istituto di Ricerche sulla Popolazione, Consiglio Nazionale delle Richerche.

Saraceno, Chiara. 1994. The Ambivalent Familism of the Italian Welfare State. *Social Politics* (Spring): 60–82.

Saraceno, Chiara. 1998. *Mutamenti della famiglia e politiche sociali in Italia*. Bologna: Il Mulino.

Sarpellon, Giovanni. 1983. *Rapporto sulla povertá in Italia: La sintesi della grande indagine Cee*. Milan: FrancoAngeli.

Schmid, Gunther, and Bernd Reissert. 1996. Unemployment Compensation and Labour Market Transitions. In *International Handbook of Labour Market Policy and Evaluation*, ed. G. Schmid, J. O'Reilly, and K. Schomann. Cheltenham, U.K., and Brookfield, Mass.: Edward Elgar.

Schmitter, Philippe. 1981. Interest Intermediation and Regime Governability in Contemporary Western Europe and North America. In *Organizing Interests in Western Europe: Pluralism, Corporatism, and the Transformation of Politics*, ed. S. Berger. Cambridge: Cambridge University Press.

Schneider, Anne, and Helen Ingram. 1993. Social Construction of Target Populations: Implications for Politics and Policy. *American Political Science Review* 87: 334–47.

Sexton, Jeremiah. 1988. *Long-Term Unemployment: Its Wider Labour Market Effects in the Countries of the European Community*. Luxembourg: Eurostat.

Sgritta, Giovanni, and Anna Zanatta. 1993. La politica familiare in Italia: Crisi economica, immobilismo politico e ideologie. *Tutela* 8 (4): 5–18.

Shefter, Martin. 1994. *Political Parties and the State: The American Historical Experience*. Princeton: Princeton University Press.

Silvestrini, Angela. 1994. Famiglia, feconditá e invecchiamento nelle politiche per la popolazione: Una lettura attraverso gli attegiamenti e le azioni dei principali partiti politici Italiani nella X e XI Legislatura. Working Paper

215

01/94. Rome: Istituto di Ricerche sulla Popolazione, Consiglio Nazionale delle Ricerche.

Skocpol, Theda. 1992. *Protecting Soldiers and Mothers: The Political Origins of Social Policy in the United States*. Cambridge, Mass.: Harvard University Press.

Soss, Joe. 1999. Lessons of Welfare: Policy Design, Political Learning, and Political Action. *American Political Science Review* 93: 363–80.

Stephens, John. 1979. *The Transition from Capitalism to Socialism*. London: Macmillan.

Stoffelsma, Ronald, and Jan Oosterhaven. 1989. Social Security Benefits and Inter-regional Income Inequalities: The Case of the Netherlands. *Annals of Regional Science* 23: 223–40.

Streeck, Wolfgang, and Kathleen Thelen. 2005. Introduction: Institutional Change in Advanced Political Economies. In *Beyond Continuity: Institutional Change in Advanced Political Economies*, ed. W. Streeck and K. Thelen. Oxford: Oxford University Press.

Sullo, Fiorentino. 1961. *Una riforma che ne prepara altre: gli assegni familiari. Discorso tenuto al senato nella seduta del 13 ottobre 1961*. Rome: Ufficio stampa del Ministero del Lavoro e della Previdenza Sociale.

de Swaan, Abraham. 1988. *In Care of the State: Health Care, Education, and Welfare in Europe and the USA in the Modern Era*. Oxford: Oxford University Press.

Swenson, Peter. 2002. *Capitalists against Markets: The Making of Labor Markets and Welfare States in the United States and Sweden*. New York: Oxford University Press.

Thelen, Kathleen. 1999. Historical Institutionalism in Comparative Politics. *Annual Review of Political Science* 2: 369–404.

Thomson, David. 1989. The Welfare State and Generation Conflict: Winners and Losers. In *Workers versus Pensioners: Intergenerational Justice in an Aging World*, ed. P. Johnson, C. Conrad, and D. Thomson. Manchester: Manchester University Press.

Thomson, David. 1993. A Lifetime of Privilege? Aging and Generations at Century's End. In *The Changing Contract across Generations*, ed. V. Bengston and W. A. Achenbaum. New York: DeGruyter.

Titmuss, Richard M. 1974. *Social Policy: An Introduction*, ed. Brian Abel-Smith and Kay Titmuss. London: Allen & Unwin.

Valiente, Celia. 1996. The Rejection of Authoritarian Policy Legacies: Family Policy in Spain (1975–1995). *South European Society and Politics* 1 (1): 95–114.

van der Valk, Loes. 1991. Poor Law and Social Security Legislation in the Netherlands. *Economic and Social History in the Netherlands* (3): 99–118.

Varley, Rita. 1986. The Government Household Transfer Data Base, 1960–1984. Working Paper 36. Paris: OECD Dept. of Economics and Statistics.

Visser, Jelle, and Anton Hemerijck. 1997. *A Dutch Miracle: Job Growth, Welfare Reform and Corporatism in the Netherlands*. Amsterdam: Amsterdam University Press.

Vlek, Ruud. 1997. *Inactieven in actie: Belangstrijd en belangenbehartiging van uitkeringsgerechtigden in de Nederlandse politiek, 1974–1994*. Amsterdam: Amsterdam University Press.

References

de Vroom, Bert, and Martin Blomsma. 1991. The Netherlands: An Extreme Case. In *Time for Retirement: Comparative Studies of Early Exit from the Labor Force*, ed. M. Kohli, M. Rein, A.-M. Guillemard, and H. v. Gunsteren. Cambridge: Cambridge University Press.

Waldo, Daniel, Sally Sonnerfeld, David McCusick, and Ross Arnett. 1989. Health Expenditure by Age Group, 1977 and 1987. *Health Care Financing Review* 10 (4): 111–21.

Weaver, R. Kent. 1986. "The Politics of Blame Avoidance." *Journal of Public Policy* 6 (4): 371–98.

Wennemo, Irene. 1994. *Sharing the Costs of Children: Studies on the Development of Family Support in OECD Countries*. Stockholm: Swedish Institute for Social Research.

Westerveld, Mies. 2001. Personal communication, July 10.

Wilensky, Harold. 1975. *The Welfare State and Equality: Structural and Ideological Roots of Public Expenditures*. Berkeley: University of California Press.

Wilensky, Harold. 1981. Leftism, Catholicism, and Democratic Corporatism: The Role of Political Parties in Recent Welfare State Development. In *The Development of Welfare States in Europe and America*, ed. P. Flora and A. Heidenheimer. New Brunswick, N.J.: Transaction Books.

Wilensky, Harold. 1990. Common Problems, Divergent Policies: An 18-Nation Study of Family Policy. *Public Affairs Report* 31 (3): 1–3.

World Bank. 1994. *Averting the Old Age Crisis: Policies to Protect the Old and Promote Growth*. New York: Published for the World Bank by Oxford University Press.

Zaller, John. 1992. *The Nature and Origins of Mass Opinion*. Cambridge: Cambridge University Press.

van Zanden, Jan. 1998. *The Economic History of the Netherlands 1914–1995*. London: Routledge.

Index

ABW (Dutch Unemployment
  Assistance Act), 131
active labor market policy, 4, 24, 108,
  119, 131–133, 135, 137
agricultural workers, 94, 96, 99, 135,
  161, 173
AKW (Dutch General Family
  Allowance Act), 81. *See also*
  family allowances
Amato, Giorgio, 161
ANF (*assegno per il nucleo familiare*),
  102. *See also* family allowances
AOW (Dutch General Old-Age
  Pensions Act), 146–148, 151,
  153–154, 169, 171
ARP (Dutch Protestant Reform Party),
  79, 83
Australia, 23, 26, 33, 34–36, 39, 65,
  181, 182
Austria, 4, 16, 23, 32, 38, 39, 185, 192,
  195

Belgium, 4, 16, 25, 38, 47, 52, 62, 64,
  82, 122, 181, 192, 202
Berlusconi, Silvio, 162
Beveridge plan, 11, 62, 94, 186

Canada, 6, 26, 32, 34, 35, 36, 38, 55,
  64, 65, 181, 182
Catholic Church, 47, 80, 91, 93, 104,
  156

CDA (Christian Democratic Appeal),
  84, 86–87
CGIL, 96, 130, 132, 136, 160, 161,
  174. *See also* unions, Italy
child care, 15, 21, 26, 35, 48, 70
Christian Democracy, 4, 8, 12, 42, 47,
  68, 86, 87, 103, 164, 165,
  190–191. *See also* CDA; DC;
  KVP
  and family allowance spending,
    73–75, 77–78, 81–83
  and unemployment benefits
    spending, 109, 133–135
CIG (Italian short-time earnings
  replacement program),
  114–115, 116, 120, 124,
  129–130, 137
CIGS, 114, 118, 120, 122, 130,
  137
CISL, 96, 170. *See also* unions, Italy
clientelism, 12, 185, 187–188
  defined, 63
  and family allowances, 89
  measurement, 63–65
  and occupationalism, 65–67
  and pensions, 172–179
  and unemployment benefits,
    127–128, 131–133, 135
CNEL (Italian National Council on
  Labor and the Economy), 155,
  160, 172, 177

Index

Index

Other Books in the Series *(continued from page iii)*